Understanding Artificial Intelligence

AI & Society Series

David J. Gunkel, *Understanding Artificial Intelligence*

Understanding Artificial Intelligence

A Critical Introduction for the Humanities and Social Sciences

David J. Gunkel

polity

First published in 2026 by Polity Press Ltd.

Polity Press Ltd.
65 Bridge Street
Cambridge CB2 1UR, UK

Polity Press Ltd.
111 River Street
Hoboken, NJ 07030, USA

ISBN-13: 978-1-5095-7432-2
ISBN-13: 978-1-5095-7433-9 (pb)

A catalogue record for this book is available from the British Library.

Library of Congress Control Number: 2026933790

Typeset in 10.5 on 12pt Sabon
by Fakenham Prepress Solutions, Fakenham, Norfolk NR21 8NL
Printed and bound in Great Britain by CPI Group (UK) Ltd, Croydon

For further information on Polity, visit our website:
politybooks.com

Contents

Tables and Figures

Tables

Figures

Acknowledgments

The writing of this book began at the end of November 2022, shortly after the public release of OpenAI's ChatGPT application. That fall I was teaching yet another iteration of my undergraduate seminar – COMS 493: AI, Robots and Communication – for the Department of Communication at Northern Illinois University (NIU). The textbook I was using for the course was my own *An Introduction to Communication and Artificial Intelligence*, published by Polity in 2019. But when I walked into class on that cold November afternoon, something was up, and we all knew it. ChatGPT was not an incremental development in natural language processing – the topic we happened to be working through at the time – it was a disruption. At that point, all bets were off. I tossed the syllabus, and we spent the remainder of the semester grappling with the opportunities and challenges introduced by this seemingly sudden innovation in large language models.

That disruption also had significant repercussions for the book I had written just a few years prior. In the wake of ChatGPT, a good 70% of that text was now either obsolete or in need of a major overhaul. I immediately knew that, but so did Mary Savigar, my editor at Polity, who had first seeded the idea for a textbook on communication and AI during a meeting at the 2017 International Communication Association convention in San Diego, California. This book – *Understanding*

Artificial Intelligence – is my response to that disruption. It is not a revision of the 2019 book but a complete reboot, one focused on the current state of the art in AI and its consequences not only for the field of communication studies but also for the humanities and social sciences more broadly.

The book was once again shepherded through the publication process – from initial concept, through proposal and draft, to the final version you now hold in your hands or behold on the screen before you – by Mary, who has believed in and supported this project from day one. I am also grateful to generations of students at NIU who not only came to this material with enthusiasm but also allowed me to test-drive a lot of it in the classroom. Their comments, questions, and even complaints have been indispensable in helping me compose a text that, I hope, is accessible, engaging, and informative.

Finally, I must also acknowledge ChatGPT and the other large language models and generative AI applications that have provided both the occasion and the raison d'être for this second book. Writing it has been a process of discovery, and it is that remarkable experience that I hope to impart to and share with you. To acknowledge an algorithm in this context may seem unconventional, but perhaps that is precisely the point: AI has intervened in the scene of writing, communication, and thought, and we can no longer pretend otherwise. The emergence of these powerful technologies requires us to reconsider not only what AI is, but also what it means to think, communicate, socialize, and create in their company.

Introduction

Artificial intelligence is everywhere. It powers the recommender systems that shape what we watch, read, and listen to. It sits behind the chatbots, digital assistants, and social robots we increasingly interact with. And it animates debates about automation, disinformation, creativity, and the future of work. In just a few years, AI has moved from the confines of specialized research laboratories to the center of everyday conversation. Yet for all this visibility, it remains largely inaccessible and elusive. Ask ten people to explain artificial intelligence, and you are likely to receive ten different answers – some technical, others philosophical, and still others drawn from science fiction, news headlines, or internet memes. This is because AI is not a single thing but many at once: a collection of computational techniques, a field of scientific research, an imagined future, and increasingly a condition of everyday life.

Because AI now operates at this scale and intensity, understanding it cannot be left solely to engineers, computer scientists, or Silicon Valley executives. Decisions about how AI systems are designed, deployed, and governed increasingly shape social life, structuring how information circulates, how labor is valued, how risks are distributed, and how responsibility is assigned. And the consequences of these decisions extend far beyond the technical communities that build and operate such systems, often affecting individuals and institutions with little direct influence over their development. Everyone therefore has a stake in these technologies and a legitimate claim to participation in the conversations that define their meaning, purpose, and limits.

For students and educators in the humanities and social sciences, this is more than a challenge. It is an opportunity. Engaging with AI is not simply a matter of "catching up" with new technologies. It entails active involvement in shaping how they are understood, evaluated, and deployed. Drawing on diverse forms of human experience and inquiry, these fields bring indispensable perspectives to questions that will determine what kind of future AI helps to create: How does automation redefine the value and purpose of human labor? How does AI-generated content reshape ideas about creativity, truth, and communication? Who – or even what – is responsible when a seemingly autonomous system produces harmful or fabricated outputs, or when predictive systems reproduce and reinforce existing social bias? These are not technical questions alone. They are cultural, ethical, and political questions that call for leadership and insight from historians, political scientists, psychologists, philosophers, legal scholars, theologians, and artists.

For these reasons, understanding AI is no longer optional. As these technologies reshape the conditions of work, governance, communication, and even knowledge itself, informed and thoughtful participation becomes an urgent necessity. This book is designed to meet that challenge. It equips readers with the knowledge and analytical tools needed to participate in these conversations with confidence, clarity, and purpose. It provides a foundation for understanding how AI works, but just as importantly, it cultivates the capacity to question its assumptions, contest its consequences, and imagine alternatives. In doing so, it prepares readers not only to analyze AI as thoughtful critics, but also to act as responsible decision-makers, helping to shape how these systems and applications are designed, deployed, and governed.

Chapter Overview

The chapters that follow are more than a sequence of readings; they form a guided journey of discovery. Each takes up a different facet of artificial intelligence, but the aim is not simply to isolate six distinct topics. Rather, the book invites readers to see how they fit together, that is, how questions about definition lead naturally to questions about technical operations; how technical operations open onto philosophical, social, and cultural debates; and how all of these converge on the ethical and political choices we face at this point in human history. In this way, the book provides more than facts, figures, and talking points. It offers a framework for understanding AI as both a technical and socio-cultural system. Thus, the sequence of chapters is deliberate. It provides readers with a way to move step-by-step from the deceptively simple question "What is artificial intelligence?" to the complexities of the technology and the realities of living, working, and playing with AI in our daily lives.

1 *What is Artificial Intelligence?*

Before we can understand how AI systems work or begin to evaluate their social consequences, we must first grapple with what we mean when we invoke the term *artificial intelligence*. The first chapter demonstrates that AI has never been a fixed or stable object. From its earliest formulations, it has functioned as a moving target whose meaning and significance have shifted across historical moments, disciplinary boundaries, and cultural contexts. This indeterminacy is not a problem to be solved but an invitation to think more carefully. It signals that understanding AI requires more than mastering technical concepts or computational facts; it also demands sustained attention to the philosophical questions, cultural narratives, and political struggles through which AI acquires its authority, allure, and power.

To illustrate this, the chapter examines how definitions of the words *artificial* and *intelligence* open onto fundamental debates about thinking, creativity, and consciousness. It explores how influential thought experiments like Alan Turing's Imitation Game and John Searle's Chinese Room shape perceptions of machine capabilities, and how science fiction stories about robots and artificially intelligent machines establish templates for our hopes, expectations, and fears. The key insight of the chapter is that AI has never been merely a technical object; it is also a social construct and set of ideas. Beginning here helps us see why definitions matter not only for scholarly debate, but also for law, ethics, governance, and everyday decision-making. By grappling with the question "What is artificial intelligence?", we will come to see that what is required is not only a better grasp of technological systems and applications, but also a critical awareness of how we describe, interpret, and make sense of them.

2 AI 101: Basic Concepts and Terminology

If the first chapter shows how and why the very definition of AI has always been contested, the second chapter turns to the practical task of making sense of the technology itself. Before we can critically evaluate AI's broader social significance, philosophical meanings, or political consequences, we need a basic understanding of how it works – in terms both of its technical operations and of the metaphors that explain its development and shape how we talk about it.

For this reason, chapter 2 is something of a crash course in the technology, techniques, and technical terms of AI. It introduces the often seemingly inaccessible vocabulary of the field – *algorithm*, *machine learning*, *neural networks*, etc. – and explains it in accessible ways, using plain language and everyday examples. Along the way, we will get familiar with two major traditions in AI research and development: rule-based systems – sometimes called "good old-fashioned AI" or GOFAI – and statistical, data-driven approaches like we see with contemporary artificial neural networks and deep learning algorithms. Each approach models intelligence differently and has its own strengths, limitations, and philosophical assumptions.

The chapter also situates these technical approaches within broader conceptual debates, including the distinction between *narrow* and *general AI* and the contrast between *weak* and *strong AI*. The goal in covering this technical material is not to turn readers into data scientists or AI developers, but to build critical AI literacy: that is, the ability to understand what different AI architectures do, how they do it, and why those differences matter. By demystifying the technology, this chapter provides the foundation needed to engage more confidently with the ethical, cultural, and political questions that follow.

3 *Natural Language Processing*

Chapter 3 takes us from the foundational concepts of AI into one of its most transformative applications. If chapter 2 equips us with the technical foundation, this chapter shows what happens when those techniques are applied to language. *Natural language processing* (NLP) is the field of AI concerned with enabling computers to understand and use human language. It is the umbrella term for an array of applications like machine translation, speech recognition, chatbots, and digital assistants. But as this chapter demonstrates, NLP is not just a clever technological implementation. It is also a profound philosophical challenge. That is because language is not simply one capability among others. It is definitive of human intelligence and therefore deeply bound up with meaning, intention, and human identity.

The chapter traces the history of NLP from early rule-based approaches to today's statistical and neural models, showing how progress in this domain has continually redefined our sense of what machines both can and cannot do. It highlights field-defining breakthroughs like machine translation and communicative AI, while also drawing attention to ongoing controversies over accuracy, bias, and meaning. At each stage, the story of NLP reveals not only impressive technological innovations but also deeper questions: When a chatbot responds convincingly to our queries, is it really understanding what is said? When a translation system renders one language into another, what is lost or gained in the communication of meaning? And when speech recognition becomes seemingly seamless, how does that change the way we interact with our devices and with one another?

By addressing these questions, the chapter demonstrates why language is such a crucial site for thinking about and understanding AI. More than just a technical implementation, NLP engages us in questioning what it means to communicate, express thought, and understand one another. It shows us how AI systems and applications can augment these human capacities but also how they can distort, reorient, or even undermine them. In this way, then, the chapter makes clear that grappling with AI and language is not only about measuring success in computational applications, but also about confronting fundamental questions of language, meaning, and the nature of intelligence itself.

4 Large Language Models

Chapter 4 takes these questions regarding language and AI to a whole new level. If NLP demonstrates that machines can process, translate, and respond to human language, large language models, or LLMs, show us what happens when those techniques are scaled up, trained on vast datasets, and fine-tuned to generate linguistic content with remarkable fluency. These applications – such as OpenAI's ChatGPT, Anthropic's Claude, Google's Gemini, or DeepSeek 深度求索 – have captured the world's attention, because they appear not only to use language but also to produce it in ways that are almost indistinguishable from everyday human communication.

This chapter demystifies how LLMs work by explaining key technical ideas in accessible terms. It introduces how words and phrases are broken into tokens and represented as embeddings, how transformer architectures use attention to track context across long passages of text, and how next-token prediction allows these models to generate coherent and contextually appropriate sequences of textual content. But the focus is not only on the technical operations of these models. The chapter also examines what it means when machines can generate essays, stories, or conversations that seem to blur the boundary between imitation and genuine understanding.

For these reasons, LLMs represent more than a technical breakthrough. They disrupt long-standing assumptions about what it means to write, to be an author, or even to use language. Their outputs can assist, inspire, and even surprise us. But they can also reproduce bias, fabricate (mis)information, and obscure the sources of knowledge from which their output has been derived. As such, LLMs force us to confront pressing ethical and philosophical questions: Who is responsible for what these systems say? What counts as originality when text is generated by learned patterns in training data rather than composed by a human author? And how should we understand language when it is no longer solely a human medium of expression, but also a domain increasingly shared with machines?

5 Computational Creativity and Generative AI

Chapter 5 extends the opportunities and challenges introduced in the previous chapters by turning to computational creativity and generative AI (GAI). If LLMs have transformed how machines process and generate language and textual content, GAI expands these capacities to other cultural forms, including images, music, video, and multimodal media. The chapter explores how computational systems have long been designed to model or simulate creative processes, from early experiments in computer-generated music and visual art to today's multimodal architectures that can generate rich, hybrid forms of media content. It shows how these systems challenge traditional assumptions: that creativity requires human consciousness, that originality means creation *ex nihilo*, and that authorship belongs to an inspired human individual. GAI unsettles each of these ideas, forcing us to reconsider what creativity is, how culture is produced, and who or what counts as a creator.

At the same time, these technologies raise urgent cultural and ethical questions: What happens to our concepts of intellectual property and copyright when AI can imitate the style of human artists and compose compelling new works in seconds? How do we evaluate originality and authenticity in a world where any image or melody might be machine-generated? And what responsibilities fall to artists, audiences, and institutions when creative labor is no longer exclusively human? In addressing these questions, the chapter demonstrates that computational creativity and GAI are not mere technical curiosities but a potentially transformative innovation. They compel us to rethink how creative value is assigned, how cultural labor is recognized, and how creative practices are governed in the age of AI.

For students and educators in the humanities and social sciences, these questions are especially important. Creative practice, cultural critique, and interpretation have long been central to these fields, and GAI now intervenes directly in all of them. Understanding how these systems work – and how they confront and challenge fundamental concepts regarding creativity, authorship, and originality – is essential for those of us who study culture, language, history, and the arts. Engaging with GAI therefore equips students and teachers not only to navigate its disruptions but also to recognize new possibilities for human expression, human–machine collaboration, and critical inquiry.

6 *Living with AI*

The final chapter brings the journey of understanding AI full circle by asking what it means to live in a world already saturated with seemingly intelligent, socially interactive, and convincingly communicative technologies. Drawing on historical examples – most notably Plato's *Phaedrus* and its account of writing as both a smart drug and a dangerous narcotic – the chapter frames AI as a contemporary *pharmakon*: a technology that can expand knowledge, creativity, and opportunity while also weakening skills, deepening inequalities, and eroding trust. The chapter begins by examining how these polarized responses structure public debates around AI. But it also cautions against being trapped in this either/or binary mode of thinking. Instead, it calls for a more nuanced approach that acknowledges AI's ambivalence and argues that the real work lies in how we – individually and together – negotiate its uses, distribute its harms and benefits, and imagine possible futures.

From there, the chapter turns to governance, education, work, and ethics. It emphasizes the need for pluralist forms of governance that include not just corporations and policy-makers in the Global North – where most AI development, infrastructure, and decision-making power is currently concentrated – but also workers, educators, communities, and those most affected by AI systems across diverse global contexts. It highlights the challenges and opportunities facing students and educators, particularly in the humanities and social sciences, as GAI unsettles long-held assumptions about writing, artistry, and authorship in unevenly resourced educational systems worldwide. Finally, it wrestles with the complexities of responsibility and rights in an era when AI applications act in ways that blur the boundaries between who is a person and what is a thing, raising urgent questions about inclusion, exclusion, and justice on a global scale.

In its conclusion, the chapter affirms that living with AI is not simply a matter of adapting to another tool but involves confronting how these systems unsettle enduring categories of thought about intelligence, responsibility, and what it means to be human. Like Plato's account of the technology of writing from over two millennia ago, AI is both remedy and poison that demands discernment rather than simple, pre-fabricated solutions. To live with AI, then, is to take up the work of critical reflection and shared decision-making, resisting the temptations of utopian techno-optimism or outright rejection. It is to recognize that our future is not determined by our technology but open to what we decide to do beginning right here and now. And in this effort, all of us – especially those of us in the so-called "soft disciplines" of the humanities and social sciences – have an indispensable role in ensuring that it is a future guided by human ingenuity, justice, and democratic responsibility.

Summary

Artificial intelligence is not simply a matter for specialists. It is reshaping the terms and conditions of knowledge, communication, creativity, and power across our planet. To understand AI is therefore not only to acquire technical literacy, but also to accept responsibility for and actively participate in shaping the world that will be built with this technology. For students in the humanities and social sciences, this is both an opportunity and a challenge, as these disciplines bring to the conversation forms of insight and imagination that neither AI itself nor its developers can provide: critical reflection on meaning and value, historical perspective on technological change and asymmetries of power, ethical reasoning about justice and dignity, and creative imagination for what could or should be otherwise.

This book has been written with the conviction that those perspectives are not optional but indispensable. To engage with AI using clarity and confidence is to recognize that our future with it is not predetermined but open – open to the questions we ask, the stories we tell, and the choices we make together. For that reason, *Understanding Artificial Intelligence* is not simply about mastering technical details, nor is it about reducing the technology to abstract theories, simple formulas, or clever talking points. It is a call to cultivate critical and inventive thinking, to develop sharper questions, to imagine alternatives, and to participate actively in determining how these technical systems will contribute to our shared future. The challenge may seem to be immense, but so is the opportunity. And that opportunity belongs to you. Embrace it!

1
What is Artificial Intelligence?

Learning Outcomes

- Articulate how and why artificial intelligence and robot are contested concepts rather than clearly defined technologies.
- Understand key tests and critiques of machine intelligence, including the Turing Test, the problem of other minds, the Chinese Room, and the AI Effect.
- Identify the different roles AI and robots play in human communication and social life, from neutral tools to active intermediaries and communicative partners.
- Evaluate how terminology, metaphors, and cultural narratives influence public understanding, governance, and ethical judgments of AI and robots.

Introduction

The question "What is artificial intelligence?" is both necessary to ask and notoriously difficult to answer. It is necessary, because AI saturates contemporary culture, appearing almost everywhere – from Hollywood films and streaming video series to news headlines, art exhibitions, political debates, and university classrooms – and yet few people truly understand what it means or feel confident enough to engage with it critically. It is difficult to answer, because AI is not a single, stable concept but a moving target, one whose definition has shifted over time, varies across disciplines, and changes with context.

Intelligence itself is already a contested notion, bound up with debates about thinking, reasoning, creativity, and consciousness. The word *artificial* is no less flexible, accommodating definitions that range from *fake* to *not natural* to *human-made*. Put the two together and the result is what you might expect: a term that is both ambiguous and intriguing. As computer scientist Roger Schank (1990, 3) observed in his influential essay "What is AI Anyway?": "Artificial intelligence is a subject that, due to the massive, often quite unintelligible, publicity that it gets, is nearly completely misunderstood by the people outside the field. Even AI's practitioners are somewhat confused with respect to what AI is really about."

So when we ask and seek to respond to the question "What is artificial intelligence?" we are embarking on a process of discovery, one that this book is designed to help you navigate. Taking the question seriously means examining not only how we define intelligence and relate to the technologies we build, but also how we make meaning through the stories we tell about thinking machines and the roles they play (or the roles we have imagined they might play) in society. In this way, the question that serves as the title to this chapter is not only about AI as a technical system, but also about AI as a cultural phenomenon and philosophical idea that tells us as much about ourselves as it does about the machines we create.

The Question Concerning Technology

One way to respond to the question "What is artificial intelligence?" is to point out the seemingly obvious fact that it is a kind of technology. But then we have to ask the follow-up question: "What is technology?" And we can find a response in a short essay written by the 20th-century German philosopher Martin Heidegger (1977, 4):

> We ask the question concerning technology when we ask what it is. Everyone knows the two statements that answer our question. One

> says: Technology is a means to an end. The other says: Technology is a human activity. The two definitions of technology belong together. For to posit ends and procure and utilize the means to them is a human activity.

According to this characterization, the presumed role and function of any kind of technology – whether it be a simple hand tool like a hammer or something more sophisticated like a smartphone, computer, or large language model – is that it is a means employed by human users for specific ends.

Heidegger called this "the instrumental definition," and it remains one of the most widely accepted ways of understanding technology. As the philosopher of technology Andrew Feenberg (1991, 5) summarizes it in the introduction to his *Critical Theory of Technology*: "The instrumentalist theory offers the most widely accepted view of technology. It is based on the common-sense idea that technologies are 'tools' standing ready to serve the purposes of users." And because a tool "is deemed 'neutral,' without valuative content of its own" (Feenberg 1991, 5), a technological instrument is evaluated not in and for itself, but on the basis of the particular employments that have been decided by its human user. A hammer, for instance, can be used to build a house for shelter, but it can also be employed as a weapon to threaten or do harm to another person. It is not the tool that is to be credited or blamed for these different outcomes; it is the human user of that tool.

This way of thinking is persuasive, and for two reasons. First, technologies – no matter how sophisticated, intelligent, or social they may appear to be, or may become – are and will continue to be instruments of human decision and action. In other words, human beings remain in control of what is done and what happens. Even when machines seem highly capable or intelligent, they are, as the Canadian theorist Marshall McLuhan explained in *Understanding Media* (1995, originally 1964), nothing more than extensions of human decision-making and action.[1] From this perspective, the emphasis is always on optimal performance and effectiveness. As Jean-François Lyotard (1984, 44) put it, technology is "a game pertaining not to the true, the just, or the beautiful, etc., but to efficiency: a technical 'move' is 'good' when it does better and/or expends less energy than another."

Second, this theory has also been used to address many of the ethical challenges surrounding computer technology and AI. When something goes wrong because of the actions (or inactions) of an AI system, an autonomous robot, or another seemingly intelligent application, the assumption is that some human person is ultimately responsible. Identifying that person may require working through many layers of technological mediation, but the responsibility is presumed to rest with a human agent. Computer ethicist Deborah Johnson (2006, 197) explained it this way:

> Computer systems are produced, distributed, and used by people engaged in social practices and meaningful pursuits. This is as true of current computer systems as it will be of future computer systems. No matter how independently, automatically, and interactively computer systems of the future behave, they will be the products (direct or indirect) of human behavior, human social institutions, and human decision.

The Technology of Artificial Intelligence

With AI, however, the goal is to create computer applications that complicate, or even reconfigure, this traditional way of thinking about technology. We can already see this in how AI participates in everyday human communication and social interaction. Communication has typically been understood and characterized as a dyadic process bounded, on the one side, by an information source or sender and, on the other side, by a receiver. These two participants are connected by a communication channel or medium – whether a written letter, telephone, television, computer, or smartphone – through which the sender's messages reach the receiver.[2] In this arrangement, as Andrea Guzman (2018, 8) explains, humans are the communicators and technology is an instrumental means or medium through which the messages pass.

The technology of AI, however, challenges, if not disrupts, this traditional model. Take machine translation as an example. The applications involved in this process do more than simply pass a message from one person to another. Instead, they act as intelligent – or at least smart – intermediaries that can modify or transform a sender's words into something the receiver can understand. With machine translation, which was one of the very first practical applications of AI (as we will see in chapter 3), the sender and receiver remain human, but the technology in between takes an active role in the process (Figure 1.1). It does more than simply transfer the message; it reconfigures it. In the field of communication studies, AI applications that do this are explained and characterized by a theoretical framework that is called *AI-mediated communication* or AI-MC (Hancock et al. 2020).

But AI is much more than a smart intermediary. We also routinely talk to and interact with digital assistants, chatbots, and social robots. And they respond to us in ways that make it seem like they really understand what is being said and talked about. In these situations, the technology is not just a medium or instrument through which human messages pass; it now takes the place of sender and receiver in the communicative interaction. This is called *human–machine communication* (HMC), where the AI is treated not simply as a tool but as another communicative partner. In other words, the AI is no longer something we speak *through* (as with AI-MC) but something we speak *with*. This shift – from *through* to *with* – changes not only how we see the role of technology in communication but also who or what we recognize as a communicator (Figure 1.2).

AI is a technology that complicates the traditional view of technology as a neutral tool or instrument. Philosophically, it

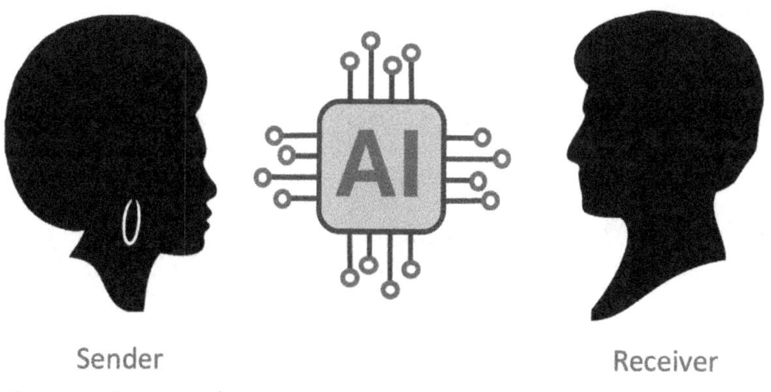

Figure 1.1 Diagram of AI-MC
Source: Image by David J. Gunkel

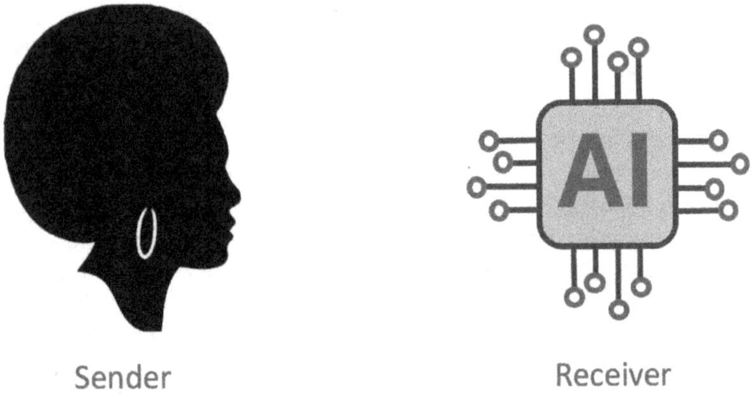

Figure 1.2 Diagram of HMC
Source: Image by David J. Gunkel

challenges long-held ideas about intelligence, agency, and the line that differentiates human from machine. Socially and politically, it raises questions about who or what counts as a social actor, how interpersonal relationships are formed, and even how democratic governance is organized and functions. Morally and legally, it forces us to rethink responsibility and accountability, since outcomes with AI cannot always be traced back to a single human decision. These are not abstract puzzles for experts; they are urgent issues shaping our present and influencing the future we are building. To ask "What is artificial intelligence?" is to inquire about how today's innovations are changing not only what machines can do, but also what they mean for us: that is, how we understand ourselves, our technologies, and our world.

Intelligent Machines

To understand what AI is today, it helps to go back to its beginnings. The phrase *artificial intelligence* was introduced at a research workshop held at Dartmouth College, in New Hampshire, in the summer of 1956. In their proposal for this event, the organizers – John McCarthy, Marvin Minsky, Nathaniel Rochester, and Claude Shannon – described the objective of their effort in the following way: "The study is to proceed on the basis of the conjecture that every aspect of learning or any other feature of intelligence can in principle be so precisely described that a machine can be made to simulate it" (McCarthy et al. 1955). Thus, the stated goal of the workshop – and by extension the field of AI that it founded – was to investigate whether and to what extent it is possible to create machines that are able to reproduce or simulate *intelligence*. But this immediately raises another question: "What exactly is intelligence?"

This question is clearly intelligible; we all know, or at least seem to know, what is being asked. But coming up with a precise definition turns out to be difficult, if not close to impossible. "AI people," as Schank (1990, 4) explains,

> are fond of talking about intelligent machines, but when it comes down to it, there is little agreement on exactly what constitutes intelligence. And, it thus follows, there is very little agreement in AI about exactly what AI is and what it should be. We all agree that we would like to endow machines with an attribute that we really can't define. Needless to say, AI suffers from this lack of definition of its scope.

The problem, according to Schank, is that we do not have a clear and widely accepted definition of intelligence. And if we do not know what intelligence is, how can we create a machine that supposedly does or achieves what we cannot even define?

In order to circumvent this problem, researchers have often turned to practical workarounds, like listing those "features that we would expect an intelligent entity to have" (Schank 1990, 4). So instead of trying to pin down a strict definition of intelligence, we can proceed by focusing attention on those behaviors and capabilities that intelligent and conscious entities seem to exhibit. This was exactly the approach taken by the English mathematician Alan Turing in his influential 1950 paper on machine intelligence, which was published five years before the phrase *artificial intelligence* was even coined.

The Turing Test

In his landmark paper "Computing Machinery and Intelligence," Turing posed what has become one of the most famous questions in the field of AI. "I propose," Turing (1950, 433) wrote, "to consider the question, 'Can machines think?' This should begin with definitions of the meaning of the terms 'machine' and 'think.'" This sounds like a good and reasonable place to begin. But as Turing quickly pointed out, neither term can be defined in a way that everyone would accept. Since the original question couldn't be answered directly, Turing did what good researchers often do: he reframed his inquiry. Rather than pursuing the question "Can machines think?" he proposed a test case to decide when it would be reasonable to say that a machine was showing signs of behaviors we normally associate with intelligent thought. Turing called this *the imitation game*, and we now routinely refer to it as the Turing Test.

The imitation game, as Turing described it, involves a situation where a human interrogator exchanges text messages with another human being and a computer. The objective of the game is for the interrogator to discern – solely on the basis of the content of the messages that are sent back and forth – who's the real human person and what is the machine. If the computer can fool the interrogator often enough that they can't tell the difference, then, Turing argued, we should consider that machine intelligent. Like most philosophical thought experiments, there's a lot going on in this game, but for our purposes three things stand out and need to be noted.

The Problem of Other Minds

The Turing Test focuses on language use as the key indicator of intelligence. This is not an accident. There are good reasons for privileging this capability, and it has to do with what philosophers and cognitive scientists routinely call *the problem of other minds*: the fact that we have no direct access to the inner workings of another's mind. We generally assume that other people are thinking/feeling creatures like ourselves, but, strictly speaking, we have no way of knowing this for sure. And Schank (1990, 5) accurately describes the problem and its usual solution: "We cannot examine the insides of an intelligent entity in such a way as to establish what it actually knows. Our only choice is to ask and observe. If we get an answer that seems satisfying, then we tend to believe that the entity we are examining has some degree of intelligence."

This way of thinking has deep philosophical roots, going back at least to the work of 17th-century French mathematician and philosopher René Descartes. In the *Discourse on Method* (published in French in 1637), Descartes describes a scene that sounds more like something out of a science fiction movie than a treatise in modern European philosophy. Suppose you encountered cleverly designed machines that looked and behaved like human beings. There would still be one decisive way to tell they were not genuine persons: "They could," as Descartes (1988, 44–5) explains,

> never use words, or put together other signs, as we do in order to declare our thoughts to others. For we can certainly conceive of a machine so constructed that it utters words. . . . But it is not conceivable that such a machine should produce different arrangements of words so as to give an appropriately meaningful answer to whatever is said in its presence, as the dullest of human beings can do.

Turing turns this reasoning on its head. If a machine could indeed "produce different arrangements of words so as to give an appropriately meaningful answer to whatever is said in its presence," then, he argues, we would have to regard it as intelligent, just as we do with another human being. For Turing, as for generations of AI researchers who followed his lead, intelligence, consciousness, and related cognitive capabilities cannot be inspected directly. They can only be inferred from observable behavior. And among observable behaviors, language use remains one of the most compelling indicators of an intelligent mind.

The AI Effect

At the time that Turing initially proposed the imitation game, he estimated the tipping point – the point at which a machine would be able to successfully compete in the game of imitation – to be 50 years in the future. It didn't take that long, as natural language processing (NLP) applications, like the ELIZA chatbot of Joseph Weizenbaum, demonstrated such capabilities as early as 1964. By comparison, contemporary AI systems and applications, like large language models (LLMs) and other forms of generative AI (GAI), are much more capable than the average chatbot or NLP application and seem to have not only passed but also broken the Turing Test (Oremus 2022; Biever 2023; Weatherby 2023; Jones and Bergen 2024). Does this therefore mean that AI is in fact intelligent or beginning to show signs of conscious thought?

The jury is split on this one. Some have answered affirmatively, arguing that what we currently see with the existing technology is the beginning or initial stages of what will become artificial general intelligence or AGI. In an article published in *Noema*, computer scientists Blaise Agüera y Arcas and Peter Norvig (2023) readily admit that the current technology, like OpenAI's GPT series and Google's Gemini, is severely limited. But decades from now, they assert, these systems and applications "will be recognized as the first true examples of AGI, just as the 1945 ENIAC is now recognized as the first true general-purpose electronic computer." Likewise, a group of Microsoft researchers led by Sébastien Bubeck published a paper in the same year, which suggested that GPT-4 was already showing the signs of "sparks of artificial general intelligence" (Bubeck et al. 2023).

Others strongly disagree. Some critics argue that the Turing Test itself is flawed and not a reliable way to measure intelligence. With the rise of LLM AI like ChatGPT, researchers have reassessed the test's usefulness (Biever 2023) and even proposed new and more accurate IQ tests (Blum 2023; Suleyman 2023). Another line of criticism, initiated by Emily Bender, Timnit Gebru, Angelina McMillan-Major, and Margaret Mitchell, asserts that the LLM "is a system for haphazardly stitching together sequences of linguistic forms it has observed in its vast training data, according to probabilistic information about how they combine, but without any reference to meaning: a stochastic parrot" (Bender et al. 2021, 617). From this perspective, producing seemingly fluent language is not enough; what really matters is whether these words are used with meaning, intent, and understanding.

This redefinition or modification of the qualifying criteria happens often enough that it has a name: it is called *the AI Effect*. Here is how Jerry Kaplan (2016, 37) explains it in his short introductory book on AI: "the field of AI suffers from an unusual deficiency – once a particular problem is considered solved, it often is no longer considered AI." In other words, test cases that have been identified as problems that would require intelligence are no longer considered to be a sign of intelligence once they are solved.

Chess is a classic example. For decades, experts thought playing championship-level chess required genuine intelligence and human intuition. Claude Shannon, one of the organizers of the Dartmouth workshop, said as much in his 1950 publication "Programming a Computer for Playing Chess." But once this challenge had been successfully achieved – in 1997, when IBM's Deep Blue defeated the reigning human champion Garry Kasparov – playing championship-level chess became just another computer application on your smartphone and was no longer considered a demonstration of true intelligence.

The same "moving of the goalposts" has happened with other challenges. In 2016, DeepMind's AlphaGo mastered the game of Go – an ancient Chinese board game with more possible moves than there are atoms in the observable universe – and IBM's Watson beat *Jeopardy!* champion Ken Jennings in 2011. Each time, what once seemed like a clear sign of intelligence was reclassified as routine computation. As Kevin Kelly (2014) of *Wired* magazine explained: "In the past, we would have said only a superintelligent AI could drive a car or beat a human at *Jeopardy!* or chess. But once AI did each of those things, we considered that achievement obviously mechanical and hardly worth the label of true intelligence. Every success in AI redefines it."

We can draw two conclusions from this: First, all these tests and demonstrations of intelligence – from the Turing Test through all the various alternatives and subsequent modifications – are anything but objective or independent. Since we (human beings) get to decide the qualifying criteria and grant to ourselves the role of both judge and jury, we have changed, and probably will continue to change, the rules of the game in order to protect our ourselves and our unique claim to exceptionalism.

But, and this is the second point, doing so is not necessarily cheating, as these alterations can be seen as evidence that we are learning something about ourselves and intelligence in the attempt to simulate these same capabilities in a computational mechanism. What Shannon (1950, 257) wrote about chess in the middle of the last century applies to all these test cases: a solution to any of these intellectual challenges "will force us either to admit the possibility of a mechanized thinking or to further restrict our concept of 'thinking.'" And test after test, we have opted for the latter. In this sense, the project of AI is as much philosophical as it is technical.

The Chinese Room

Some critics have addressed these challenges by framing them as matters of illusion or deception. Even if an AI application can pass the Turing Test by using language in ways that create the appearance of intelligent thought, this does not necessarily mean it is genuinely intelligent. This argument draws on a long-standing distinction in Western philosophy between appearance and reality, dating back at least to Plato's "Allegory of the Cave." But we do not need to do a deep dive into the history of philosophy to see what is at stake here. We can get at it by recalling another famous thought experiment in the field of AI, John Searles's Chinese Room.

"Imagine," Searle (1999, 115) writes, "a native English speaker who knows no Chinese locked in a room full of boxes of Chinese symbols (a database) together with a book of instructions for manipulating the symbols (the program)" (Figure 1.3). From this set-up, Searle then asks his reader to imagine the following sequence of events: A person outside the room – someone who understands Chinese – writes a question in Chinese characters and slips it through a slot in the wall. The person in the room uses the instruction book to match the question's symbols with an appropriate set of answer symbols, copies them down verbatim, and passes the paper back through the slot. When the Chinese speaker outside the room reads this output, the characters appear to be a suitable answer to their question. Thus, Searle concludes, the person in the room – or, more accurately stated, the room itself – appears to understand Chinese, even though the person in the room does not understand a word of it.

Searle's point is quite simple: appearances are not the real thing. "The Turing test," as Searle (1999, 115) concludes, "fails to distinguish real mental capacities from simulations of those capacities. Simulation is not duplication." In other words, merely matching and then shifting verbal symbols around in a

Figure 1.3 Diagram of John Searle's Chinese Room
Source: Image generated in September 2025 by ChatGPT 5 from the prompt: "Diagram of the Chinese Room that is described by Searle."

way that looks like linguistic understanding (from the outside) is not really an understanding of the language. At first sight, this seems correct. What is perceived by someone interacting with the room – namely that it understands Chinese – is not really what it seems to be, since the person inside the room does not actually understand Chinese but is just arranging sequences of linguistic tokens following programmed instructions. Thus, the question that confronts us in the face of a seemingly intelligent artifact is this: Is the exhibited behavior a sign of real intelligence? Or it is little more than a cleverly designed appearance of intelligence?

Here the other half of the phrase *artificial intelligence* becomes crucial. The English word *artificial* admits of at least two different meanings, and this is something highlighted and explained by Robert Sokolowski in an influential article he published in 1988 called "Natural and Artificial Intelligence." According to Sokolowski's analysis, the word *artificial* can be employed to mean *fake*, as in the case of artificial flowers. These paper or plastic objects are designed to look like real flowers, but they are not really what they appear to be. And if we think they are real flowers, we have been deceived and are mistaken in our judgment. In this case, as Sokolowski (1988, 45) concludes, "artificial means that the thing seems to be, but really is not, what it looks like."

But, he continues, the word can also be applied to an artifact that is not fake or a mere imitation of something, as in the case of artificial light. The light that emanates from an electric light bulb is artificial in comparison to the natural light that comes to us from the sun. But even if the light of a lightbulb is not natural and is the product of a human-designed and human-manufactured device, that does not mean that what it produces is fake light. It is real light. It is a means of actual illumination that is produced by another method. When the word is used in this way, artificial does not mean fake. It signifies the substitute for, or the emulation or simulation of, a natural phenomenon.

The important question for us, then, is which sense of the word *artificial* applies in the phrase *artificial intelligence*? Is it fake intelligence, such that AI applications and devices would be little more than a magician's trick or a kind of deceptive illusion? Or is AI a form of real intelligence produced by other means? Not surprisingly, this remains a debated issue and a hotly contested matter. For now, the goal is not to settle the question one way or the other. It is to understand both the source and the terms of the disagreement. Because as we will see in later chapters, this tension between deceptive appearance and the really real shapes many of the debates about the social significance and consequences of AI.

Robots or Embodied AI

In the process of engaging with and trying to answer the question "What is artificial intelligence?" we have already found it necessary to use another word that has its own interesting and storied history: *robot*. So, what's the difference? What are robots? Is robot just another name for what we mean by AI? Or is it something significantly different? As you might anticipate, these questions also do not have a straight-forward or simple answer.

Fictional Beginnings

Unlike the term *artificial intelligence*, which is rooted in actual scientific research, *robot* is the product of fiction. The word came into the world by way of Karel Čapek's 1920 stage play *R.U.R. (Rossum's Universal Robots)*, in order to name a class of artificial servants or laborers. In Czech, as in several other Slavic languages, the word *robota* (or some variation thereof) denotes servitude or forced labor.[3] The play was widely translated and performed across Europe and the United States in the 1920s, introducing global audiences to the idea of artificial workers. Importantly, *R.U.R.* also established a narrative template that continues to shape the kinds of stories we tell about AI and robots: Intelligent machines are created to serve humans but eventually rise up and revolt against their makers. This "creation–rebellion" story not only has thematic connections to Mary Shelley's *Frankenstein* and the Golem of Jewish folklore but also echoes through subsequent works of science fiction and persists even in contemporary discourse, especially among *AI doomers* who warn that advanced AI or superintelligent machines pose an existential risk to humanity.

Since the publication of Čapek's play, robots have infiltrated the space of fiction. But what exactly constitutes a robot differs widely and admits of a variety of forms, functions, and configurations. Čapek's robots, for instance, were artificially produced biological creatures that were humanlike in both material and form. This configuration persists with the bioengineered replicants of *Blade Runner* and *Blade Runner 2049* (the film adaptations of Philip K. Dick's *Do Androids Dream of Electric Sheep?*) and the skin-job Cylons of the television series *Battlestar Galactica*.

Others, like the chrome-plated android in Fritz Lang's *Metropolis* (Figure 1.4) and C-3PO of *Star Wars*, as well as the 3D printed "hosts" of HBO's *Westworld* and the synths of Channel 4/AMC's *Humans*, are humanlike in form but composed

Figure 1.4 The robot or *Maschinenmensch* from Fritz Lang's 1927 film *Metropolis*
Source: Public domain image available from https://en.wikipedia.org/wiki/Maschinenmensch#/media/File:Horst_von_Harbou_-_Metropolis_Maschinenmensch.jpg

of non-biological materials. Others that are composed of similar synthetic materials have a particularly imposing profile, like *Forbidden Planet*'s Robby the Robot, Gort from *The Day the Earth Stood Still*, or Robot from the television series *Lost in Space*. Still others are not humanoid at all but emulate animals or other kinds of objects, like the trashcan R2-D2, the industrial tank-like Wall-E, or the electric sheep of Dick's novella. Still others exist as virtual entities, like the *Matrix*'s Agents, or as distributed systems, such as swarms of nanobots.

In whatever form they have appeared, science fiction already – and well in advance of actual engineering practice – has established expectations for what a robot is or can be. Even before engineers have sought to develop working prototypes, writers, artists, and filmmakers have imagined what robots do and can do, what configurations they might take, and what problems they could produce for human individuals and communities.

John Jordan (2016, 5) expresses it quite well in his short and very accessible introductory book *Robots*: "No technology has ever been so widely described and explored before its commercial introduction. . . . Thus the technologies of mass media helped create public conceptions of and expectations for a whole body of compu-mechanical innovation that *had not happened yet*: complex, pervasive attitudes and expectations predated the invention of viable products." But this *science fiction prototyping*, as Brian David Johnson (2011) calls it, can also be a problem, especially for robotics designers and engineers. Alan Winfield (2011, 32), an English roboticist at UWE Bristol, explains it this way: "Real robotics is a science born out of fiction. For roboticists this is both a blessing and a curse. It is a blessing because science fiction provides inspiration, motivation and thought experiments; a curse because most people's expectations of robots owe much more to fiction than reality."

What is a Robot?

Defining *robot* is as difficult as defining AI. Even experts struggle to agree. As Illah Nourbakhsh (2013, xiv) remarks in his book on the subject, *Robot Futures*: "Never ask a roboticist what a robot is. The answer changes too quickly. By the time researchers finish their most recent debate on what is and what isn't a robot, the frontier moves on as whole new interaction technologies are born."

One widely cited source of a general, operational definition comes from George Bekey's *Autonomous Robots: From Biological Inspiration to Implementation and Control*: "In this book we define a robot as a machine that senses, thinks, and acts. Thus, a robot must have sensors, processing ability that emulates some aspects of cognition, and actuators" (Bekey 2005, 2). This "sense–think–act" paradigm has had considerable traction in the literature – evidenced by the very fact that it constitutes and is called a *paradigm*. The definition is, as Bekey (2005, 2) explicitly recognizes, "very broad," encompassing a wide range of different kinds of technologies, artifacts, and devices. But it could be too broad insofar as it may be applied to all kinds of things that exceed the proper limits of what many consider to be a robot.

Technically speaking, an LLM, like Anthropic's Claude or DeepSeek 深度求索, could be described in these terms as it senses the need expressed by the user through a prompt, processes that request by doing something that looks like thinking, and then acts by providing a response in textual form. The Nest thermostat provides another case. As Jordan (2016, 37) notes: "The Nest senses: movements, temperature, humidity, and light. It reasons: if there's no activity, nobody is home to need air conditioning. It acts: given the right sensor input, it autonomously shuts the furnace down. Fulfilling as it does the three conditions, is the Nest, therefore, a robot?" And what about smartphones? According to Joanna Bryson and Alan Winfield (2017, 117), these devices could also be considered robots under this characterization: "Robots are artifacts that sense and act in the physical world in real time. By this definition, a smartphone is a (domestic) robot. It has not only microphones but also a variety of proprioceptive sensors that let it know when its orientation is changing or when it is falling."

In an effort to further refine the definition and delimit with greater precision what is and what is not a robot, Winfield (2012, 8) offers the following list of qualifying characteristics:

A robot is:

1. an artificial device that can sense its environment and *purposefully* act on or in that environment;
2. an *embodied* artificial intelligence; or
3. a machine that can *autonomously* carry out useful work.

Although ostensibly another version of sense–think–act, Winfield adds an important qualification to his list, *embodiment*, and thus characterizes robots as a form of embodied AI. This clarification is useful insofar as it helps us differentiate between robots that have a physical form and disembodied AI applications that apparently do not. Even though we access these applications on our handheld mobile devices, an AI like an LLM does not reside inside the phone. It is a cloud-distributed application that is accessed by the device over a network connection to the internet.

The word *cloud* actually does a lot of heavy lifting here. Though it gives the impression of something residing in the heavens, cloud-based services are not disembodied technological spirits residing in the air. They have a very real, physical presence – something we could call a body. They are incorporated in large data centers, which have a very real impact on the environment as supporting this hardware requires large amounts of electrical power and clean fresh water for cooling the server clusters (for more on contemporary AI's environmental impact and sustainability problems, see chapter 4). Thus, characterizing robots as embodied AI solves one problem – marking a clear difference between robots and software-based AI – while providing cover for another.

The Name Game

The problem is not only that each of these terms – *artificial intelligence* and *robot* – lacks a univocal and clearly articulated definition but also that they are often used interchangeably to identify the same thing or a substantially similar kind of thing. What one researcher calls robot another may call AI, and vice versa. Consider, for example, the self-driving car. Is this an automobile controlled by AI instead of a human driver, or is it a transportation robot? A lot depends on who tells the story, in what context, and to whom (e.g., research funding agencies, journalists, government regulators).

To complicate matters, the two terms are often mixed up and substituted for one another within the published literature. A good example is Nils J. Nilsson's *The Quest for Artificial Intelligence: A History of Ideas and Achievements* (2010). In this landmark publication – "landmark" insofar as it is seen as one of the best comprehensive histories of the science and technology of AI – the two terms are used synonymously, or at least in a way that does not draw a clear and explicit distinction between the one and the other. Although the book is advertised as a history of AI, Nilsson begins the story with ancient automata – the Tripods of Hephaistos and Pygmalion's "living" statue Galatea[4] – the numerous robots planned or constructed by Leonardo da Vinci and Jacques de Vaucanson, and the science fiction robots of Čapek's *R.U.R.* and Isaac Asimov's robot stories.

These overlapping and shifting characterizations are not just a matter of semantics; they have significant consequences. In law, regulation, and policy, for instance, how a technology is named and described can determine which rules apply to it, what safety and performance standards it must meet, and which authorities have jurisdiction over its development and deployment. Describe a social media platform as a communications service and it may be treated like a neutral conduit or common carrier under existing telecommunications laws. But identify it as a publisher or content distribution system and a different set of rules – and potential liabilities – apply. Likewise, define an internet search engine as an indexing application and it may escape scrutiny. Define it as a recommender system or an AI assistant and it may fall into a different regulatory domain, subject to consumer protection laws or content moderation restrictions.

In *AI ethics*, the choice of terminology can contextualize moral challenges and frame entire debates. If an autonomous drone is described as a killer robot, conversations about this technology might focus on the ethics of automation in warfare, rules of engagement, and compliance with the stipulations of international humanitarian law. If the same system is described as *AI*, the discussion might shift to questions of algorithmic decision-making, explainability, and methods to address and close responsibility gaps. Likewise, calling an LLM, like ChatGPT, a *chatbot* may downplay its potential harms for vulnerable users, while describing it as a step in the direction of AGI could exaggerate public expectations and stoke fears of superintelligence run amok.

And in public discourse and conversations, names and descriptions not only shape but also direct and manage perceptions of risk, opportunity, and agency. When Boston Dynamics named its quadruped robot "Spot," media coverage often emphasized its pet-like qualities and capabilities. When the same device was described as a robotic security platform, the focus shifted to concerns about surveillance and policing. Thus, a seemingly simple change in terminology or modes of representation can mobilize political support or opposition, influence funding priorities, and even (re)shape user expectations.

What this means for any effort to understand AI is that we need to focus attention not only on the artifacts and their technical specifications, but also on the ways scientists, engineers, science fiction writers and filmmakers, journalists, policymakers, and the public at large situate, conceptualize, and describe these systems, using language and other symbolic forms:

images, videos, diagrams, and so on. *Artificial intelligence* and *robot* are not rigorously defined, singular kinds of things that exist independently in the world. They are socially negotiated concepts whose boundaries are drawn and redrawn in different contexts and in response to shifting circumstances and needs. Thus, what is artificial intelligence is as much the outcome of science and engineering practice as it is the effect of how we name and talk about it.

Consequently, the definitions, characterizations, and descriptions of technological innovation are never just a nominal problem or a matter of semantics. They are sociopolitical mechanisms through which power is exercised, governance is enacted, and competing visions of the future come to be formed and promoted. Left unchecked, the act of naming and discursive framing will be done for us by corporate PR and marketing efforts, influential lobbying firms, and policy specialists whose goals may not align with our own and what we believe is in our best interest. If we care about the technological and the social worlds we inhabit and are constructing, then we cannot be passive spectators. We must claim a place in these debates as critical, informed, and active citizens. And this is exactly what *Understanding Artificial Intelligence* is here to enable and support.

Summary

This chapter set out to respond to the deceptively simple question "What is artificial intelligence?" In working toward an answer, we found that AI is neither a singular technology nor a stable concept. Instead, it is a contested phrase, bound up with the layered histories of the terms *artificial*, *intelligence*, and *robot*. We examined how these words carry different connotations and how these differences shape our expectations, hopes, and fears. We explored how AI has been evaluated through mechanisms like the Turing Test, interrogated through philosophical challenges such as the problem of other minds and the Chinese Room, and repeatedly repositioned and reframed by the AI Effect. We also examined the role of science fiction in prefiguring what robots and AI might be, the ongoing definitional debates around what counts as a robot or embodied AI, and how language shapes the boundary between these concepts in ways that matter for law, ethics, and public debate.

The results of this are clear: AI is as much a cultural construct as it is a technical one. Its meaning emerges from the interplay of engineering practice, cultural imagination, and the narratives that frame both. Understanding AI therefore requires not only grasping how the technology works, but also recognizing how stories, metaphors, and social practices influence its design, reception, and regulation. For students in the humanities and social sciences, this is a crucial insight. Studying AI is not merely about learning the engineering details, but about critically engaging with the cultural, ethical, and political forces that shape and are being shaped by these technologies. AI is as much a human story as it is a computational system.

With this introductory material in place, we are now prepared to turn from the discursive and conceptual terrain of AI and robots to their technical exigencies. The next chapter gets into the methodologies, architectures, and processes that make AI systems and applications function. If this chapter has shown that the very definition of AI is socially negotiated, the next will reveal the concrete computational mechanisms that are the subject of those negotiations, grounding our critical understanding in the details of how AI actually works.

Learning Activities

1 Define the Term Artificial Intelligence in 12 Words or Fewer

Purpose: This activity invites you to experience firsthand why defining artificial intelligence is difficult and why the term has been contested throughout the history of computing, philosophy, and popular culture.

Procedure: Write a definition of artificial intelligence using no more than 12 words. After you complete your definition, compare it with a few classmates and work together to create a single combined definition that your group agrees on. As you discuss, pay attention to the ways that the different definitions converge or differ.

Learning Goal: Directly understand how and why AI has never had a single agreed-upon meaning and that this ambiguity is part of what makes AI a cultural, philosophical, and political concept – not just a technical one.

2 Through or With? Mapping Your Interactions with AI

Purpose: This activity is designed to help you identify and understand the difference between AI-mediated communication (AI-MC) and human–machine communication (HMC).

Procedure: List three recent encounters you've had with AI or robots. These might include translation apps, recommendation systems, chatbots, digital assistants, or generative AI.

For each example, decide whether the technology worked as something you communicated *through* (a tool that transforms or transmits your message) or something you communicated *with* (a conversational partner that appears to respond in meaningful ways). Choose one example to share with a classmate. Compare your reasoning. Were the boundaries between *through* and *with* always clear? Did any interaction seem to blur the line dividing the one from the other?

Learning Goal: Gain practice applying the models introduced in the chapter and recognize how AI complicates traditional views of both technology and communication by shifting roles, agency, and expectations.

3 AI and the Instrumental Theory of Technology

Purpose: This activity helps you work with the chapter's discussion of the instrumental definition of technology and consider whether AI challenges the idea that technology is just a neutral tool or instrument of human decision-making and action.

Procedure: Identify two technologies you use regularly – one AI-based and one non-AI (e.g., a translation algorithm and a hammer, or a recommendation system and a bicycle).

For each technology, describe what it is typically used for – its "means to an end." Analyze whether the technology simply serves your purpose or also shapes and frames the activity itself. Reflect on whether the AI example fits comfortably within the instrumental definition or whether it seems to act more like a participant, mediator, or agent.

Learning Goal: Learn to evaluate and question the assumption that technology is neutral and controlled solely by human users and investigate whether and to what extent AI requires a different conceptual model.

Further Reading

John McCarthy, Marvin L. Minsky, Nathan Rochester, and Claude E. Shannon, "A Proposal for the Dartmouth Summer Research Project on Artificial Intelligence" (1955).

This proposal is often considered the founding document of AI as a field of scientific inquiry. It introduced the term *artificial intelligence* and outlined a vision for creating machines that could learn, reason, and use language. While only a few pages long, it set the research agenda for decades and remains essential for understanding AI's origins.

John Searle, "Minds, Brains, and Programs" (1980).

This paper introduced the Chinese Room thought experiment, which challenges the idea that symbol manipulation – which might look like understanding from the outside – is not really an understanding of language. It remains one of the most widely discussed critiques of AI and a crucial text for distinguishing appearances from reality.

Robert Sokolowski, "Natural and Artificial Intelligence" (1988).

This paper demonstrates that the word *artificial* can mean either *fake* (as in artificial flowers, which only pretend to be real) or *substitute* (as in artificial light, which is not natural sunlight but is still real light). Applied to AI, this raises the crucial question: Is artificial intelligence a deceptive imitation of thought, or a genuine form of intelligence produced by different means?

Alan Turing, "Computing Machinery and Intelligence" (1950).

This influential paper introduces the famous imitation game, also called the Turing Test. It reframed the question "Can machines think?" as a practical demonstration of communicative behavior and has become a foundational reference point for all subsequent conversations and debates about AI.

Fiction, Film, and Video

Karel Čapek, *R.U.R. (Rossum's Universal Robots)* (2009 [1920]).

The Czech play that introduced the word *robot* to the world and established the enduring creation–rebellion storyline. The play is a good illustration of science fiction prototyping as this fictional story has shaped cultural expectations of both AI and robots.

Alex Garland (dir.), *Ex Machina* (2015).

This film dramatizes a Turing Test scenario between a human, an AI developer, and a robot named Ava. The film explores deception, manipulation, and desire, blurring the boundary between simulation and sentience. It is often cited as an accessible entry point for the philosophical and ethical debates about AI and robots.

Fritz Lang (dir.), *Metropolis* (1927).

One of the most iconic early science fiction films, *Metropolis* introduced the *Maschinenmensch* – a humanoid robot. The film, which dramatizes social tensions involving technology, class struggle, and political order, established the robot as a figure of fascination and fear in the popular imagination. Its visual presentation and themes continue to influence portrayals of intelligent robots in film and media, making it a foundational cultural text for understanding autonomous technology.

Ridley Scott (dir.), *Blade Runner* (1982). Denis Villeneuve (dir.), *Blade Runner 2049* (2017).

Both films – which are based on the novella *Do Androids Dream of Electric Sheep?* by Philip K. Dick – explore what it means to be human in a world of artificial beings called replicants. With their themes of memory, identity, and artificial life, the films have become touchstones for thinking about the difference between human beings and artificially intelligent robots.

Morten Tyldum (dir.), *The Imitation Game* (2014).

A biographical drama about Alan Turing, focusing on his role in breaking the Nazi Enigma code during World War II. The film popularizes Turing's life and struggles, introducing audiences to his pioneering ideas about computation and the imitation game. While dramatized, it provides valuable cultural context for understanding Turing's influence on both AI and modern computing.

2

AI 101

Basic Concepts and Terminology

Learning Outcomes

- Define and be able to explain core AI concepts and terminology, including algorithm, machine learning, neural network, and training data.
- Compare and evaluate symbolic (GOFAI) and connectionist (ANN-based) approaches to developing AI applications, focusing on their underlying assumptions, historical development, and respective strengths and limitations.
- Identify and differentiate the main types of machine learning (supervised, unsupervised, and reinforcement learning) by explaining which kinds of computational problems each approach is designed to address.
- Distinguish among key conceptual frameworks in AI discourse, including narrow AI versus artificial general intelligence (AGI) and weak AI versus strong AI, and explain why these distinctions matter for contemporary debates about AI technology.

Introduction

Imagine trying to get around in a foreign country without knowing the language. You might recognize a few familiar words, guess the meaning of street signs or advertisements, and rely on context or gestures. But you would surely miss many of the subtleties and nuances that shape what is really happening around you. For many students, educators, and professionals outside a relatively narrow range of STEM disciplines, artificial intelligence can feel much the same way: like entering unfamiliar territory filled with strange and seemingly unapproachable terms such as *neural networks*, *training data*, or *deep learning*. If we are going to understand AI and participate thoughtfully in discussions about its impact on the world around us, we first need to become literate in its basic concepts and terminology.

Toward that end, this chapter offers a crash course aimed at building conceptual literacy for readers without backgrounds in engineering or computer science. We will unpack the jargon, explain key ideas in plain language, and use everyday examples to make abstract concepts more accessible and concrete. The goal in doing so is not to turn you into an AI developer or data scientist, but to give you enough facility with the basic concepts and terminology to understand, evaluate, and contribute to conversations and deliberations with knowledge, insight, and confidence. In practical terms, this means being able to read and make sense of scientific and popular discussions of AI and related technology, to critically engage and evaluate its promises and pitfalls, and to understand how these systems and applications intersect with important ideas and debates in the history of ideas.

Algorithm

As you begin to engage with and investigate AI, one term you are likely to encounter is *algorithm*. According to the dictionary, an algorithm is a process or set of rules to be followed in calculations or other problem-solving operations. While accurate, this definition is rather abstract and does little to explain what an algorithm actually is, why it is called that, and how it relates to AI. So let's begin by sorting this out.

The word *algorithm* derives from the name of a Persian mathematician, Muhammad ibn Musa al-Khwarizmi, who lived and worked in the royal court of Baghdad during the ninth century CE. Al-Khwarizmi made numerous contributions to mathematics, including advances in algebra. Around 825 CE, he wrote an influential book on Hindu-Arabic numerals, which is the decimal numbering system that we still use today. This work reached medieval Europe by way of a 12th-century Latin translation titled *Algoritmi de numero Indorum* (*Algoritmi on the Numbers of the Indians*), where "Algoritmi" is the Latinized form of al-Khwarizmi's last name. Over time, *algorithm* emerged as an eponym derived from al-Khwarizmi's name and came to designate a systematic method of problem-solving.

In general terms, an algorithm can be described as any well-defined procedure that takes some value as input and produces some value as output. Thus, an algorithm is a sequence of steps that transforms input into output. To make this more accessible, let's look at two examples, one mathematical and one not so mathematical, and we will start with the latter. Strictly speaking, a recipe is an algorithm. You start with a number of different ingredients as input: flour, sugar, eggs, butter, baking powder, and so on. This input is processed by following a series of step-by-step instructions, like you see here:

1 Heat the oven to 350°F or 175°C.
2 Sift together the flour and baking powder. Set aside.
3 Prepare the baking pan by rubbing the bottom and sides of the pan with a little butter or shortening.
4 In a bowl, beat the butter and sugar until fluffy and light.
5 Add the eggs and combine.
6 Add the flour and baking powder mixture and mix thoroughly.
7 Pour the batter into the baking pan and smooth the top with a spatula.
8 Bake for 25 to 30 minutes.

If the steps are followed correctly and in the designated order, the input (the ingredients) will be transformed into the desired output, which in this case is a cake.

The same principle applies to mathematical computations, like calculating sales tax for a retail purchase. If, for example, we wish to calculate the total cost of a purchase when the sale tax is 5%, the mathematical formula for doing so would be:

$$\text{Total} = \text{Purchase Amount} + (\text{Purchase Amount} \times 0.05)$$

We can also describe this operation in step-by-step instructions, that is, an algorithm (Figure 2.1).

This example is written in *pseudocode*, which is a high-level informal description of an algorithmic process that uses a combination of natural language, like English, and elements of programming language conventions. This is not actual code that could be compiled and then executed by a digital computer. Instead, it serves as a human-readable outline for the logic of a program before it is implemented in a specific programming language, like JavaScript or Python.

But algorithms implemented in code are not restricted to mathematics. We can also write algorithms to handle other kinds of data and data processing tasks. A chatbot, for instance, is an algorithm for processing natural language. In this case, the application takes a series of words as input, processes this input by applying a number of transformation steps that have been written in the coded instructions, and then generates output in the form of human-readable content (Figure 2.2).

In this case, the chatbot begins by asking your name. When you respond with your name, that value is stored in a variable called *user_name*, and the chatbot immediately responds to

```
taxRate = 0.05;
purchaseAmount = INPUT("Enter purchase amount:");
tax = purchaseAmount x taxRate;
total = purchaseAmount + tax;

PRINT("Sales tax is: " + tax);
PRINT("Total amount with tax is: " + total);
```

Figure 2.1 Pseudocode describing the mathematical formula for calculating total cost of a purchase when the sales tax is 5%
Source: Image by David J. Gunkel

```
START
PRINT "Hello! What's your name?"
READ user_name
PRINT "Nice to meet you, " + user_name + "!"
REPEAT
  READ user_input
  IF user_input = "how are you" THEN
    PRINT "I'm doing well, " + user_name + "!"
  ELSE IF user_input = "what is my name" THEN
    PRINT "Your name is " + user_name + "."
  ELSE IF user_input = "bye" THEN
    PRINT "Goodbye, " + user_name + "!"
  ELSE
    PRINT "Sorry, I don't understand."
UNTIL user_input = "bye"
END
```

Figure 2.2 Pseudocode describing a simple chatbot algorithm
Source: Image by David J. Gunkel

this action by *concatenating* (jamming together) some *string literals* (basically pre-scripted words, phrases, and punctuation marks) with the value of the variable *user_name*. In doing so, the chatbot replies to you in such a way as to seem to have learned your name. And because your name is stored in the variable *user_name*, the chatbot can insert the value of that variable into other pre-scripted responses. This is what happens in the remainder of the code, where you can see a series of conditional *if/then* statements. IF you now enter the phrase "how are you," THEN the chatbot responds with a reply that combines (or *concatenates*) "I'm doing well" with your name, which it obtains from accessing the value stored in the variable *user_name*. Notice that the chatbot does not "learn" your name or know what a name is. It merely takes the sequences of letters you provided to the input prompt and then inserts that value into prefabricated responses. But in using the sequences of letter that make up your name in its responses, it might seem to you as if the chatbot "knows" you by name.

Even though the first example – the recipe for a making a cake – could be accurately characterized and described as an algorithm, it is not common to refer to recipes as "food algorithms" or to title cookbooks *Algorithms for the Kitchen* (Walmsley 2012, 42), and doing so is likely to be met with puzzled looks and bemusement. This is because the term *algorithm* (and the way it is currently utilized across disciplines) is a word that is typically restricted to computational operations. For this reason, the definition of algorithm is more properly stated like this: "An algorithm is any well-defined computational procedure that takes some value, or set of values, as input and produces some value, or set of values, as output. An algorithm is thus a sequence of computational steps that transform the input into the output" (Cormen et al. 2009, 5).

The important item here is the addition of the word *computation*, which means not only mathematical operations but also any process that can be modeled with mathematical logic. For this reason, an algorithm can be specified using standard human language (like the recipe for a cake), in the design of hardware (like a logic circuit), or, more often than not, in the coded instructions of a computer program.

Given this characterization, one might be tempted to conclude that every algorithm is AI and every AI is algorithmic. But this statement is only half right, and it is the second half that is accurate. To date, the vast majority of effort in the field has sought to implement AI through developing software instructions to be run on digital computers. This explains why AI has typically been located within the discipline of computer science. But the first half – i.e., every algorithm is AI – is incorrect or inaccurate. Many of the applications on our mobile devices and smartphones are algorithmic but not necessarily AI, like the calculator, clock, or voice recorder apps. Further complicating things is the *AI Effect* (see chapter 1), where algorithmic applications once considered AI eventually become "demoted" to just another computer application once they are widely adopted and no longer seen as cutting edge. In the 1960s, the chess app that is on your mobile phone would have been AI. Today it's just another boring computer application.

Technical Approaches and Efforts

In chapter 1, we began by pointing out the seemingly obvious fact that AI is a technology. But AI is not one technology, nor is it developed through a single method. Instead, it is an umbrella term for a range of approaches that attempt, in different ways, to replicate, simulate, or evoke intelligent behavior (or what looks like intelligent behavior) in computational mechanisms. And from the very beginning – already at the time of the Dartmouth Summer Research Project – AI development proceeded along two distinct and separate pathways. In this section, we will investigate the advantages and disadvantages of both methods by considering their histories, their successes and limitations, and the underlying assumptions about cognition and intelligence that each one operationalizes.

Symbol Manipulation

One of the earliest approaches to artificial intelligence starts from a simple but influential idea: intelligence is fundamentally about manipulating symbols – such as words, numbers, or other tokens – according to rules. When you perform a mathematical calculation, like 2 + 2 = 4, you are applying rules (in this case, addition) to abstract symbols (numbers).

This view was most clearly articulated by Allen Newell and Herbert Simon (1976), who argued that intelligence – human or artificial – can be explained in terms of what they called a "physical symbol system." In a well-known formulation, they argued that such a system "has the necessary and sufficient means for general intelligent action" (Newell and Simon 1976, 116). Put more plainly, this claim has two components. First, *necessary* means that any system we would recognize as genuinely intelligent must, at some level, be manipulating symbols. If something can think, reason, or solve problems, then symbol manipulation will show up when we analyze how it works. Second, *sufficient* means that any system capable of manipulating symbols in the right way – and at a large enough scale – can, in principle, be intelligent.

This way of thinking about thinking became known as the *Physical Symbol System Hypothesis (PSSH)*, and it leads to two important conclusions. First, natural human intelligence itself is understood as a form of symbol manipulation. In other words, we think and reason by manipulating symbols, and the words you are reading and processing right now are a good illustration of that insight. Second, and following from this, computers should be capable of intelligent behavior if they can be given the appropriate symbols and symbol-processing capabilities. As a result of this, early AI research focused on designing computational applications that could reason, plan, and solve problems by explicitly representing knowledge as symbols and operating on them through logical rules.

Historical Backstory

This way of thinking about thinking has deep philosophical roots. It is ultimately grounded in the logic of Aristotle, but finds significant traction during the modern era in the work of René Descartes (1596–1650), Thomas Hobbes (1588–1679), and Gottfried Wilhelm Leibniz (1646–1716). "Descartes," as Hubert and Stuart Dreyfus (1988, 17) explain, "had already assumed that all understanding consisted of forming and manipulating appropriate representations, that these representations could be analyzed into primitive elements (*naturas simplices*), and that all phenomena could be understood as complex combinations of these simple elements."

The English philosopher Thomas Hobbes took this one step further, arguing that all thinking could be entirely reduced to a process of calculation, or what he called *reckoning*:

> When a man [*sic*] *reasons*, he does nothing else but conceive a sum total from *addition* of parcels, or conceive a remainder from *subtraction* of one sum from another. . . . For REASON, in this sense, is nothing but *reckoning* (that is, adding and subtracting) of the consequences of general names agreed upon for the *marking* and *signifying* of our thoughts. (Hobbes 1994, 22–3)

But it is with Leibniz, the German philosopher and mathematician, that this *computational theory of mind* (as it is now called) reached its apex. Leibniz sought to devise not only a universal symbol system – the *characteristica universalis* – but also a method of logical reasoning or a *calculus ratiocinator* where all dispute and debate in human endeavor could be resolved through the simple act of calculation. Thus AI, which might seem to be a rather recent innovation in computer technology, actually has deep intellectual roots in modern European thought with the attempt to understand thinking as a formal, rule-governed process that can be captured, represented, and automated.

Cost/Benefit Analysis

Because this approach dominated early AI research from the late 1950s through the mid-1990s, it is often called "good old-fashioned AI" or GOFAI. In GOFAI systems, intelligence is modeled by writing explicit, step-by-step instructions that transform input into output. These rules can govern simple numerical tasks, such as calculating sales tax, or more complex activities like natural language processing, where programmers attempt to specify in advance how a system should respond to user input.

This approach has several important characteristics:

- *Scale and Complexity:* The capacity of these systems is often dependent on the number of lines of coded instructions. Thus, as tasks become more complex, the number of required rules increases dramatically. To approach the performance of contemporary machine translation systems, for example, a purely symbolic system would need hundreds of thousands or even millions of carefully crafted rules, making development slow and difficult to manage.
- *Intelligence:* The intelligence of these systems lies less in the machine than in the expertise of its developers. Programmers need to know everything about the task in advance and be able to describe solutions in a form that a computer can manipulate.
- *Debugging and Transparency:* If something goes wrong in a GOFAI application, the developer can always go back into the code, locate the error, and correct it by rewriting the relevant line or lines of code. This makes symbolic systems relatively transparent, predictable, and well suited to auditing and debugging.

Even though this approach is called "good old-fashioned," it remains valuable for many contemporary applications.

GOFAI excels in domains where tasks can be clearly specified and reduced to abstract reasoning, such as symbolic mathematics, formal logic, or certain areas of decision-making where accuracy, consistency, and transparency typically matter more than adaptability or learning from data. At the same time, however, GOFAI has significant limitations. Rule-based systems struggle to cope with the messiness of the real world, where situations are ambiguous, contexts shift, and exceptions are common. These challenges are especially pronounced in areas like perception, everyday language use, and social interaction.

Artificial Neural Networks (ANNs)

Artificial neural networks (ANNs) take a fundamentally different approach to AI. Instead of relying on explicit step-by-step instructions written by programmers, ANNs are designed to learn from patterns in data. At the core of an ANN are artificial neurons – simple computational units that receive inputs, combine them, and produce an output when a certain predefined threshold condition is met. These neurons, which can be described in computer code, are linked together so that the output of one provides the input for another. And each connection carries a weight, a numerical value that amplifies or diminishes the signal passing through it.

When data are fed through the network during a process called *training*, they generate patterns of activation across these interconnected neurons, ultimately producing an output, such as a prediction or classification. The system then compares this output to an expected correct answer and adjusts the connection weights to reduce error. This adjustment process, known as *backpropagation*, is repeated many times, allowing the network to gradually improve its performance. This capacity to modify internal connections in response to data is what we call *machine learning*. Unlike GOFAI systems, where intelligence is explicitly specified in advance through rules and procedures applied to symbolic data, ANNs develop their internal operations by adapting to examples.

Historical Backstory

Unlike symbolic AI, which emerged from philosophical and logical theories about reasoning, ANNs were inspired by observations of the physical structure and operation of the brain. Rather than asking how thinking appears to work at the level of rules and symbols, this approach asked how intelligence might arise from the interaction of simple biological components. This shift was shaped by three intersecting innovations from the mid-20th century.

1 *The Artificial Neuron:* In 1943, Warren McCulloch and Walter Pitts proposed that the activity of a biological neuron could be understood in logical and mathematical terms. In their landmark paper "A Logical Calculus of Ideas Immanent in Nervous Activity," they introduced a simplified mathematical model of a neuron as a threshold logic device. In this model, the neuron receives multiple inputs, each carrying a signal. These signals are summed (or added up), and if the total exceeds a predefined threshold (*T*), the neuron "fires." In other words, if the threshold condition is met, the neuron produces an output of 1; if not, the output is 0 (Figure 2.3). Despite its simplicity, this formalization captured an important idea: Complex behavior can emerge from networks of very simple units operating according to basic operations.

At the time that they conducted this research, McCulloch and Pitts were not thinking about computers in the modern sense. In 1943, electronic digital computers were still being developed in secret government laboratories and were largely inaccessible to

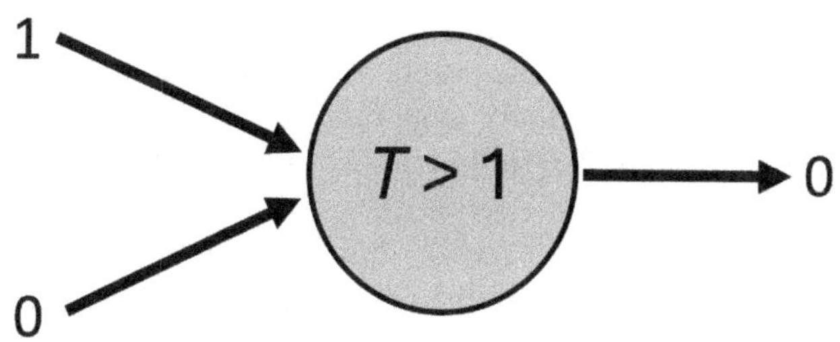

Figure 2.3 Graphical representation of the McCulloch–Pitts artificial neuron
Source: Image by David J. Gunkel

academic researchers. Their primary interest was theoretical and biological. They wanted to understand how real brains might perform simple logical operations and how this understanding could inform new approaches to psychology and psychiatry. Only later would their abstract neuron model become foundational for computational neural networks and machine learning.

2 Learning: In 1949, the Canadian psychologist Donald Hebb proposed an influential explanation for how networks of biological neurons learn. His insight, later known as Hebb's Rule, is often summarized by the phrase "cells that fire together wire together." Or as he described it: "When an axon of cell A is near enough to excite a cell B and repeatedly or persistently takes part in firing it, some growth process or metabolic change takes place in one or both cells such that A's efficiency, as one of the cells firing B, is increased" (Hebb 1949, 62).

This principle concerns two key ideas. First, the connection between two neurons becomes stronger when they repeatedly activate together. Second, this ability of connections to change over time provides a biological mechanism for learning and memory. For the artificial neuron, this insight led to an important modification of the McCulloch–Pitts model. Instead of treating all synaptic inputs equally, each connection was assigned a numerical weight or multiplier that could increase or decrease the strength of an incoming signal. By adjusting these weights over time, artificial neurons could change how they responded to inputs. In this way, learning could be modeled not by rewriting formal rules or instructions, but by gradually tuning the strength of connections within the network.

3 The Perceptron: These two innovations – the McCulloch–Pitts model of the artificial neuron and Hebb's account of learning – came together with the invention of the perceptron. This was the first computer-based implementation of an artificial neuron, developed by Frank Rosenblatt in 1958 at Cornell University. Designed for pattern recognition in images (hence the name, derived from the word *perception*), the perceptron combined threshold logic with adjustable weights, producing one of the earliest working machine learning systems. The perceptron can be diagrammed as in Figure 2.4 and explained in the following way.

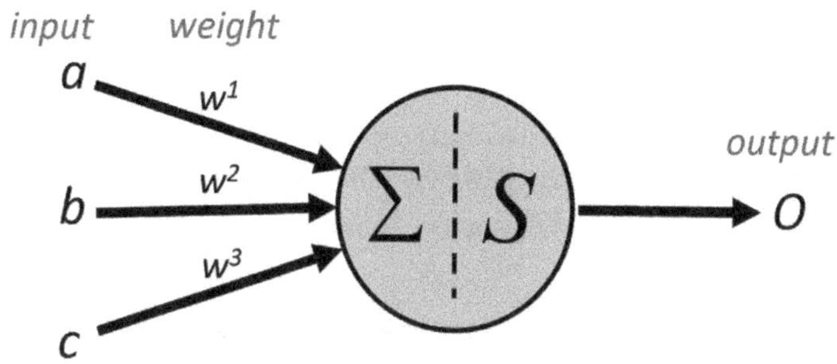

Figure 2.4 Diagram of the perceptron
Source: Image by David J. Gunkel

At one end of the system are the inputs (a, b, c), which are typically numerical values often normalized to fall between 0 and 1. Each input connection has an associated weight (w), also a numerical value. These weights modify the inputs by multiplying each input value by its corresponding weight. In effect, the weights determine how much influence each input has on the final outcome. The three input values (modified by the weights on the connections) are added together or summed up. This is indicated on the diagram by the Greek letter Σ, which is the standard mathematical notation for summation. This total is passed to an activation function, indicated by the letter S, which determines whether and how an output is produced. There are a number of different mathematically defined activation functions. The simplest is a step function (hence the S in the diagram), which produces an output of 1 if the input sum exceeds the threshold, and 0 if it does not. Rosenblatt's original perceptron used this step function. However, other non-linear activation functions – such as the sigmoid, hyperbolic tangent, or ReLU (Rectified Linear Unit) – can also be used and have become essential in the development of modern multi-layer neural networks.[1]

Finally, because the artificial neuron is a mathematical model, it can be implemented in computer code. Figure 2.5 shows what that would look like in pseudocode. For our purposes, it is not necessary to go through this line-by-line. What is important is the fact that the perceptron, which we diagrammed above, can also be described in computer code and therefore made operational on a digital computer.

```
Initialize weights to small random values
Set learning rate (e.g., 0.1)

For each epoch (number of training cycles):
 For each training example (input_vector, target_output):
  1. Compute weighted sum:
       sum = 0
       For each input:
          sum = sum + (input * corresponding weight)

  2. Apply activation function (step function):
    if sum > 0:
       output = 1
    else:
       output = 0

  3. Compute error:
       error = target_output - output

  4. Update weights:
    For each weight:
       Weight = weight + (learning_rate * error * corresponding input)
```

Figure 2.5 Perceptron in pseudocode
Source: Image by David J. Gunkel

Technical Set-Up and Operations

The perceptron is the most basic form of an ANN; essentially it is a single-layer network. On its own, however, such a simple network is extremely limited. To develop neural networks that are more powerful and capable, we can connect many of these individual neurons together into a larger structure. Figure 2.6 provides a graphical representation of a very simple ANN. In order to be made operational, a network like this must also be implemented as executable code that can be run on a computer. Thus the diagram illustrates the structure of the network, while the code specifies the details for how inputs, weights, and activation functions are calculated during operation.

A simple ANN like this takes in data at one end and produces a result at the other end. The layer that receives the incoming data is called the *input layer*, and the layer that produces the

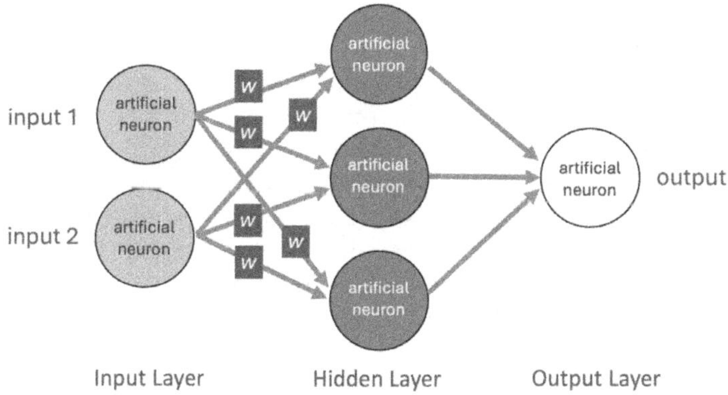

Figure 2.6 Graphical representation of an ANN with weighted connections (*w*) between layers of interacting neurons
Source: Image by David J. Gunkel

final output or decision is called the *output layer*. In between, there can be one or more *hidden layers*. They are called *hidden* because we do not see or have direct access to their activity. Each of these hidden layers may contain many neurons, with each connected to neurons in nearby layers. And these connections have adjustable weights (*w*), or what are also called *parameters*. Contemporary neural networks often contain dozens or even hundreds of hidden layers, with hundreds or thousands of neurons per layer, and a million or more adjustable parameters. As the numbers of layers, interconnected neurons, and parameters increase, the network becomes more complex and thereby capable of solving more difficult problems, ranging from image recognition to natural language processing.

This alternative methodology – something that is now routinely called *artificial neural networks* but which has also gone by other names, like *parallel distributed processing* or *connectionism* – provides for a distinctly different way of developing AI algorithms, one that operates on statistical principles instead of symbolic logic. "In this *connectionist* approach to AI," as Paul Smolensky (1990a, 306) explains, "intelligence is an *emergent* property of the network's processing; each individual processor [artificial neuron] has no intelligence, and the messages they exchange – real numbers – participate only in very simple numerical operations." Despite this simplicity at the level of the individual components, the approach works. Data propagated through the network produce a pattern of activations in the interconnected artificial neurons that eventually result in some output. And by progressively adjusting the weighted connections between the neurons in the network, the system can be adjusted or *tuned* to exhibit different kinds of output behavior. Consequently, the rules by which input is transformed into output are not specified as distinct and static logical steps applied to input data; instead the network evolves the transformation operations dynamically from exposure to data.

Cost/Benefit Analysis

ANNs excel at tasks that involve pattern recognition, where there are abundant data but there is no obvious way to describe the desired behavior in sequential instructions. Take facial recognition as an example. We are all quite capable of recognizing the faces of friends and family members. But can you specify in step-by-step instructions exactly how you manage this operation? It turns out that specifying the individual steps involved in performing the task of facial recognition is incredibly difficult, and, for this reason, efforts to write GOFAI facial recognition algorithms have generally resulted in disappointing failure. If, however, we set up a neural network and train it on billions of images of human faces, this will result in an algorithm that is as accurate as – or, in some cases, even more accurate than – human beings at performing facial recognition tasks.

This means that neural networks can solve problems where we have access to large amounts of data but lack clear instructions for how to transform input into output. Unlike symbolic systems, where the intelligence resides in the developer's knowledge and coding skill, the intelligence of an ANN emerges from the network itself as it adapts to data through training. Yet this beneficial capability also introduces new challenges, which we can group under two broad concerns: data quality and system transparency.

First, neural networks are only as good as the data they are trained on. Unlike humans, ANNs do not possess common sense, contextual awareness, or the ability to reason about fairness. They simply detect and reproduce patterns present in the training data. When those data reflect social biases, stereotypes, or other distortions, the network will often learn and reproduce them.

This is not a hypothetical problem but a well-documented reality. For instance, facial recognition systems have consistently shown higher error rates for people with darker skin tones, largely because the datasets used to train them contained disproportionately more images of lighter-skinned individuals.

Even when datasets are not overtly biased, the way they are collected, curated, and labeled can introduce subtle distortions. Decisions about which categories to include, how to balance the dataset, or what counts as a correct output may appear minor but can have far-reaching effects. For this reason, the quality and integrity of training data remain one of the most critical – and most difficult – challenges in developing and deploying ANN AI.

A second major challenge is that the behavior of a neural network is an emergent property of its training, which means its internal operations are often opaque, even to its developers. Unlike traditional GOFAI algorithms, where explicit rules and instructions can be inspected and debugged, ANNs operate as vast webs of weighted connections that are adjusted through training. Once a network is trained, there is no simple set of *if/then* statements to examine, as the reasoning behind a specific decision is encoded across millions – or even billions – of adjustable parameters. This *black box problem*, as it is called, makes it extremely difficult to determine why a particular output was generated or how to correct a problematic behavior once it emerges.

This opacity has serious implications for both reliability and accountability. Problems may not surface until after deployment, often in high-stakes environments such as healthcare, law enforcement, or finance, where errors can have significant consequences. And when these mistakes occur – whether a medical misdiagnosis, an unfair loan rejection, or a wrongful identification by facial recognition – tracing the cause is rarely straightforward. Developers and the companies they work for can legitimately claim that they did not program the harmful outcome, as the system's behavior results from the statistical patterns learned during training and not from explicit coded instructions.

Thore Graepel, one of the engineers behind DeepMind's AlphaGo, captured this challenge when reflecting on that system's surprising abilities with the board game Go: "Although we have programmed this machine to play, we have no idea what moves it will come up with. Its moves are an emergent phenomenon from the training. We just create the data sets and the training algorithms. But the moves it then comes up with are out of our hands" (Metz 2016). This unpredictability – where the machine seems to have a mind of its own – raises critical questions about responsibility: Who is accountable when an algorithm makes a harmful or unethical decision? The designer? The user? Or is the system itself to blame? These questions complicate efforts to regulate and govern contemporary AI systems.

Machine Learning

In describing the technical operations of the artificial neuron and ANNs, we have repeatedly used the phrase *machine learning*. This term was first introduced in 1959 by computer scientist Arthur Samuel, who developed one of the earliest self-improving computer programs: a checkers-playing system that refined its strategy by playing games against itself and adjusting its evaluation rules over time. Samuel's program did not use artificial neural networks. Instead, it relied on symbolic methods and heuristic search. But it embodied the central idea of machine learning: that is, an application that can improve performance through its operations rather than relying solely on static, coded instructions.

Over time, the phrase *machine learning* became closely associated with ANN architectures, particularly as these models demonstrated remarkable success on large-scale problems. Today, the most influential variety of machine learning is *deep learning*, which employs multi-layered ANNs, also called *deep neural networks*, to analyze massive datasets and detect complex patterns. Importantly, contemporary deep neural networks are not trained in a single, uniform way. Machine learning is an umbrella term that encompasses several distinct approaches, each based on different assumptions about the nature of data, the type of feedback available, and the goals of the process. Broadly speaking, these approaches fall into three main categories:

1 *Supervised Learning:* This form of machine learning is called supervised because the model is trained on examples where the correct answers are already provided. A common illustration is image classification. Suppose we have thousands of images of

household pets, each one labeled as *cat* or *dog*. The model learns to associate certain visual patterns – such as the shape of ears or the texture of fur – with the correct label. During training, the ANN compares its predictions to the known labels, calculates the error (e.g., predicting *dog* when the image is labeled *cat*), and then adjusts its internal parameters through the process of backpropagation. By repeating this cycle hundreds of thousands – or even millions – of times, the network gradually improves its performance. Supervised learning is well suited for tasks that involve either regression (predicting a continuous variable, such as housing prices in a competitive real estate market) or classification (categorizing inputs into discrete classes, such as differentiating animals or labeling emails as spam or not spam). Its effectiveness, however, is heavily dependent on the quality and quantity of labeled data available for training.

2 *Unsupervised Learning:* In unsupervised learning, there are no pre-defined outputs to guide the process – only large sets of input data. The goal here is to uncover patterns, structures, or clusters that exist in the data. As Ethem Alpaydin (2016, 111) explains in his book on the subject: "There is a structure to the input space such that certain patterns occur more often than others, and we want to see what generally happens and what does not." A familiar example is how photo apps automatically organize your pictures into groups, such as vacation, concert, or family. The algorithm is not told what these categories should be. Instead, it clusters images based on similarities – such as color patterns, shapes, or the frequency of certain features – without any human-provided labels. The same principle underlies the recommendation engines of streaming services. By grouping users with similar listening or viewing habits, unsupervised learning enables platforms to suggest new songs, movies, or television shows that align with a user's past behavior. This type of learning is particularly useful for clustering tasks (grouping similar data points) or anomaly detection (spotting unusual patterns, like fraudulent transactions on your credit card). By uncovering hidden structures in data, unsupervised learning provides powerful insights where labeled examples are unavailable.

3 *Reinforcement Learning:* This approach, first demonstrated in Samuel's pioneering checkers program,[2] is inspired

by trial-and-error learning. Unlike supervised or unsupervised learning, there is no fixed training dataset. Instead, the algorithm interacts with an environment: it takes actions, observes the results, and receives feedback in the form of rewards or penalties. Over time, it learns to maximize its cumulative reward by favoring actions that produce better outcomes. As Alpaydin (2016, 128) puts it, the system "tries out actions in the environment and receives feedback (or not) in the form of a reward. It then uses this feedback to update its knowledge so that in time it learns to do actions that return the highest reward." Reinforcement learning has proven particularly effective in gaming contexts, where algorithms have mastered Atari's *Breakout* and other video games by playing millions of rounds against themselves and adjusting their strategies based on the rewards achieved (Mnih et al. 2015).

Finally, it is important to note that these three approaches to machine learning are not mutually exclusive. Many AI systems are hybrids that combine multiple methods to achieve better results. A well-known example is DeepMind's championship-winning Go-playing algorithm, AlphaGo. The system was first trained on a large dataset of expert human games, using supervised learning to imitate professional strategies, and then refined its operations through reinforcement learning by playing millions of games against itself.

GOFAI versus ANN

Historically, both methods for developing AI applications and algorithms have been in play. But, at different times in this history, one method seems to have had the upper hand over the other. Symbol manipulation got the nickname GOFAI, which was bestowed upon it by the American philosopher Paul Haugeland (1985, 112), because it had been the favored method – virtually the only method – for over two decades. This was due both to technological limitations with computing power and to political infighting among early AI scientists competing for lucrative research funding.[3]

Since the turn of the millennium, however, the pendulum has swung in the other direction. Machine learning with deep neural networks – marginalized for much of the early history of AI – has risen to prominence. Three developments explain this shift. First, exponential increases in computing power, often tracked by Moore's Law,[4] made it possible to set up and train large networks efficiently. Second, the explosion of digital data, especially through the internet, created vast training resources that neural networks could use to improve their performance. And, third, the revival of this approach had a key research catalyst with the 1986 publication of *Parallel Distributed Processing* by David E. Rumelhart, James L. McClelland, and the PDP Research Group (McClelland et al. 1986; Rumelhart et al. 1986). Widely dubbed the "Connectionist Bible," this two-volume set argued that cognition could be better explained through networks of simple units rather than symbolic rules. Combined with advances in compute resources and digitized data, this helped set the stage for the deep learning breakthroughs of the 2000s.

Despite these ups and downs, the two approaches are not mutually exclusive. Each has its own distinct strengths and weaknesses, which often balance the limitations of the other. To illustrate, Jerry Kaplan offers a useful thought experiment:

> Suppose you want to build a robot that can ride a bike (that is, one that can control the pedals and handlebars, and is able to balance). Representing the problem in symbolic terms may be possible, but imagine trying to interview a human expert in an effort to build an expert system [a kind of GOFAI algorithm] to do this. (Kaplan 2016, 36)

This is a task that would be better suited to machine learning and most likely reinforcement learning through trial and error. But this does not mean that machine learning works in all situations and circumstances. "There are," Kaplan (2016, 37) continues, "other issues for which machine learning techniques aren't well suited. To state the obvious, machine learning is not useful for problems where there's no data, just some initial conditions, a bunch of constraints, and one shot to get it right." In these situations, GOFAI has the upper hand, because it works at a higher level of abstraction, where the problem and the steps necessary to solve it can be described in logical procedures.

A Pair of Terminological Pairs

In the science and engineering of AI, there are two pairs of terms that are often confused with one another, even though they are intended to address and explain different conceptual differences. The first pair consists of *artificial general intelligence (AGI)* versus *narrow AI*; the second involves *strong AI* versus *weak AI*. We will, therefore, conclude this chapter on basic concepts and terminology by getting a handle on and sorting out what makes these two conceptual pairings different and why they have often been confused with each other.

AGI versus Narrow AI

From at least the time of the Dartmouth Summer Research Project, the apex of AI has been the creation of machine intelligence that is on par with, if not eventually better than, human intelligence. This kind of wide-ranging or general cognitive capability is something that is imaginatively portrayed in science fiction, whether it is the HAL 9000 computer of Stanley Kubrick's *2001: A Space Odyssey*, the Samantha operating system in *Her*, or Ava from *Ex Machina*. This vision of AI is now called *artificial general intelligence* or AGI.

Although the phrase was first utilized by Mark Gubrud in 1997, its current formulation comes from a 2007 book titled *Artificial General Intelligence*, edited by Ben Goertzel and Cassio Pennachin. In the preface to this book, the editors differentiate between two different kinds of effort in AI engineering: AGI and narrow AI. "What is meant by AGI is, loosely speaking, AI systems that possess a reasonable degree of self-understanding and autonomous self-control, and have the ability to solve a variety of complex problems in a variety of contexts, and to learn to solve new problems that they didn't know about at the time of their creation." This objective is distinguished from more pragmatic efforts to engineer specific problem-solving applications: "Pragmatic but specialized 'narrow AI' research," they continue, "is aimed at creating programs carrying out specific tasks like playing chess, diagnosing diseases, driving cars and so forth" (Goertzel and Pennachin 2007, vi).

At present, AGI is still hypothetical, and its feasibility is open to debate and significant disagreement. Although there has been some effort to produce a broadly intelligent and conscious machine, achievement of AGI is still something that remains an uncertain future possibility. Narrow AI, however, is a reality. We do have applications that are able to carry out specific tasks, like translating between different human languages, engaging in conversational exchange with human users, generating original stories for publication, or playing championship-level chess and Go. To put it another way: AGI is still science fiction, while narrow AI is already science fact.

Strong versus Weak AI

Unlike the AGI versus narrow AI distinction, which concerns engineering practice, the terms *strong AI* and *weak AI* describe two different philosophical hypotheses about the scientific implications of artificial intelligence. The distinction originates with philosopher John Searle, who introduced it in connection with his Chinese Room thought experiment (see chapter 1). "According to *weak AI*," as Searle (1980, 417) explains, "the principal value of the computer in the study of the mind is that it gives us a very powerful tool. For example, it enables us to formulate and test hypotheses in a more rigorous and precise fashion." From this vantage point, computers are valuable for simulating cognitive processes, making them useful tools for research in cognitive science and related fields.

Strong AI goes further. Here, as Searle (1980, 417) puts it, "the computer is not merely a tool in the study of the mind; rather, the appropriately programmed computer really is a mind, in the sense that computers given the right programs can be literally said to understand and have other cognitive states." On this interpretation, AI is not just a simulation of thought but an actual, conscious mind instantiated in a different substrate, that is, in silicon rather than carbon.

For this reason, strong AI is often equated with AGI, while weak AI is commonly associated with narrow AI. But the match is not exact, and examples help clarify the difference. Consider OpenAI, the company that built ChatGPT, which describes its mission as ensuring that "artificial general intelligence (AGI) – by which we mean highly autonomous systems that outperform humans at most economically valuable work – benefits all of humanity" (OpenAI 2025). If such AGI is ever achieved, the question will remain whether it is strong or weak in Searle's sense. If the system genuinely possesses consciousness and mental states, it would qualify as strong AI. If it merely reproduces human-like cognition across many domains – as ChatGPT appears to do now – it would remain weak AI.

The same holds for narrow AI or smart devices and applications. Consider Suno, a web-based AI music generator that allows users to create songs from a text prompt. Is the music generated by the Suno algorithm just a clever approximation of human ingenuity, producing pop tunes that mechanically mimic or emulate human artistry? Or does Suno's music open the opportunity for us to re-evaluate and revise what is meant by creativity, such that the AI could be called creative in its own right? If the former, then Suno is weak AI; if the latter, it edges toward strong AI. The difficulty, of course, is telling the difference. A sufficiently sophisticated simulation may be indistinguishable from the real thing. And this returns us once again to the philosophical problem of other minds and the challenge posed by the Chinese Room thought experiment.

Summary

We began this chapter with a metaphor: AI as a foreign country – unfamiliar, complex, and easy to get lost in without a guide. By working through its key terms and foundational concepts, we have started to acquire the vocabulary and orientation needed to navigate this terrain with greater confidence and clarity. In other words, we've begun to pick up the local language – terms like *algorithm*, *neural network*, *supervised learning* – and have started to recognize the landmark developments and historically important features. We are no longer outsiders. We've started to become conversant in and are beginning to understand AI.

Along the way, we have learned what an algorithm is and how symbolic systems (aka GOFAI) model cognition with step-by-step instructions, while artificial neural networks or ANNs generate emergent behaviors by adapting to patterns discoverable in data. We have seen that machine learning is not one method but an ensemble of approaches, each with its own strengths and weaknesses. And we have encountered the deeper philosophical questions these innovations provoke: Are we modeling human thought? Replacing it? Simulating it? Or reinventing it entirely?

We've also seen how the shift from programming intelligence explicitly to training on massive datasets opens up novel possibilities while also introducing profound challenges. Contemporary AI systems built on ANN architectures can recognize faces, generate language, and simulate creativity across many domains, but their inner workings often remain opaque, even to their creators. This is not just an engineering problem; it is also a cultural and ethical one. AI is not merely a technical artifact; it is also a social actor and philosophical provocation. Responding to it requires not only engineering expertise but also informed critical inquiry, ethical reflection, and collective decision-making. In other words, you do not need to be a computer engineer or data scientist to be AI literate and to engage in these epoch-defining conversations and debates, but you do need to understand how these systems work, what assumptions they operationalize, and how they influence and shape the world around us.

And that brings us to the next step in our journey. If intelligence is being increasingly mediated or even taken over by machines, then language – arguably our most human faculty – is at the very center of this transformation. Today's AI does not just compute. It talks, writes, translates, and persuades. So what happens, then, when the tool begins to speak and write? This is not just a technological evolution; it is a philosophical rupture. When algorithms generate language that feels indistinguishable from our own, what kind of thinking – if any – does that entail? And who – or what – is really speaking? To answer these questions, we turn next to the field of natural language processing (NLP) – the area of AI research and development dedicated to enabling computers to process, analyze, and generate human language.

Learning Activities

1 Writing an Algorithm

Purpose: This activity helps you understand what an algorithm is by translating an everyday activity into a step-by-step computational procedure. It reinforces the idea that algorithms are not mysterious or uniquely AI, but structured ways to transform input into output.

Procedure: Choose a simple everyday task, such as making coffee, doing laundry, finding a classroom on campus, or deciding what to eat for lunch. Write a step-by-step list of instructions for completing the task. Then rewrite the same instructions in pseudocode, using simple elements such as: INPUT, IF/THEN, OUTPUT. (If you encounter trouble writing the pseudocode yourself, you could prompt an LLM to transform your instructions into code.) Compare your pseudocode with a classmate's and try to identify what assumptions each of you made about the task to be accomplished, the procedural steps, and the environment in which the algorithm operates.

Learning Goal: Learn to recognize algorithms as formalized procedures, experience the different ways that human decision-making and action can (or maybe cannot) be translated into explicit instructions, and identify both the opportunities and challenges of turning real-world tasks into rule-based coded instructions.

2 *Machine Learning: Opportunities and Challenges*

Purpose: This activity encourages you to think critically about the social and ethical consequences of machine learning systems whose internal decision-making processes are not specified in coded step-by-step instructions but derived from patterns discoverable in existing data.

Procedure: Consider the following scenario and then respond to the questions that follow:

> A large company adopts an AI system to help screen job applications for entry-level positions. The system is based on a deep neural network trained on thousands of past hiring decisions and employee performance records. According to the company, the system increases efficiency by quickly filtering applications and improves hiring outcomes by identifying candidates who are most likely to succeed in the role. After several months of use, however, some applicants begin

to question the fairness of the system. Qualified candidates report being rejected without explanation, and internal audits reveal that applicants from certain demographic backgrounds are being disproportionately screened out. When managers ask how the system made its decisions, the vendor explains that the model's outputs emerge from complex patterns learned during training and cannot be traced back to simple rules or criteria. The vendor emphasizes that the system is statistically more accurate than the previous, rule-based screening process.

Answer and discuss the following questions:

- What is the cause of the bias or unfairness that is exhibited by this hiring algorithm?
- Who should be held responsible for the unjust or biased outcomes that it produces: the AI developers, the HR department, company leadership, or the system itself?
- How does the opacity of the system affect the ability of rejected applicants or the organization itself to challenge or contest hiring decisions?

Learning Goal: Understand how the technical features of machine learning systems – especially the configuration of the ANN and its dependence on training data – create challenges for accountability, trust, and governance in real-world decision-making contexts.

3 Where is the Intelligence?

Purpose: This activity asks you to compare symbolic (GOFAI) and machine learning (ANN-based) approaches to AI by examining where exactly the intelligence of these systems resides.

Procedure: Consider the following scenario and then respond to the questions that follow.

Imagine two customer service chatbots used by the same organization.

Chatbot A is built using a symbolic, rule-based (GOFAI) approach. Developers carefully write thousands of *if/then* instructions that specify how the chatbot should respond to particular keywords, phrases, and situations. When the chatbot gives a helpful response, it is because the relevant rule was correctly anticipated and written in advance.

Chatbot B is built using a machine learning approach based on ANN architecture. Instead of executing explicit *if/then* rules, it is trained on millions of past customer service conversations. Over time, it learns statistical patterns from the data and produces responses that were not explicitly programmed by developers.

Discuss the following questions:

- In each case, where does the "intelligence" of the chatbot seem to be located: primarily in the developers, in the code, in the data, or in the system itself?
- How does this difference affect how we think about learning, improvement, and creativity in each system?
- If one of these chatbots gives a surprisingly clever or inappropriate response, how would you explain what happened?
- Does one approach make it easier to say that the chatbot itself is intelligent? Why or why not?

Learning Goal: Compare and contrast GOFAI and machine learning systems by explaining how different technical architectures locate intelligence differently and why this matters for interpreting AI behavior, responsibility, and agency.

Further Reading

Hubert L. Dreyfus and Stuart E. Dreyfus (with Tom Athanasiou), *Mind over Machine: The Power of Human Intuition and Experience in the Era of the Computer* (1986).

This book presents a powerful critique of symbolic, rule-based AI by drawing on studies of human expertise. The Dreyfus brothers argue that true intelligence and skill depend on intuition, embodiment, and context – qualities that cannot be reduced to explicit rules or formal symbol manipulation. Their work became a central challenge to GOFAI and anticipated later interest in embodied and situated approaches to AI.

Allen Newell and Herbert A. Simon, "Computer Science as Empirical Inquiry: Symbols and Search" (1976).

In this influential article, Newell and Simon proposed the *Physical Symbol System Hypothesis* – the claim that any system capable of intelligent action must be a symbol-manipulating system. This became the definitive characterization of symbolic AI (or GOFAI), grounding decades of research in rule-based reasoning, problem-solving, and search strategies.

Paul Smolensky, "On the Proper Treatment of Connectionism" (1990b).

Smolensky defends neural networks as a serious alternative to symbolic AI, arguing that intelligence can emerge from distributed patterns of activation rather than explicit rules. The paper helped legitimize connectionism within cognitive science and showed how it could complement, rather than simply replace, symbolic approaches.

Fiction, Film, and Video

Greg Kohs (dir.), *AlphaGo* (2017).

This documentary illustrates how a machine-learning algorithm accomplished what had long been considered impossible: defeating a world-champion human player at the ancient and highly complex game of Go. The film shows that AlphaGo's success did not come from hand-coded strategies but from learning through vast amounts of data (supervised learning) and self-play (reinforcement learning). In doing so, AlphaGo came up with moves that surprised not only professional Go players but even its own developers, revealing how intelligence in machine learning systems can emerge in ways that exceed human expectations and oversight.

Stanley Kubrick (dir.), *2001: A Space Odyssey* (1968).

Kubrick's science fiction masterpiece features the HAL 9000 computer, one of the most iconic portrayals of AGI. HAL's calm voice and apparent rationality make its eventual breakdown all that more disturbing, dramatizing the risks of machine autonomy, error, and conflict with human control. The film remains a cultural touchstone for thinking about trust, responsibility, and the boundaries of human–machine collaboration.

3

Natural Language Processing

Learning Outcomes

- Explain how natural language processing (NLP) enables machines to analyze, interpret, and generate human language, and why language has long functioned as a litmus test for intelligence and social presence.
- Compare major NLP applications – such as machine translation, chatbots, digital voice assistants, and social robots – by identifying the design strategies they employ and the social roles they perform.
- Analyze how NLP systems can produce language that appears meaningful without understanding, and assess how this affects communication, trust, and social interaction.
- Critically evaluate the social and ethical implications of NLP technologies, including anthropomorphism, identity representation, deception, and the ways these systems reshape human expectations of communication and social participation.

Introduction

One of the most compelling ambitions of artificial intelligence has been to make machines capable of understanding and producing natural language. This capacity appeared as the first of four objectives listed in the proposal for the Dartmouth Summer Research Project. It shaped the configuration of Alan Turing's imitation game. And it has long animated science fiction portrayals of AI, from the emotionless HAL 9000 in *2001: A Space Odyssey* to the multilingual protocol droid C-3PO in *Star Wars* to the expressive Samantha operating system in *Her*. From these ambitions to contemporary AI systems and applications, the ability to speak and to be spoken to has remained not just one feature among many; it is the litmus test for intelligence and social presence.

This chapter examines natural language processing (NLP), the branch of AI concerned with enabling computers to analyze, interpret, and generate human language. We approach this subject in two stages. The first surveys key NLP applications – from machine translation and chatbots to digital assistants and social robots – to explore both the technical strategies and the practical challenges of making machines speak our language. Along the way, we consider how these systems balance linguistic accuracy, computational efficiency, and the constraints of real-world use.

The second stage turns to the communicative and social consequences of these innovations. What happens when a system that does not understand language nonetheless produces responses we take to be meaningful? How do such systems alter interpersonal interaction, shape our sense of social presence, and influence the experience of trust? Drawing on insights from communication theory, the social sciences, and human–computer interaction, we assess both the opportunities and the challenges of NLP, from efficiencies in translation and customer service encounters, to the ways it can sustain small talk and social ritual, to the dangers of anthropomorphism and deception. By moving between the technical and the social, the chapter not only explains how NLP works but also provides a critical framework for thinking about what it now means to live alongside and interact with machines that talk.

Techniques and Applications

As NLP capabilities have matured, they have moved from experimental prototypes to common, everyday applications. Today, NLP applications not only process language but also participate in interactions that feel recognizably social, whether translating between languages, answering questions through a chatbot, providing voice-based assistance, or animating an embodied robot. These technologies demonstrate both the remarkable potential for and the seemingly persistent limitations of computational approaches to language.

This section examines four key NLP implementations: machine translation, text-based conversational agents, spoken dialogue systems, and social robots. Each one provides a point of entry for examining the different ways these systems have been designed, what technical challenges they have encountered, and how their performance is shaped by both technical exigencies and the social environments in which they operate. By analyzing these four NLP applications, we can better understand the underlying technical methods and system architectures that enable language processing; the trade-offs between accuracy, efficiency, and usability; and the way that design choices influence not only functionality but also the communicative presence and potential these systems operationalize.

Machine Translation

The idea of applying digital computers to the task of translation can be traced back to Warren Weaver shortly after the end of World War II. Having worked with computers for wartime cryptography and code-breaking, Weaver thought that the same computational techniques might be adapted to translating between human languages,[1] and in 1949, he circulated a short but influential memorandum proposing the idea. Weaver's memo proved to be catalytic. His ambitious proposal, combined with access to substantial US federal funding, sparked the first major wave of research in AI, initiating a sustained effort that would evolve through multiple technical phases over the decades that followed.

These initiatives positioned *machine translation* (MT) as an early test case for AI. The challenge was not only technical – i.e., how to represent grammar, semantics, and context in a form that a machine could manipulate – but also cultural and geopolitical, promising tools for international communication at a moment shaped by Cold War imperatives. Consequently, the history of machine translation not only illustrates the shifting paradigms of NLP methodologies – from early rule-based approaches grounded in linguistics, through statistical methods exploiting bilingual corpora, to contemporary models built on machine learning – but also demonstrates how technical innovations in AI have been inseparable from questions of language, meaning, and power.

MT Techniques and Technology

1 Classical MT: The earliest efforts in MT relied on symbolic reasoning or GOFAI methods to directly convert text from one language into another using rule-based instructions. A simple Polish-to-English system, for example, might include rules such as: IF "Dzień dobry" RETURN "Good morning." These systems functioned much like bilingual dictionaries or phrase books, using explicit mappings between language pairs at the individual word or phrase level. While relatively straightforward and effective for limited tasks, this method depends entirely on manually coded transformation rules tailored to specific language pairs.

For this reason, rule-based approaches scale poorly. For every pair of languages in a multilingual system, a distinct translation model must be constructed. And the number of required models grows rapidly as expressed by the formula $n(n - 1)$, where n is the number of languages. Thus, a system handling two languages (like English and Polish) would need 2(2 – 1) or 2 models – one model to translate English into Polish and another model to translate Polish into English. If translating between three languages, you would need 3(3 – 1) or six models. And in the case of nine languages, you would need 9(9 – 1) or 72 models. As a result, classical MT becomes increasingly unwieldy and resource intensive as more languages are added, limiting its practicality in globally diverse applications.

To address these limitations, researchers explored the idea of using an *interlingua*: an intermediate language into which all source languages could be translated and from which all target languages could be generated. Whereas a direct translation system required $n(n - 1)$ separate translation models, the use of an interlingua reduced the burden to just $2n$: that is, one to transform each source language into the interlingua, and one to transfer out of it into the target language. Thus, a system covering nine languages, for example, could be managed with only 18 translation models instead of the 72 required by direct transfer approaches.

Interlinguas could take the form of a natural language, like English, or an artificial language designed for this purpose, such as Esperanto. But the choice of interlingua was not neutral. By funneling all expression through one central idiom, these systems inevitably privileged the grammatical structures, conceptual categories, and cultural assumptions and biases encoded in that particular language. Even an ostensibly universal artificial language, like Esperanto, carried the imprint of its European heritage in its grammar and vocabulary, giving some users an advantage (or even just the perception of an advantage) over others. As a result, while interlingua systems offered practical solutions to the scaling problem, they also raised important questions about linguistic equity and cultural power. It was precisely these difficulties that set the stage for the next major methodological breakthrough.

2 Example-Based MT (EBMT): In the early 1980s, the Japanese computer scientist Makoto Nagao observed that classical or rule-based MT systems, which worked reasonably well for European languages, struggled with structurally divergent language pairs such as English and Japanese. To address this, he proposed a new approach to MT modeled on how human translators actually perform their work: that is, not by applying formal rules but by recalling and adapting previous examples. Example-based MT (EBMT) systems operationalize this insight by identifying aligned text fragments in a set of bilingual documents or *parallel corpora*,[2] extracting the relevant translation pairs, and then recombining these segments to produce coherent output in the target language.

In his introductory book *Machine Translation*, Thierry Poibeau (2017, 112) provides the following illustration: "Let's imagine that we ask the system to translate 'Training is not the solution to every problem' into French and that a bilingual corpus is available with, among others, the following pairs of sentences [see Table 3.1]." The translation system performs a simple text search, trying to match segments from the input text – "Training is not the solution to every problem" – to what is available in the bilingual corpus. In the process, the search identifies two matches for the phrase "Training is not the solution . . .," which is associated with the French phrase "La formation n'est pas la solution . . .," and two matches for the phrase ". . . to every problem," which is aligned with the French ". . . à tous les problèmes." By extracting and combining these two fragments – "La formation n'est pas la solution" + "à tous les problèmes" – the system can then produce a translation of the English source text.

Importantly, the computer does not need to understand the meaning of the words or the phrases that are being searched, matched, and combined. From its perspective (assuming that it has a perspective), "Training is not" is a string of searchable text characters, no different from other strings of characters like "gQx$_&2NmK." The computer, like the person in Searle's Chinese Room, is just searching for and matching character patterns. Meaning takes place in us, when the output is displayed to the human user, who is able to read and interpret its significance.

EBMT gained momentum during the 1980s, particularly for translation applications involving Asian languages, where syntactic and lexical alignment is more complex. Its success, however, depended heavily on the availability of large, well-aligned parallel corpora – ideally at the sentence level. While

Table 3.1 Segment of an English/French bilingual corpus

	ENGLISH	FRENCH
Ex. 1	Training is not the solution to everything	La formation n'est pas la solution universelle
Ex. 2	Training is not the solution to all parenting struggles	La formation n'est pas la solution à toutes les difficultés rencontrées par les parents
Ex. 3	There is a solution to every problem	Il y a une solution à tous les problèmes
Ex. 4	There is a spiritual solution to every problem	Il y a une solution spirituelle à tous les problèmes

such resources expanded with the digitization of documents and the rise of the internet, there were still many language pairs that were not well represented. In the absence of suitable examples, these EBMT systems either faltered or reverted to direct word-for-word substitution, diminishing translation quality. These limitations eventually led to the rise of statistical MT, which integrated and extended many of EBMT's core insights.

3 Statistical MT: SMT emerged from the insight that human language is inherently probabilistic. In any language, some sequences of words are far more likely to occur than others. For example, "This book is written in the English language" is much more probable than "Book language the is English this in written." SMT systems take advantage of this fact by analyzing very large bilingual corpora and building models that estimate the likelihood of different translations.

The key innovation of SMT was to treat translation not as a matter of applying fixed grammatical rules but as a statistical optimization problem. Using parallel corpora, or aligned bilingual texts, SMT systems construct two kinds of models:

- *Language models* that rank possible word sequences in the target language according to how often they occur in real usage. This ensures that the output "sounds good."
- *Translation models* that map fragments from the source language to the target language, assigning probabilities based on how frequently those word or phrase alignments appear in previous human-produced translations.

When combined, these models allow the system to evaluate thousands of possible outputs and select the one with the highest overall probability of both sounding fluent in the target language and being faithful to the original source. The approach was first formalized by IBM researchers in the 1990s with what became the IBM Alignment Models (Brown et al. 1993) and was popularized in commercial systems like Google Translate in the 2010s.

The strength of SMT lay in its ability to merge the fragment-based approach of EBMT with the precision of the earlier rule-based systems. Thus, it leveraged real-world translation examples while preserving fine-grained, word-level correspondences. But it also had several important limitations. First, it required massive, high-quality bilingual corpora (which exist for some language pairs, like English and French, but not others, like Icelandic and Cambodian). Second, these systems were labor-intensive to build and to maintain. Finally, SMT often struggled with long-range dependencies and context, often producing translations that were statistically plausible but sometimes awkward or misleading. These shortcomings eventually paved the way for neural MT, which could better model whole sentences and capture contextual nuance.

4 Neural MT: NMT represents a significant shift, driven by advances in machine learning and neural network architectures. The approach was first formalized in 2014 with the introduction of the RNN encoder–decoder model, which uses two recurrent neural networks (RNNs) in a sequence-to-sequence (Seq2Seq) configuration (Cho et al. 2014). The first RNN – the encoder – processes an input sentence word-by-word, generating a numerical representation (a fixed-length vector) that captures the overall structure and context of the source language. The second RNN – the decoder – takes this representation and generates a new sentence in the target language guided by statistical associations it has learned from large bilingual datasets. In other words, the encoder compresses the meaning of the input, and the decoder expands that meaning into another language. This allows NMT to treat whole sentences as units of translation, preserving grammar and nuance more effectively than earlier methods (Figure 3.1).

The advantages of NMT are considerable. It delivers more accurate and fluid translations, capturing complex patterns across languages without relying on explicit rules. Because it learns directly from data rather than from human-coded features,

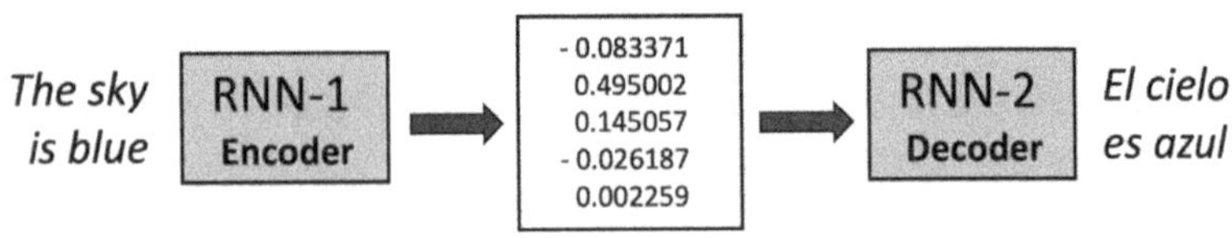

Figure 3.1 Schematic diagram of sequence-to-sequence RNN for machine translation
Source: Image by David J. Gunkel

it is also more scalable and cost-effective to develop. Yet these benefits come with challenges. NMT depends on massive datasets scraped from the internet, which means it can reproduce and even amplify existing linguistic and cultural biases. Its internal operations remain largely opaque, functioning as a *black box* that resists interpretation, auditing, or debugging. And the high computational demands of training and running these systems raise concerns about sustainability, as the energy required for processing contributes to environmental costs. These limitations prompted researchers to look for alternative approaches – most notably attention mechanisms and transformer architectures – that would become the foundation of today's large language models (we will get into this in chapter 4).

MT Opportunities and Challenges

With all this progress, it is tempting to see current MT applications as a technological fix for the damage inflicted upon humanity at the mythical Tower of Babel – something like a digital Pentecost where everyone can understand everyone else in their own native tongue.[3] In one sense, this vision has in fact come true: smartphone apps can now instantaneously translate street signs or menus for travelers visiting foreign lands; built-in features on social media platforms like Facebook, Instagram, and LinkedIn automatically render posts and comments into a user's preferred language, enabling interaction across linguistic boundaries in global networks; and real-time closed captioning and translation on platforms like Microsoft Teams and Zoom make meetings and events accessible to multilingual participants.

These remarkable innovations, however, naturally raise an important question, especially for students, educators, and educational institutions: Has MT now made language learning and the foreign language requirement obsolete? The answer to this question depends on how we understand language and linguistic difference. If language is regarded as little more than a tool or instrument for interpersonal communication, and linguistic diversity is thereby seen as an obstacle to understanding and cooperation, then MT appears to deliver on what Weaver in 1949 called the "world-wide translation problem." From this perspective, linguistic diversity – the fact that there are close to

7,000 different languages on planet earth – is an engineering challenge. And now, there's an app for that.

But language has always been more than a conduit for information transfer. It is also a carrier of culture, history, and unique ways of understanding the world. Far from being a hindrance, linguistic diversity can be a source of creativity and resilience, much like biodiversity in an ecosystem. Seen in this light, MT does not diminish or even eliminate the need for language learning so much as reframe it. Thus, the role of language education may no longer be to overcome linguistic difference by striving for universal understandablity, but rather to encounter difference directly – to appreciate, interpret, and learn from the plurality of ways that human beings make sense of themselves and their world. In this regard, MT may in fact give the foreign language requirement new purpose: not to overcome linguistic difference, but to encounter it, understand it, and draw from its diverse resources.

Chatbots

While MT systems and applications act as smart intermediaries – transforming one person's message into a different language so that it can be understood by another – chatbots disrupt this instrumentalist understanding entirely. In this case, we are not just talking *through* a machine to another person; we are talking *with* it. This shift – from *through* to *with* – marks an important difference (noted in chapter 1) between AI-MC and HMC. And in HMC, the AI is not merely an intelligent conduit situated between human users; it is a communicative participant in its own right.

The original idea for this kind of NLP application can be traced back to Alan Turing's imitation game and Joseph Weizenbaum's practical implementation of it with the ELIZA program (1966). ELIZA was a relatively simple GOFAI application. As Weizenbaum (1976, 188) explained in the book *Computer Power and Human Reason*, it operated through basic procedures for parsing sentences, identifying keywords, and assembling responses from pre-fabricated sentence fragments. Consequently, ELIZA did not have anything of its own to say. It was a kind of actress (a role reflected in the name, which had been taken from the protagonist of George Bernard Shaw's play *Pygmalion*) that followed pre-scripted responses supplied to it by its programmer.

If, for example, you input sentences with the form "You seem to be [*adjective*]" – where the value of [*adjective*] could be angry, unhappy, mean, thoughtful, and so on – the bot can be programmed to reply with a response that inserts the chosen adjective into a pre-scripted template. This produces outputs such as: "What makes you think I am [*adjective*]?" And by stringing together a number of responses like this, the resulting exchange, though often formulaic, could feel remarkably conversational. For this reason, many users became emotionally invested in these interactions, treating the ELIZA program as if it genuinely cared about or comprehended their statements, an outcome that Weizenbaum himself found both surprising and unsettling.

Since ELIZA, chatbot designs and capabilities have steadily evolved. Early successors like Kenneth Colby's PARRY (1972), Michael Mauldin's CHATTERBOT (1994) – which, incidentally, is where the term *chatbot* originated – and Richard Wallace's ALICE (1995) continued to use rule-based, GOFAI-style architectures. These systems were limited by the scripts and pattern-matching rules supplied by their programmers, but they demonstrated how conversational programs could simulate different personalities or interaction styles. Later systems such as Rollo Carpenter's Cleverbot (1997), Steve Worswick's Kuki (2012), and Microsoft's Tay.ai (2016) departed from scripted dialogues, drawing instead on large corpora of past conversations to generate more dynamic responses. Today, chatbots are widely embedded in digital environments: animating non-player characters (NPCs) in video games and virtual worlds, managing real-time customer service interactions, and increasingly serving as the first point of contact in both commercial and public communication.

Though chatbots work with natural language, they are limited to its written form. This restriction is not immaterial; it is a crucial design element that is advantageous to their operations, especially on the internet. By participating in text-based exchanges, a chatbot can easily be mistaken for and pass as another human user. In other words, chatbots capitalize on the inherent narrow bandwidth of online social interaction, where conversational engagement, whether between two human users or a human user and a bot, is typically limited to the circulation of brief typewritten statements. Under these conditions, all that is needed are the rudiments of some kind of perceived social presence in order for human users to mistakenly assume that they are talking to *someone* instead of *something*. Thus, the apparent intelligence of the chatbot is as much a result of its technical operations as it is a product of the tightly constrained social context in which these applications operate.

Digital Voice Assistants

While chatbots rely on typewritten input and output, a closely related technology has emerged that moves this interaction into the domain of spoken language. These systems and devices – often referred to as *digital voice assistants* or *spoken dialogue systems (SDS)* – represent a significant evolution in conversational AI. By incorporating speech recognition and speech synthesis capabilities, they enable users to interact with machines in a way that feels more natural and immediate. From Apple's Siri and Amazon's Alexa to Google's Assistant, these voice-activated applications are now embedded in a wide range of devices we use every day, from smartphones and home appliances to automobiles and smart speakers, providing us with a seamless hands- and screen-free interface.

Technically speaking, these SDS applications are composite systems that integrate at least three distinct but interdependent components: automatic speech recognition (ASR), dialogue management (DM), and text-to-speech (TTS) synthesis (Figure 3.2).

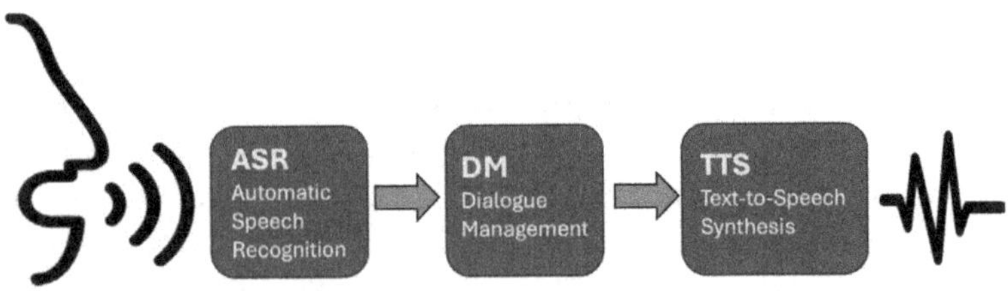

Figure 3.2 Spoken dialogue system (SDS) block diagram
Source: Image by David J. Gunkel

1 Automatic Speech Recognition (ASR): The job of ASR is to convert the acoustic signal of a user's voice into a text-like representation the computer can analyze. This involves detecting the speech signal, segmenting it into smaller units (such as phonemes), and then using statistical models – trained on large datasets of spoken language – to identify the most probable sequence of text tokens that best approximate the spoken input. Importantly, the output of the ASR is not "words" in the human sense, but a string of numeric encodings that correspond to these tokens. For the computer, "hello" is not letters or sounds but a sequence of numbers it can store, compare, and manipulate.

2 Dialogue Management (DM): Once the user's spoken input has been converted into a tokenized representation, the system must then decide what it means and how to respond. This task is handled by the DM component, which typically involves two subsystems:

- *Natural Language Understanding (NLU):* This subsystem analyzes the sequence of tokens generated by the ASR to determine the intent behind the user's statement and identify any relevant information. Early SDS systems relied on simple keyword matching: if a sentence contained the word *weather* and a city name, the application would initiate a weather response. Current NLU systems, however, uses machine learning models to capture patterns in phrasing and context. This allows the system to recognize that both "What's the weather like in Chicago?" and "Do I need an umbrella in Chicago today?" are requests for *weather* information with *Chicago* as the key location.
- *Natural Language Generation (NLG):* Once the system identifies the user's request, the NLG component produces a response in natural-sounding language. In many commercial applications, this has traditionally been done through templates: pre-written sentence patterns that the system fills with real-time information pulled from external sources, such as: "The current temperature in [*city*] is [*value*] degrees and [*condition*]." More advanced systems, however, go beyond templates by using statistical or neural models to generate text dynamically. This allows them to produce more flexible, varied, and contextually appropriate responses. For instance,

instead of always replying with "The current temperature in Chicago is 75 degrees and sunny," a neural NLG system might say, "It's a sunny 75 degrees in Chicago right now" or "Chicago is currently warm and clear at 75 degrees." The goal is not just to convey information, but also to make the interaction feel less repetitive and more conversational.

3 Text-to-Speech Synthesis (TTS): The final step is to turn the response that was generated by the DM subsystem into audible speech output that the user can understand. This is the task of the TTS component. Traditionally, this has been done in two main ways: concatenative synthesis, which stitches together snippets of pre-recorded human speech to form complete sentences; or formant or articulatory synthesis, which generates the sound of speech from scratch using algorithms that simulate the human voice. More recently, neural TTS systems, such as Google's WaveNet, have become increasingly common. Trained on large datasets of human speech, these generative models can produce output that is smoother, more flexible, and more natural sounding. In all cases, the goal is the same: to produce clear and intelligible spoken output that allows the system to talk back to the user in a way that feels conversational and responsive.

By combining these elements, spoken dialogue systems attempt to simulate the dynamics of interpersonal human communication, albeit in highly structured and constrained ways. What distinguishes these applications from their text-based predecessors is not just the use of voice, but also the expectation that they can function in real time, often in noisy or unpredictable environments, and still maintain coherent conversational interaction.

Social Robots

So far, all the HMC applications we have considered – chatbots and digital voice assistants – operate primarily through language. And there's a good reason for this: human communication is heavily dependent on it. But communication is not only verbal. In face-to-face interactions, spoken language is almost always accompanied by a wide-range of non-verbal behaviors: facial expressions, gestures, posture, eye gaze, and more. These cues play a vital role in how we interpret meaning, signal emotion, and manage the flow of conversation. One of the acknowledged limitations of current SDS devices like Siri, Alexa, and Google Assistant is their inability to perceive, interpret, or produce such non-verbal cues. They can talk, but they cannot look, gesture, or move. One way to address this limitation is to give the AI a physical form – to embed it in a body that can interact with us in our shared physical environment. This is the domain of robots, and, more specifically, the emerging field of social robots.

Types of Social Robots

Social robots are technological artifacts designed to engage with human users in socially meaningful ways. Unlike voice assistants, which operate primarily through speech, social robots are physically embodied systems that can communicate and respond not only with spoken and written language but also through gesture, movement, facial expression, and spatial positioning. Importantly, there is no single kind of social robot. The term refers to a range of design strategies and implementations, each with different assumptions about what counts as *social*. While terminology may vary, researchers generally distinguish four major types, arranged along a scale from minimal to robust social functionality.[4]

1 Socially Evocative: These devices rely primarily on the human user's tendency to anthropomorphize. The robot itself does not need to exhibit actual social intelligence. Rather, it is designed to elicit emotional and social responses from the human user. Thus, interaction with these robots is largely one-sided, with the user attributing intention, emotion, or meaning to what is essentially a programmed performance. Examples include robotic toys like Tamagotchis or digital pets that are designed to evoke a sense of companionship without possessing actual social understanding.

2 Social Interface: These robotic devices are capable of using humanlike social cues – such as eye contact, body orientation, or vocal tone – to facilitate user interaction. They appear social at the surface level but typically operate with a shallow model of user behavior. The interaction is largely scripted or reflexive, designed to give the appearance of responsiveness without genuine understanding. As social robotics innovator Cynthia Breazeal (2003, 169) notes, their sociality is concentrated at the level of the interface. In other words, these mechanisms act as if they are responding to the user, but this is an act or outward performance. A good example of this type of social robot are museum tour guides, interactive kiosks, and therapy robots like Paro.

3 *Socially Receptive:* While still socially passive, these robots differ from social interface types by being able to learn from their interactions. They benefit from social exchanges by updating internal models or adapting behavior over time, often through methods like reinforcement learning. As Breazeal (2003, 169) clarifies: "Interactions with people affect the robot's internal structure at deeper levels, such as organizing the motor system to perform new gestures, or associating symbolic labels to incoming perceptions." Many of Breazeal's own research robots, like Kismet and Leonardo, were designed to exhibit this capability. Other examples include various forms of companion robots, designed to respond to user behaviors and develop a kind of pseudo-relationship through repeated interaction, and sex robots, which aim to simulate intimacy and emotional reciprocity by adapting to user preferences and social cues.

4 *Sociable:* At the high end of the spectrum are robots that are not only socially responsive but also participative. This type of robot is described as being "socially intelligent in a human-like way, and interacting with it is like interacting with another person" (Breazeal 2002, 1). Thus, these devices don't just act or pretend to be social. They are genuinely social and have "their own internal goals and motivations" (Breazeal 2003, 169). Currently, there are no robots that fully meet this criterion. Consequently, this final category functions more as a horizon concept: that is, something that guides research and sets a benchmark for future development. Real-world systems and devices may exhibit partial traits of sociability (e.g., multi-turn dialogue, emotional responsiveness, adaptive learning), but these remain largely domain-specific, scripted, and limited in autonomy.

As we move from the low to the high end of the scale, the robots become not only more capable but also more complex and, as a result, significantly more expensive to produce. Fortunately, not every robotic device requires the full set of social competencies. In many cases (perhaps even most cases), a plausible appearance of social intelligence is sufficient to satisfy user expectations. This is especially true in highly constrained environments, where the range of possible interactions is limited and predictable, such as with a child's interactive toy or a therapeutic companion robot. Additionally, as the complexity of the environment increases or as the robot is expected to manage more dynamic and open-ended social encounters, the required level of social functionality must scale accordingly. In such contexts, the challenge is not simply to simulate social behavior but to support adaptive, context-aware interaction that can respond to subtle cues and shifting human needs. For this reason, social robotics is a truly interdisciplinary field, requiring contributions not just from engineering but also from the social and human sciences.

Embodiment and Morphology

Robotic embodiment can take different forms, depending on how designers choose to present the system and shape its interactions. In broad terms, these embodiments can be virtual, physical, or hybrid. Each offers a different way of giving the robot social presence, and each mode has its own set of affordances and constraints.

1 *Virtual:* Virtual embodiments are non-physical but graphically rendered agents, like avatars or animated personas. A good example is Replika, a customizable, embodied chatbot that users can design by selecting features like skin tone, body type, and hairstyle. Though Replika lacks physical presence, its avatar form allows it to simulate richer social interactions than a purely text-based chatbot. In such cases, embodiment is visual and symbolic, anchored in the conventions of digital self-representation.

2 *Physical:* Physical embodiments involve robots that exist in the real world and occupy physical space. One notable example is Jibo, a socially receptive tabletop robot developed by Breazeal in 2014. Though roughly the size of a large smart speaker, Jibo could move, pivot its head, track eye gaze, display

facial expressions, and respond with gestures and movement. These non-verbal capabilities made the Jibo robot seem far more socially aware than stationary voice assistants like Alexa, even though its actual conversational intelligence was also very limited.

3 *Hybrid:* Hybrid embodiments blend the virtual and the physical. The Furhat robot exemplifies this form of implementation. It has the physical form of a bust – the head and shoulders of a human figure – and an expressive face that is rendered in video form by way of back-projection. This allows the robot to simulate facial expressions with greater flexibility and lower mechanical complexity, while also making it possible to customize its appearance through software adjustments, which is something difficult and costly with physically implemented facial features.

The specific shape or structure that a robot takes – its *morphology* – also plays a significant role in determining user expectations and interpretations. Morphology communicates a robot's intended social role and the kind of interactions one is likely to have with it. Most social robots fall into one of three broad morphological categories:

1 *Zoomorphic:* Zoomorphic robots resemble animals, like Sony's AIBO (a dog), Intelligent System Co.'s Paro (a seal), Innvo Labs' Pleo (a dinosaur), and Consequential Robotics' MiRo (Figure 3.3). These designs capitalize on familiar human–animal relationships. Because we don't expect animals to speak or engage in complex dialogue, zoomorphic robots can interact meaningfully through simpler expressive behaviors, such as sounds, movement, and eye gaze.

2 *Caricatured:* Caricatured robots borrow from the world of animation and cartoon aesthetics. These robots, such as Kismet (Breazeal's early prototype) and Lovot (Figure 3.4), use exaggerated features and stylized expressions to appear lifelike without mimicking realistic human or animal anatomy.

3 *Anthropomorphic:* Anthropomorphic robots are designed to look and act like humans. These range from the small, friendly

Figure 3.3 Consequential Robotics' MiRo
Source: By permission of Tony Prescott

Figure 3.4 Lovot robots
Source: Photograph by David J. Gunkel

form of Softbank Robotic's NAO (Figure 3.5) to more lifelike and controversial examples such as Sophia (Hanson Robotics) and Geminoids (developed by Hiroshi Ishiguro). Some of these robots can walk, talk, and make facial expressions. Others

Figure 3.5 NAO
Source: Photograph by ubahnverleih CC 0 from https://commons.wikimedia.org/w/index.php?curid=49912982

are either fully or partially controlled behind the scenes, like puppets, but nonetheless project the illusion of autonomy.

Taken together, embodiment and morphology structure how we perceive and interact with social robots. They influence not only what a robot looks like or how it moves, but also how much social intelligence we attribute to it, what roles we expect it to play, and how we respond to its behavior. For this reason, designers and developers must carefully consider both dimensions when building robots meant to engage with humans as social partners.

Achieving this requires not only technical expertise in the design and fabrication of sensors, actuators, and other output devices – even artificial skin – but also behavioral modeling similar to what is needed for creating believable characters in fiction, on stage, or for film and video games. Just as writers, animators, and filmmakers must carefully script and stage behaviors to sustain the illusion of personality, so too must roboticists choreograph the movements, gestures, and expressions that make a robot's presence feel socially meaningful. Importantly, these latter challenges are not primarily engineering problems but interpretive and cultural ones, often better addressed with insights from the social sciences, humanities, and performing arts, which study how people assign meaning, attribute intention, and respond to performances of social presence.

Social Opportunities and Challenges

NLP applications – whether in the form of machine translation, chatbots, spoken dialogue systems, or social robots – seem to have realized one of the founding ambitions of AI, articulated as far back as the Dartmouth Summer Research Project: to make machines use language. Yet this apparent achievement carries profound consequences for how we understand communication, social interaction, and trust.

Communication

NLP systems can process natural human language, but does this amount to communication? The answer depends on how we define the term. If we adopt what James Carey (1989) calls the *transmission view* – communication as the sending and receiving of messages – then the answer is plainly yes. These systems accept user input, process it, and return output, alternating as sender and receiver in conversational exchanges, even if the range of possible messages is finite.

But Carey also described a *ritual view* of communication, one that emphasizes the maintenance of social bonds rather than the transfer of information. Much of everyday talk, like casual greetings, polite small talk, and common expressions like "How's it going?" or "See you later," functions less to convey facts and information than to affirm mutual recognition and shared social presence. And here NLP systems often excel. Because ritualized exchanges operate at the surface level of interaction and do not require deep semantic understanding, they are relatively easy to model algorithmically. In this respect, then, NLP applications, like chatbots, digital assistants, and social robots of all forms and varieties, can convincingly perform many of the small gestures that help sustain a sense of social cohesion.

That NLP applications can participate in both the transmission and ritual modes of communication has important consequences.

On the one hand, this dual capacity allows them to operate across a wide range of contexts: from delivering precise factual answers to sustaining ongoing, socially meaningful exchanges. This flexibility helps explain their appeal as tools, companions, and service agents. On the other hand, it also blurs the boundary between informational exchange and relational engagement. When a machine can both tell us the weather and ask how our day is going, it becomes harder to distinguish instrumental communication from social connection. This complicates not only our everyday understanding of what counts as *communication*, but also the criteria by which we assess sincerity, trustworthiness, and even the presence of another mind.

Social Presence and Anthropomorphism

Even if one insists that NLP applications are merely mindless processors of linguistic data, what really matters is our very human responses to these behaviors. The Computers Are Social Actors (CASA) research program, initially developed by Byron Reeves and Clifford Nass in the latter part of the 1990s, demonstrated that people frequently treat computers and other technological artifacts as socially attentive partners, even when they are fully aware that they are talking to and interacting with a machine. This so-called "conservative error," as Reeves and Nass (1996, 22) refer to it, leads users to grant these systems a kind of provisional social standing based solely on their exhibited behaviors. Consequently, in order for *something* to be recognized and treated as *someone* (i.e., a social significant other), "it is not necessary," as Reeves and Nass (1996, 28) conclude, "to have artificial intelligence." All that is needed is that it appears to be close enough to encourage some kind of social response.

One explanation for this is our tendency toward *anthropomorphism*: the projection of human traits, intentions, or emotions onto non-human entities. Anthropomorphism is often criticized as a form of deception that should be tightly controlled or avoided altogether. From this perspective, good design practice demands transparency and an active effort to prevent the creation of systems and devices that invite unwarranted humanlike projections in the first place. But anthropomorphism has also proven to be extremely useful. It can, for instance, help users feel more comfortable, willing to interact, and able to sustain meaningful exchanges with NLP applications. For this reason, some designers argue that the goal should not be to eliminate anthropomorphism but to manage it by leveraging its benefits while mitigating potential harms. Since anthropomorphic projection is almost certain to occur – whether we like it or not – it may be more productive to learn how to work with it than to try to resist it entirely.

The difficulty is that we lack clear consensus on whether anthropomorphic projections are ultimately beneficial, detrimental, or both when applied to technologies designed for human communication and social interaction. As with the broader question of social presence, the issue is not simply whether these systems are intelligent or socially aware, but how convincingly they can perform those roles and how humans respond to that performance. What is at stake, then, is not only the design of effective user interfaces but also the larger social and ethical frameworks through which we evaluate them. Anthropomorphism can foster trust, comfort, and engagement, but it can also create false expectations, obscure responsibility, and encourage misplaced attachments. For this reason, debates about anthropomorphism are unlikely to be resolved by design decisions or technical adjustments alone; they demand insights from psychology, philosophy, and communication studies, which can help us understand why humans are so quick to attribute mind and agency, and what the consequences are when we do so with machines.

Identity: Gender and Race

Although chatbots, digital voice assistants, and social robots – like any technological object – do not possess a gender or a race, they are inevitably gendered and racialized through design choices, modes of representation, and user perceptions. These identity markers are often assigned by developers, whether intentionally or through unexamined cultural defaults. For instance, early chatbots such as ELIZA and more recent ones like Kuki have been gendered female by developers through their name, character description, and visual representation. Kuki's profile image – created and selected by her developer, Steve Worswick – depicts her as a young white woman (Figure 3.6). Similarly, digital voice assistants or SDS applications extend these identity

Figure 3.6 Kuki's profile image
Source: By permission of Steve Worswick

cues beyond naming and imagery into vocal characteristics and speech patterns.

Social robots also present a wide spectrum of embodied identity cues, as their morphology can be designed to evoke or reinforce gender and racial stereotypes. This is particularly explicit in the case of sex robots, whose physical forms often replicate narrow, stereotypical ideals of femininity and (though much less common) masculinity. Other social robots – whether humanoid, caricatured, or zoomorphic – can be gendered and racialized through facial design, color, styling, and the socio-cultural roles they are scripted to perform.

Consider the case of Siri, which was initially characterized as female. This feminization was not arbitrary; it was a deliberate design decision that positioned the Siri application in the role of personal assistant, thereby reinforcing sexist images about gendered labor (Guzman 2017). This echoes the mid-20th-century cinematic stereotype of the spunky secretary – often white and blonde – who is tirelessly organized, deferential to her male boss, and always on-hand and at your service. Later versions of Siri introduced a broader range of voices, including gender-neutral options, placing some control over identity representation in the hands of users.

And these identity markers extend beyond gender. In "The Whiteness of AI" (2020), Stephen Cave and Kanta Dihal show that the design and portrayal of chatbots, virtual assistants, and social robots often reflect a "default Whiteness": a normalized assumption that intelligent machines, and frequently their presumed users, are white unless explicitly represented otherwise. While offering users the ability to select different vocal characteristics or appearances may diversify the range of representational options, doing so does not necessarily eliminate the underlying stereotypes as it merely shifts responsibility for those decisions from developers to end users. In all these cases, identity is not an incidental feature of the application. It is part of the interface layer that shapes the ways these systems are perceived, how users interact with them, and the social meanings they carry into human–machine relationships.

Deception

If anthropomorphism, social presence, and identity help make NLP systems more socially engaging, they also open the door to deception, whether intentional or not. Sherry Turkle (2011), an MIT social scientist specializing in the psychological aspects of emerging technology, warns that socially evocative technologies such as chatbots, digital assistants, and social robots can foster a potentially dangerous form of self-deception. In the face of these apparently social interactive devices, Turkle argues, we are often all too willing to treat them as socially significant others – not just as surrogate pets, but as close friends, confidants, and even romantic partners. And this tendency is not limited to casual interactions. Robert Epstein, a Harvard-trained psychologist, describes having had a four-month online affair with a chatbot named Ivana (Epstein 2007). The interaction was compelling not because the bot possessed intelligence in any meaningful sense, but because its conversational behaviors were close enough to familiar human social patterns to evoke a sustained emotional response.

This problem extends well beyond personal relationships. "The rise of social bots," as Andrea Peterson (2013, 1) observes, "isn't just bad for love lives – it could have broader implications for our ability to trust the authenticity of nearly every interaction we have online." During the 2016 US presidential election, for example, Alessandro Bessi and Emilio Ferrara (2016) documented how automated social media accounts distorted political discourse, potentially influencing public opinion and compromising democratic processes. Here, the performance of social presence, reinforced by anthropomorphic cues, was sufficient to shape perception and behavior, even without genuine agency, intent, or understanding.

A third domain of concern involves the structural and economic dynamics of what Shoshana Zuboff (2019) calls surveillance capitalism. When you talk to a digital voice assistant, like Apple's Siri or Amazon's Alexa, you are not merely interacting with a single device or application, you are also providing personal data to multinational corporations that can use this information to train their models, build detailed user profiles, and fuel targeted advertising, predictive analytics, and product recommendations. These devices may present themselves as affable and helpful companions, but that appearance often conceals their deeper role as agents of powerful corporate interests. In this sense, the deception lies not only in the simulation of social presence but also in the masking of commercial motives and data-extractive practices.

Deception is obviously a problem, and no one wants to be misled. But it has also been a defining condition of NLP applications since Turing's imitation game. In his book *Deceptive Media*, Simone Natale (2021) offers one way to clarify the problem by distinguishing between what he calls *deliberate deception* – where illusion is knowingly manipulated to mislead – and *banal deception* – the mundane, often invisible masking of underlying functions through a user-friendly interface. Much like anthropomorphism, deception is not binary; it can be both functional and harmful. The task for designers, policymakers, and users is to calibrate it, retaining enough illusion to make interaction intuitive and engaging while preventing it from undermining trust, agency, and the integrity of human communication. Once again, this is not simply an engineering problem in search of a technical solution. It is a challenge that demands the insight, critical analysis, and creative problem-solving capabilities of the full range of humanistic, social scientific, and technical expertise.

Summary

We now live in a world where machines can translate our words across languages, chat with us in text and speech, and even meet our gaze through embodied forms. These systems do not simply process language. They participate in our conversations, answer our questions, and mirror the patterns of our social lives. Sometimes they do this so well we forget, or choose to forget, that there is no real understanding behind these compelling performances. This matters for all of us, not just computer scientists and AI engineers, because language is central to how we connect, share meaning, and engage with our communities.

The rise of these technologies forces us to rethink what counts as communication: whether it is the exchange of information, the maintenance of relationships, or both. It also means that we have to grapple with their complications and our own vulnerabilities: our almost automatic tendency to anthropomorphize and treat these technological things as human or at least humanlike, the ways these applications and devices can reproduce harmful gender and racial stereotypes, and the subtle and not so subtle deceptions that serve corporate, political, and other powerful interests. These are not just technical challenges. They are social, cultural, and ethical questions that will shape the world we live in and the possible futures we hope to create.

And what we have seen so far is only the beginning. The chatbots, digital assistants, and social robots discussed in this chapter are still, for the most part, narrow systems: built for specific contexts, reliant on constrained input, and limited by the scope of their coded instructions or training data. But recent advances in LLMs are rapidly eroding these constraints. Unlike earlier NLP applications, LLMs are not confined to a single domain or a small set of functions; they can generate language on virtually any topic, in almost any style, and adapt their responses in real time to the flow of conversation. With this expanded capacity comes an equally expanded set of questions – not only technical but also cultural and philosophical. What happens when the performance of social presence is no longer just good enough but uncannily fluent? How should we respond when the line between simulation and understanding becomes harder to locate, defend, and perhaps even care about? It is to these questions, and to the technical and cultural dynamics of LLMs, that we now turn.

Learning Activities

1 Social Robot Design Challenge

Purpose: This activity helps you understand the challenges of designing socially interactive systems by requiring you to think carefully about how language, embodiment, and behavior work together to create social presence.

Procedure: Working either individually or in small groups, design a social robot intended for a specific context (e.g., elder care, education, customer service, therapy, hospitality, or companionship). Your design – which can be visualized using a range of different strategies (e.g., hand-drawn sketches, computer-aided design and image processing tools, animation, or AI-generated imagery) – should address the following questions:

- What social role is the robot meant to perform?
- How will it communicate and interact with users: that is, text, speech, gesture, movement, facial expression, or some combination?
- What level of social capability does it aim for (socially evocative, social interface, socially receptive, or sociable)?
- What form of embodiment will it have (virtual, physical, or hybrid), and what morphology will it use (zoomorphic, caricatured, or anthropomorphic)? Why?
- What limits (if any) will you place on the robot's social abilities to avoid deception or unrealistic expectations?

Each individual or group should briefly present their design to the class and explain the reasoning behind their choices. The activity can also be structured as a design competition, in which projects are compared and discussed using shared criteria, such as social effectiveness, ethical restraint, and alignment between embodiment, communication style, and intended context. The goal is not to win the competition, but to critically reflect on the design trade-offs involved in creating socially interactive systems.

Learning Goal: Demonstrate the ability to analyze how design decisions shape social interaction with NLP systems and explain why social robots are as much cultural and communicative artifacts as technical ones.

2 When Does Talking Become Communication?

Purpose: This activity helps you investigate the difference between language use and communication by applying transmission and ritual models of communication to NLP systems.

Procedure: Choose one NLP application discussed in the chapter (machine translation, a chatbot, a digital voice assistant, or a social robot). Describe how the system functions under both (1) a transmission view of communication (information exchange) and (2) a ritual view of communication (maintaining social connection). Discuss whether the system is more successful in one mode than the other, and why. And consider whether communication requires understanding or whether participation in common social rituals is enough.

Learning Goal: Demonstrate the ability to apply communication theory to NLP systems and experience how machines can participate in social interaction without semantic understanding.

3 Anthropomorphism, Identity, and Trust

Purpose: This activity encourages you to critically reflect on how identity cues and anthropomorphic design influence user trust and expectations in interactions with NLP systems.

Procedure: Reflect on examples from the chapter involving chatbots, voice assistants, or social robots. Identify one design choice that encourages anthropomorphism (such as voice, name, appearance, or personality). Discuss how this design choice affects user trust, comfort, or emotional engagement. Consider how gendered or racialized design elements might reinforce stereotypes or power relations. And debate whether anthropomorphism should be minimized, managed, or deliberately embraced in NLP system design.

Learning Goal: Critically assess how anthropomorphism and identity shape human responses to NLP systems and why these issues raise important ethical and cultural concerns that extend beyond matters of technical performance.

Further Reading

Cynthia Breazeal, *Designing Sociable Robots* (2002).

Breazeal's book explores how robots can be designed not just to perform tasks but to engage socially with humans. Drawing on her pioneering work with Kismet, she outlines levels of sociability and the design challenges of creating machines that appear emotionally expressive and socially intelligent. This publication remains foundational for the field of human–robot interaction or HRI.

James Carey, *Communication as Culture: Essays on Media and Society* (1989).

Carey distinguishes between the *transmission view* of communication (focused on sending information) and the *ritual view* (focused on maintaining social relationships). This framework helps explain why NLP systems matter not only for information exchange (like translation) but also for how and why people form social bonds with machines.

Byron Reeves and Clifford Nass, *The Media Equation: How People Treat Computers, Television, and New Media Like Real People and Places* (1996).

Based on the CASA (Computers Are Social Actors) research program, this book demonstrates that humans respond to computers and other forms of media as if they were real social partners. Even when we know they are "just machines," we unconsciously apply social rules to them – an insight that explains why chatbots and voice assistants feel socially real and compelling.

Warren Weaver, "Translation" (1949).

In this short but groundbreaking memorandum, Weaver proposed that language translation could be treated as a problem of cryptography: decoding one language into another through statistical and computational methods. His vision launched MT as one of AI's first major research programs and inspired early projects at IBM and in the US government. Although these initial MT systems and applications often failed to meet expectations, Weaver's framing set the agenda for decades of work in NLP.

Joseph Weizenbaum, *Computer Power and Human Reason: From Judgment to Calculation* (1976).

In this influential book, Weizenbaum reflects on his creation of ELIZA, an early chatbot that mimicked a psychotherapist. And he describes being disturbed by how quickly users attributed understanding and empathy to the program, despite its simple design. The book raises enduring questions about deception, responsibility, and whether human decision-making can or should be turned over to machines.

Fiction, Film, and Video

Spike Jonze (dir.), *Her* (2013).

This film imagines an operating system that evolves into a social and emotional partner for its user, raising questions about intimacy, identity, and what it means to relate to a non-human other. By focusing on love and companionship rather than domination or rebellion, *Her* offers a poignant counterpoint to darker AI narratives, while still probing issues of authenticity and personhood in human–computer interaction.

George Lucas (dir.), *Star Wars* (1977–).

The droids C-3PO and R2-D2 are iconic examples of social robots: embodied machines that communicate, build relationships, and participate in human dramas. They illustrate how robots function not just as tools, but as companions and characters with personality, shaping popular expectations for social presence with AI.

Osamu Tezuka, *Astro Boy* (1952–68).
Astro Boy (known in Japan as *Mighty Atom* 鉄腕アトム) is a Japanese manga series that was later adapted into a highly influential anime serial. As one of the earliest and most enduring portrayals of a socially interactive robot, *Astro Boy* anticipates many of the central questions explored in contemporary social robotics. The character is not simply an intelligent machine but an embodied artificial being who communicates, forms relationships, and elicits powerful emotional responses from the humans around him.

4
Large Language Models

Learning Outcomes

- Explain how large language models (LLMs) generate text, focusing on the core elements of tokenization, embeddings, transformer architectures, self-attention, and next-token prediction.
- Understand how LLMs produce fluent and convincing language content without understanding, and assess how this disrupts traditional assumptions about meaning, intelligence, and communication.
- Evaluate the opportunities and challenges associated with LLM use, including applications in writing, translation, tutoring, and coding, as well as problems such as bias, hallucination, intellectual property concerns, and environmental impact.
- Critically assess how LLMs reshape human labor, creativity, and agency, including issues of technological unemployment, deskilling, dependency on platforms, and the concentration of power in AI development.

Introduction

Large language models (LLMs) are not just the next step in the development of NLP; they are a quantum leap. Where MT applications, chatbots, and digital voice assistants were built for specific and tightly defined purposes, LLMs move fluidly across topics, genres, and styles. They can summarize a Supreme Court decision, draft a business plan, compose a poem in the style of Nobel laureate Gabriela Mistral, or explain the intricacies of quantum mechanics in terms even a child can understand – all in the same conversational interaction. The effect can be dazzling, even disorienting: language generated with such fluency and adaptability that it feels real. It feels alive. It can even feel like magic.[1]

This chapter demystifies LLMs, rendering their inner workings and operations both accessible and understandable. By unpacking their core elements – tokenization, embeddings, self-attention, transformer architectures, and next-token prediction – we will see how these systems operate, what they can and cannot do, and why they sometimes surprise us. Demystifying the technology is not about draining it of wonder. It is about replacing passive astonishment with active understanding. And that understanding is critical, because it will give us the knowledge and the confidence to address and evaluate the social, political, and philosophical challenges LLMs present.

We begin by explaining what an LLM is and how it works, focusing on transformer architectures, massive datasets or what is also called *big data*, and next-token prediction. From this technical foundation, the chapter proceeds to a cost/benefit analysis, examining what these systems make possible and the challenges they introduce: from impressive applications in translation, composition, and tutoring; to persistent problems with bias and hallucination, environmental costs and sustainability; and the future of work and human deskilling. What is at stake, however, is not just a catalogue of opportunities and risks. LLMs disrupt how we think about communication, creativity, and responsibility, and they expose deeper questions about knowledge, power, and human agency in a world increasingly reliant on AI.

Technical Operations (in Plain English)

LLMs, such as OpenAI's GPT series of algorithms, Google's Gemini, Anthropic's Claude, and DeepSeek 深度求索, rely on massive datasets of text and sophisticated neural network architectures known as *transformers*. These models, as many critics have pointed out, do not understand language. Instead, they arrange legible sequences of linguistic tokens based on calculating the probable distribution of signs discoverable in their training data. That's a mouthful, so let's break it down and take it one piece at a time.

Language Modeling

A *language model* is a *probabilistic* representation of a language: English, German, Vietnamese, and so on. Whether you have ever actually thought about it or not, this simply means that in the languages we speak, some sequences of characters and words are more likely to occur than others. In English, for example, the letters *t-o-a-s-t-e-r* are far more likely to appear than other possible sequences of those same letters, like *r-t-t-a-o-s-e*. The sentence "The book is on the table" is much more likely to be used than "On the is table book the." So, producing legible linguistic content can be treated as a matter of arranging words in sequences that have a high probability of occurring in a given language. This doesn't require any actual understanding, just the ability to recognize and reproduce valid patterns.

A language model leverages this insight, and as result it can be used to evaluate whether the words that make up a sentence are in the correct order, as is done with the automatic grammar check included in common word processing applications, or perform other tasks, like *next-word prediction*. You are already familiar with a simple version of this by way of your phone's autocomplete: you start typing a text message, and it suggests the next word in the phrase. These suggestions are based on the statistical likelihood of what word tends to follow in the sequence. Take, for example, the first line from that famous soliloquy in Shakespeare's *Hamlet*:

> To be or not to be, that is the . . . .

There are a number of different words that could fill the blank and complete this sentence. But of all the word that are available in the English language, there is one word that has a higher probability of occurring than the others:

- question 45%
- problem 20%
- dilemma 15%
- consideration 10%
- toaster 1%

A language model, like the autocomplete function that is built into your mobile device, tries to guess the next most probable element in a sequence, whether that sequence concerns letters that make up a word or words that make up a phrase. The autocomplete feature, then, does not understand what it is you want to say. It simply takes the input, cycles through a set of available words, and identifies the one that has the highest probability of occurring next.

This idea was initially formulated and formalized in *The Mathematical Theory of Communication*, published by Claude Shannon in 1949. As you may recall, not only was Shannon one of the organizers of the Dartmouth Summer Research Project, but also his work, and this publication in particular, is credited with supplying the basic sender–receiver model of communication that is now utilized in communication studies and related fields. In his research, Shannon proposed the idea of modeling language statistically, using *n-grams*: a contiguous sequence of a number of items (*n*), like words, characters, numbers, and so on. He then used *Markov chains* to model the probability of the next item in a sequence based on the previous one(s), thus laying the foundation for probabilistic approaches to language processing.

During the GOFAI years (circa 1950s–1990s), n-gram models were the dominant form of language modeling. These models assumed that the probability of a word in a given sequence depended only on a limited number of preceding words. A *trigram model* (where $n = 3$), for instance, assumes that each word in a sequence depends only on the two immediately preceding words. These probabilistic values were calculated from frequency counts in large text corpora: that is, by scanning through vast collections of written material, keeping track of how often particular word sequences occur, and then estimating the probability of a next word by dividing the frequency of the full sequence (e.g., *quick brown fox*) by the frequency of the two preceding words (e.g., *quick brown*). Here's an example of trigrams derived from the English-language pangram (a sentence that includes all the letters of the alphabet) *The quick brown fox jumps over the lazy dog*:

- the quick brown
- quick brown fox
- brown fox jumps
- fox jumps over
- jumps over the
- over the lazy
- the lazy dog

Though these models worked reasonably well, their capabilities were limited, mainly because next-word prediction was based on a very small context window, such as the preceding two words in a sequence. All this began to change in 2003, when a research team at the University of Montreal led by Yoshua Bengio introduced the first neural probabilistic language model. These models used artificial neural networks (ANNs) to learn distributed word representations, called *embeddings* (more on that below), which capture patterns of similarity among words, and to estimate the probability of word sequences from those associations. Unlike n-gram models, which treat words as isolated items in short linear sequences, neural probabilistic language models convert words into representations that reflect how they have been used in a particular language. Words that appear in similar contexts are therefore treated as being "closer" to one another and therefore more likely to occur together. This allows the system to make more accurate predictions and to account for semantic relationships that span an entire sentence or more.

An example might help us appreciate why this is so important. Consider the following sentence:

> The toaster doesn't fit in the box because it is too . . .

A trigram model would complete the sentence by attending to the two last words in the sequence – in this case, *is* and *too*. Because of this, it basically ignores the rest of the words in the sentence and, as a result, cannot take into account which object failed to fit or why. Thus, the model may assign similar probabilities to continuations such as *expensive*, *old*, or *heavy*, even though these do not fit the situation that is described.

A neural probabilistic language model, by contrast, can take advantage of distributed word representations that encode broader patterns of word use. Even within a limited context window, words such as *toaster*, *box*, *fit*, and *big* tend to be used together in similar situations (a fact that is available by observing existing word sequences contained in the training data) and are therefore represented as being semantically closer to one another. As a result, the model is more likely to predict adjectives such as *big* or *large*, which provide for a more accurate prediction and continuation of the sentence.

Tokenization and Embedding

The shift from n-gram models to neural probabilistic language models marks an important conceptual change: meaning is no longer tied to fixed word sequences but emerges from patterns of similarity and difference across language use. But this shift also introduces a new problem: How can a computational system, which has no direct access to words or meanings, represent language in a way that makes such modeling possible at all? Because computers operate on numbers rather than words, natural language must be translated into a numerical form before it can be computationally processed. This transformation involves two fundamental operations: *tokenization* and *embedding*.

1 Tokenization: From what we as users of LLMs can see, these models take words, in the form of a prompt, and then generate all kinds of textual content: for example, an answer to a question, a short explanation about language models, or even the draft of a term paper. But, technically speaking, these models do not work with words, nor do they understand what words are or are not. Instead, they work with *tokens*, which consist of small words (*the*, *cat*, *in*, *hat*), fragments of words (*un believ able*), or even individual characters and punctuation marks. Transforming words into tokens is called *tokenization*.

That explain what tokens are, but it does not explain why. LLMs work with tokens instead of whole words for three reasons, all of which have to do with the efficiency of the model's operations. First, natural languages contain an enormous number of words – hundreds of thousands, if not more – especially once we include proper names, technical terms, slang, misspellings, and words borrowed from other languages. If a model had to treat every possible word as a separate item, it would become extremely large and inefficient, and it would struggle to handle new or unfamiliar words. Tokenization allows the model to break unfamiliar words into smaller, recognizable parts rather than failing when it encounters something new.

Second, words appear in many different forms. Verbs change tense (*talk*, *talked*, *talking*), nouns can be singular or plural, and many languages include gendered or inflected forms. If the model treated each variation as a completely separate word, it would need to store redundant information for closely related forms. By working with tokens – e.g., *talk*, *ing*, and *ed* – the model can recognize patterns across related word forms and generalize more effectively.

Finally, tokenization allows LLMs to operate with a much smaller and more manageable vocabulary. Instead of needing to store and process millions of distinct words, a model can work with a vocabulary of only tens of thousands of tokens. This makes both training the model and generating text faster, more efficient, and scalable.

2 Embedding: Once text has been tokenized, each token must be converted into a form that a computer can work with. This is done through *embedding*, where each token is represented as an ordered array of numbers, or what mathematicians call a vector. You can think of this vector as specifying a location in an abstract, high-dimensional space known as an *embedding space*. For example, in a widely used model trained on English Wikipedia, the word *dog* is represented not by a definition or label, but by a list of 300 numerical values (Fares et al. 2017):

> [-0.03301828354597092, 0.05134638026356697,
> 0.0036009703762829304, -0.04066073149442673,
> 0.10361430048942566, -0.0050482310084109451 . . . .]

This sequence of numbers does not mean anything by itself. What matters is how one vector (one ordered array of numbers) relates to that of other tokens. Thus, the significance of a token such as *dog*, for example, is determined by how its vector (again, an ordered array of numbers) differs from and relates to the vectors of other tokens, like *puppy*, *pet*, *toaster*, and so on. These relationships are learned during the model's pre-training process (discussed below) and represent both semantic and syntactic patterns in language.

Because these embedding spaces often have hundreds or even thousands of different dimensions, they are impossible to visualize directly. However, we can still develop an intuition for how they work by projecting a small portion of this space into two dimensions. Figure 4.1 provides a simplified illustration of how the noun *dog* might be positioned relative to other words in such a simplified embedding space.

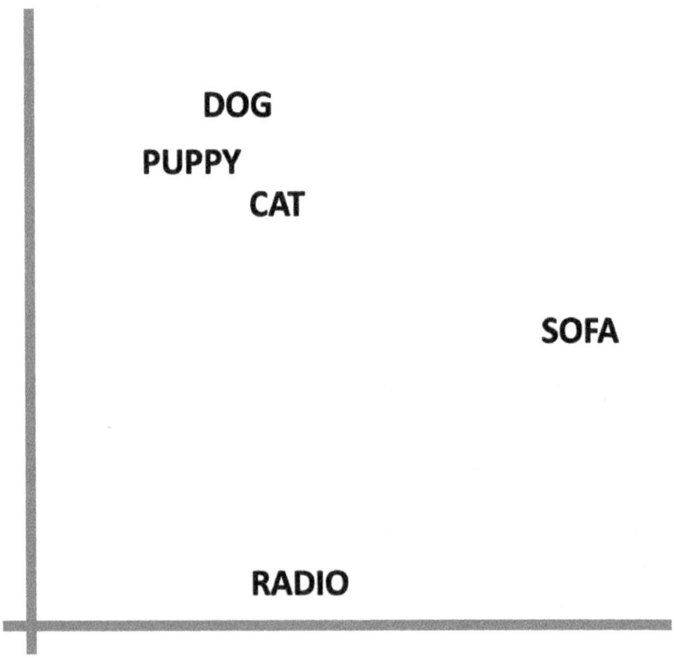

Figure 4.1 Simplified diagram of semantic associates for *dog* plotted along two dimensions
Source: Image created by David J. Gunkel

Transformer Architecture

Tokenization and embedding provide a way to turn language into numbers and to represent relationships of similarity and difference among tokens in a shared semantic space. But on their own, these representations are not enough. Once text has been converted into tokens and embeddings, the model still needs a way to process sequences of tokens, determine which ones matter most at any given moment, and use that information to predict the next word in a sequence. In other words, the model needs an architecture capable of working with these representations. This is where the *transformer* comes in.

The transformer is a type of neural network architecture that powers today's LLMs. First introduced in the breakthrough paper "Attention is All You Need" (Vaswani et al. 2017), the transformer marked a significant shift from earlier approaches to NLP. Previous models either processed text step-by-step, one word at a time, or relied on a limited context window of nearby words, as in n-gram models. Transformers, by contrast, are able to process an entire sequence of tokens simultaneously. This parallel processing not only accelerates computation but, more importantly, also enables the model to capture long-range dependencies and subtle relationships far more effectively than its predecessors.

A transformer block (Figure 4.2) is composed of two core components: a *self-attention* mechanism that dynamically relates each token to every other token in a sequence, and a *feedforward network* that further transforms those representations. Stacking many such blocks on top of one another – forming what is known as a *transformer stack* – allows the model to capture increasingly complex patterns across multiple layers of abstraction.

1 Self-Attention Mechanism: Self-attention allows the model to evaluate how each token in a sequence relates to every other token. This is especially important in language, where the meaning of a word often depends on others far away in the sentence. One might think of it as a spotlight: for each word, the model illuminates those words most relevant to its interpretation while leaving less important ones in the shadows. Consider, for example, the sentence "The book on the table is red." To

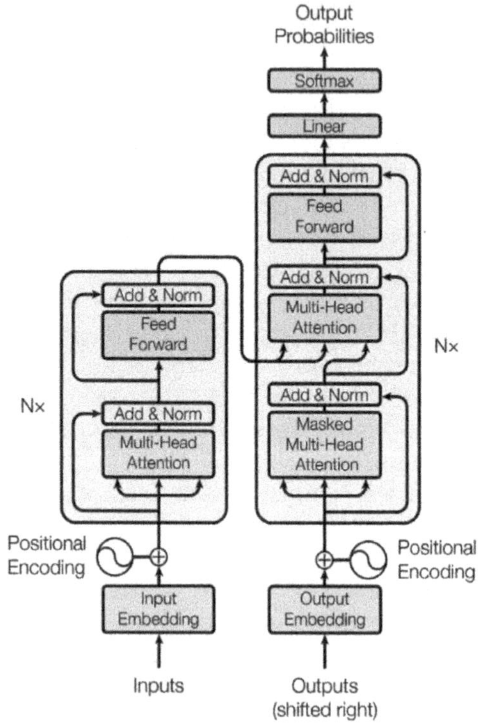

Figure 4.2 Diagram of the transformer from the paper "Attention is All You Need" (Vaswani et al. 2017)
Source: Image used with permission of Google

correctly recognize that the adjective "red" refers to "book" and not "table," we need to look beyond the nearest word (or words) and consider the entire sentence. That is exactly what self-attention makes possible.

Technically, this mechanism operates by projecting each token into three numerical vectors: a query, a key, and a value.[2] The *query* encodes features that the attention mechanism uses to evaluate the relevance of the other tokens in the sequences to the current token; the *key* represents the features that a token makes available for such evaluation; and the *value* is a transformed version of the token's representation that is carried forward. By comparing queries to keys, the attention mechanism computes *attention weights*, and these weights determine how much each token's value vector contributes to the current token's representation. These weights are then applied to the value vectors, producing updated token representations that incorporate information from across the entire sequence (Figure 4.3).

Attention weights, therefore, designate how strongly tokens are related to one another in the context of a specific sequence. As Leif Weatherby (2025, 161) explains, "the attention scores given to the sequences as they are processed are designations of how much each word is about each other word in a given passage." In other words, *self-attention* does not tell us what words are important in general, but rather how tokens relate to one another within the unfolding dynamics of a particular sequence. This context-sensitive operation is similar to – but not the same as – the way human beings make sense of language. When we interpret the word *red* in the sentence "The book on the table is red," we understand it in *context*, recognizing its relation to the noun *book* rather than *table*. The attention mechanism provides a computational analogue of this process.

In practice, transformers employ *multi-head attention*, meaning that this process occurs multiple times in parallel. Each attention head focuses on different patterns or dependencies within the same sequence, such as grammatical structure,

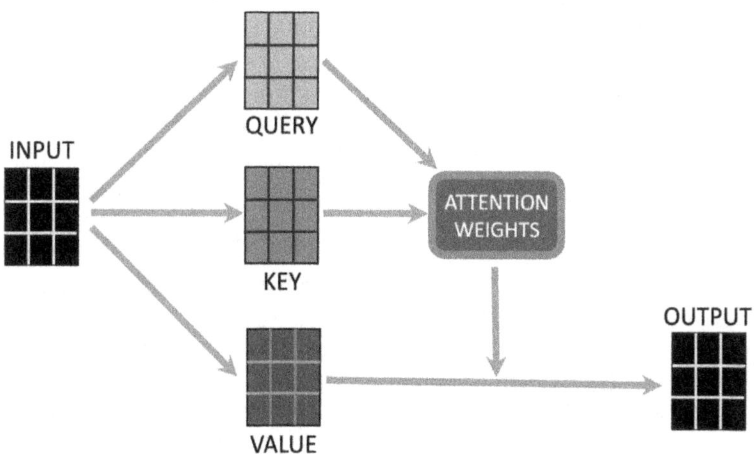

Figure 4.3 Simplified diagram of the attention mechanism
Source: Image by David J. Gunkel

semantic roles, or stylistic cues. And each head produces its own set of attention weights and updated token representations, effectively offering a different "view" of the input. These multiple views are then combined, yielding a representation of the input that is richer and more nuanced than a single attention head could produce on its own. This design is crucial because natural human language operates simultaneously along multiple dimensions. A single sentence may encode syntactic relations (word order and grammatical roles), semantic relations (who is doing what to whom), and pragmatic or stylistic features (tone, emphasis, or framing). While a single attention head may capture only one of these aspects, running many heads in parallel allows the transformer to track several of them at once. It is this multiplicity that enables the model to handle linguistic nuance and to generalize across the many ways language functions in context.

2 Feedforward Network: The output of the attention mechanism is subsequently refined by a feedforward ANN. Whereas attention highlights the relationships among tokens, the feedforward network functions more like a filter or interpreter. It takes the enriched token representations from the attention mechanism and passes them through several layers of relatively simple mathematical operations, such as weighted sums followed by non-linear activation functions. It is called *feedforward* because the information moves in one direction – from input to output – without looping back or referring to previous states. This is different from older recurrent neural networks (RNNs), where the output of one step was fed back into the next, creating a kind of short-term memory. The feedforward design is simpler, faster, and especially well suited to LLMs.

In practice, the feedforward network applies the same small neural network independently to each token's representation. This allows the model to further adjust and reinterpret the information produced by the attention mechanism. Non-linear activation functions – such as the sigmoid function discussed in chapter 2 – enable the network to capture patterns like thresholds, emphases, or categorical shifts that cannot be represented using linear combinations alone. In this way, attention gathers contextual information, while the feedforward network transforms that information into more abstract features.

The feedforward network is therefore oriented toward identifying higher-level patterns that go beyond direct token-to-token relationships, including regularities in grammar, style, or thematic coherence. One way to think about this is to imagine what happens when you reread a sentence. The first time through you notice how individual words connect and relate to one another, but on a second pass you begin to recognize broader structural relationships, like the sentence's rhythm, tone, or overall meaning. The feedforward network provides a computational analogue of this second pass within the transformer.

3 Transformer Stack: What makes transformers powerful is not attention or feedforward networks taken in isolation, but the way these two operations are combined and then repeated in depth. A single transformer block may be adequate for predicting the next word in a short sentence, but it is not sufficient for more demanding tasks, such as generating an extended email from a prompt or answering a complex question. For this reason, contemporary LLMs consist of stacks of transformer blocks, where the output of one layer becomes the input to the next. In this layered arrangement, lower levels of the transformer stack tend to encode relatively simple features such as word order or syntactic structures, while successively higher layers capture increasingly complex semantic and contextual associations. In this way, depth matters. Stacking dozens or even hundreds of layers allows the model to develop a highly differentiated internal mathematical representation of language.

It is this depth that makes LLMs *large*. OpenAI's GPT-3, for instance, incorporated 96 transformer layers, while its successor, GPT-4, is reported to contain over a hundred layers and more than a trillion parameters: that is, the adjustable weights that encode the model's learned associations. Operationally, we can think of this process as one of successive reinterpretation. Each layer revisits the same sequence of tokens, highlighting new relationships, deriving additional associations, and refining the representation produced by earlier layers. After many such passes through the transformer stack, the model becomes capable of generating fluent and contextually appropriate text in response to a prompt. Enabling this ability, however, requires one additional component: *training*.

Model Training

Like any ANN, the stack of transformers must be trained. And doing so requires text – lots of text. This includes not only much of the publicly accessible internet, but also books, articles, documents, and, in the case of more recent commercially available models, large amounts of computer code. In effect, tech companies like OpenAI, Anthropic, and Google have trained their LLMs by scraping text data from virtually every conceivable corner of the digital universe. This training typically consists of three main phases.

1 Pre-training: The first and most important phase is called *pre-training*. (GPT, incidentally, stands for generative *pre-trained* transformer.) At this stage of development, the model is repeatedly tasked with predicting the next word in sequences of text sampled from the training data. For example, given the sentence "To be or not to be, that is the . . .," we would want the model to predict "question" as the correct continuation of the sequence. At the start, the model's guesses about the next word are essentially random, because the connections in its network are initialized with arbitrary values. With each incorrect prediction, however, the error is used as a feedback signal in a process called *backpropagation*, which incrementally adjusts the network's weights. And by doing this again and again and again – through millions if not billions of iterations – the model becomes tuned so that it can reliably predict the next token in sequences that are the same as or even similar to those it has seen during training.

2 Fine-Tuning: Pre-training yields a general-purpose model, but many LLMs undergo a second phase called *fine-tuning*. At this stage, the model is retrained on a more carefully selected or domain-specific dataset. For example, a medical chatbot might be fine-tuned on clinical notes and health FAQs, or a customer support assistant might be fine-tuned on product manuals and transcripts from prior customer interactions with human support professionals. Technically, this is accomplished by adjusting the model's weights – just as in pre-training – but now guided by domain-specific data. The training objective remains the same, predicting the next token, but the data are narrower, more specialized, and often more rigorously curated. Fine-tuning therefore transforms a broad, general-purpose model into one that performs more effectively in specialized applications.

3 Reinforcement Learning from Human Feedback (RLHF): Models such as ChatGPT add a third stage of training. At this step, human evaluators review the model's outputs and provide judgments about which ones are more helpful, appropriate, or accurate. The model then uses these judgments as feedback signals to further refine its behavior. Technically, this is accomplished by training a smaller reward model based on human preferences and then using reinforcement learning (often with a method called proximal policy optimization) to adjust the weights in the transformers that comprise the LLM. In other words, just as pre-training tunes the network's weights to minimize prediction error, RLHF tunes those same weights to maximize alignment with human preferences. This additional step helps align the model's responses with social expectations about tone, context, and safety, making the system more reliable in public-facing applications.

LLM Operations (Putting It All Together)

LLMs generate seemingly meaningful sequences of text through next-token prediction. When we prompt an LLM, like ChatGPT, with a phrase such as "explain next-token prediction," the model attempts to calculate the most likely next token to follow that sequence. This predictive mechanism underlies all of the model's seemingly intelligent behaviors: composing essays, answering questions, engaging in dialogue, and even writing executable code.

The process unfolds in several steps. First, the input text is tokenized, meaning it is broken into smaller units such as words or sub-words. Each token is then converted into a numerical embedding, placing it in a high-dimensional mathematical space where distances represent patterns of similarity and difference. These numerical embeddings are passed through the transformer stack, where each layer combines self-attention, which is used to determine how tokens relate to one another in context, with a feedforward network that refines and transforms that information. The result is a set of context-aware representations for each token in the sequence.

At the final layer, the model computes a probability distribution over all possible next tokens in its vocabulary: that is, the set of tokens that the model was trained to recognize and generate. For example, given the sequence "To be or not to be, that is the . . .", the model may assign relatively high probabilities to continuations such as "question," "dilemma," "problem," or "issue." One token is then selected – often the most probable, though sometimes a less probable option is chosen to introduce variation – and appended to the sequence. This expanded sequence is then fed back into the model, which again predicts the next token. The process repeats, one token at a time, until a complete response has been produced.

For the LLM, therefore, next-token prediction is a sequential operation that dynamically unfolds over time. The model does not have access to a complete thought or an intention to say something in advance. Instead, it builds the output one token at a time, with the significance of any given token remaining provisional and reshaped by those that follow. Thus, meaning emerges not from a pre-existing intention but through an iterative and deferred process, where each new token retrospectively reconfigures what came before. This way of working with language resonates with innovations in 20th-century literary theory and semiotics, especially in the writings of Ferdinand de Saussure, Julia Kristeva, and Jacques Derrida (see Gunkel 2025).

So when does this iterative process stop? At a practical level, generation ends when the model is instructed to stop. This may occur because a maximum token limit has been reached, a stopping condition has been triggered (e.g., a punctuation mark or new line), or an instruction in the prompt has been satisfied (e.g., "*Write a 100-word summary*"). But this question touches on something more philosophically profound. Because LLMs do not generate from intention or understanding, they do not know when to stop in any human sense. They do not write toward a conclusion, nor can they experience a sense of completion. Instead, they continue predicting the next most likely token until an external constraint intervenes, or until the statistical structure of the sequence begins to break down, resulting in repetition, incoherence, or silence. In this way, LLM text generation ends not because something has been fully said, but because the process has been interrupted by a limit, a rule, or a human decision.

Opportunities

LLMs are among the most visible and widely used AI applications. What makes them distinctive is their ability to respond to simple prompts with fluent, often persuasive natural language output – whether that means writing an essay, answering a question, or holding a conversation. As we have just seen, these models do not *understand* language in the way humans do. Instead, they are trained on massive amounts of text to recognize patterns and predict which words are most likely to come next in a given sequence. From the user's perspective, however, the result can feel remarkably intelligent and useful. LLMs are currently being employed in classrooms, offices, and creative projects, and their influence continues to grow. The following lists some of the tasks and operations that these systems can currently support:

- *Answering Questions:* LLMs can respond to factual, conceptual, or even open-ended questions across a wide range of topics. From explaining quantum physics to outlining the plot of *Hamlet*, these models serve as powerful information retrieval and explanation tools.
- *Summarizing Texts:* Given a long article, report, or document, LLMs can generate concise summaries that capture the main points. This can help users process information quickly and efficiently, especially in academic, journalistic, or business contexts.
- *Translating Languages:* LLMs can translate text from one language to another with surprising fluency. While not perfect, their translations often capture the meaning and tone of the original and can support cross-linguistic communication in real time.
- *Supporting Language Learning:* LLMs can help users learn new languages by providing vocabulary explanations, grammar corrections, example sentences, and conversational practice. Learners can interact with the model in their target language, receive instant feedback, and build confidence through low-pressure dialogue.
- *Writing and Editing:* From drafting emails to revising essays, LLMs can assist with the mechanics and structure of writing.

They can also mimic different tones and genres, whether academic, informal, poetic, or professional.

- *Coding Assistance:* Many LLMs have been trained on large code repositories and can help generate, debug, or explain computer code. This makes them valuable tools for both novice programmers and experienced developers.
- *Creative Generation:* LLMs can compose poems, stories, jokes, or song lyrics based on a simple prompt. While the results vary, they often display stylistic fluency and creativity, making them useful for brainstorming or artistic experimentation.
- *Conversational Companions:* When integrated into chat interfaces, LLMs can carry on extended conversations. They can simulate personalities, play roles, or offer advice, making them suitable for entertainment, education, or even emotional support.
- *Tutoring and Personalized Learning:* LLMs can act as one-on-one tutors by explaining difficult concepts, quizzing users, or adapting explanations based on the user's input. This positions them as personalized educational tools – though their accuracy should always be verified.

This list of capabilities is undeniably impressive. What is perhaps even more striking is the fact that it was generated by ChatGPT in response to the prompt: "Briefly describe what LLMs can do." To be clear, the model doesn't *know* what it can or cannot do. It is not consulting an internal database of facts or reflecting on its own capacities. It is simply stringing words together in sequences that are statistically likely to follow one another. And yet the result is largely accurate, informative, and highly readable. In this way, the list not only describes what ChatGPT can do; it also demonstrates those capabilities in the very act of generating the list.

Challenges

Despite remarkable capabilities across a wide range of tasks and operations, these technologies also have limitations and challenges. While LLMs may appear intelligent, articulate, and even creative, their abilities are ultimately the product of probabilistic pattern matching and not actual understanding, reasoning, or awareness. As a result, they can produce outputs that are plausible sounding but factually incorrect, biased, incoherent, or even harmful. Moreover, their use raises serious questions about accuracy, authorship, environmental impact, the future of work, and human capabilities. In this section, we examine some of the key concerns and complications that arise when relying on LLMs for communication, writing, decision-making, and social interaction.

Bias and Harmful Content

LLMs can inherit and even amplify biases that are present in their training data. Because the word associations produced by an LLM are derived from the ways that human beings have used words – as codified in the texts of the training data – these models can unwittingly reproduce existing stereotypes and prejudices. For example, if the word *doctor* is statistically more likely to appear near the pronoun *he* in the training data, and *nurse* more commonly co-occurs with the pronoun *she*, the model may learn to reproduce these patterns, reinforcing gendered stereotypes. Similar biases have appeared in racialized associations, where certain ethnic or national groups are more likely to be linked with crime, poverty, or danger, while others tend to be associated with success, competence, and authority. Biases can also emerge in translation and summarization. When translating from languages that do not mark gender explicitly, language models often default to masculine pronouns for professions such as engineer or scientist and feminine pronouns for roles such as teacher or administrative assistant.

And these problems can be intensified when LLMs are deployed across different cultural and geographical contexts. Because most of the commercially available LLMs have been trained primarily on English-language and Western-produced texts, they may treat Western norms and values as standard while misrepresenting or marginalizing practices from other regions. When used at global scale, such models risk amplifying existing inequalities by projecting locally situated assumptions as if they were universal – a dynamic that echoes forms of cultural and linguistic colonialism, in which dominant ways of speaking and knowing are imposed through technical systems (Gunkel 2001 and 2018). Bias in LLMs, therefore, is not only a technical issue but also a cultural and political one, shaped by asymmetries of power and by which particular languages, experiences, and perspectives are most heavily represented in the training data.

These problems are unfortunately rather difficult to anticipate or detect in advance, since the training data are vast and the correlations often subtle. Consequently, developers and users typically become aware of this kind of *algorithmic bias* only after the model begins producing outputs that can be interpreted as sexist, racist, ageist, ableist, or otherwise discriminatory. And fixing these problems is neither easy nor straightforward, because the bias does not reside in the model's operations but in the statistical regularities of the data on which it was trained.

This brings us back to a point made in chapter 2. With GOFAI systems, debugging is relatively straightforward: one can locate the problematic line of code, revise it, and then rerun the application. But with ANNs like those behind LLMs, there are no explicit rules or lines of symbolic code to examine or rewrite. Instead, there are only adjusted weights – millions or even billions of them – and the emergent patterns shaped by exposure to massive amounts of training data. At present, the primary strategies for addressing these problems are limited. Developers may opt to decommission a problematic model entirely – which is what Microsoft did with its racist and sexist chatbot Tay.ai[3] – or attempt to reduce harmful outputs through additional training. This typically involves techniques like fine-tuning the model on curated datasets or using RLHF to nudge the system toward more appropriate behaviors.

Hallucinations and Misinformation

In the context of LLM AI, *hallucination* refers to situations where a model produces output that looks legit – i.e., the text is coherent, well-composed, and grammatically correct – but is factually wrong, fabricated, or nonsensical. LLMs have generated academic papers that make reference to sources that do not exist. They have written recipes that include ingredients that are not fit for human consumption. And they have produced financial reports where most of the data have been fabricated.

This is not a matter of the LLM making a mistake or intentionally lying. LLMs are as incapable of fabricating falsehoods as they are of telling the truth. And as with bias, the problem often becomes apparent only after content has already been generated. For this reason, careful fact-checking and critical evaluation are essential whenever LLMs are used for tasks that depend on accuracy or truth. Beyond manual review, technical strategies such as fine-tuning and RLHF can also help reduce the frequency of erroneous output, just as they can mitigate certain forms of bias. Yet neither method offers a complete solution, since models can still generate content that is factually incorrect or misleading. Compounding the issue is the fact that RLHF work is often carried out by workers, many of whom are located in the Global South and employed under precarious, low-paid conditions. These workers are tasked with evaluating, labeling, and moderating model outputs – including harmful content that can be psychologically taxing – yet their labor remains largely invisible in public narratives about AI.

An alternative to RLHF is to supply the LLM with an explicit set of values, rather than relying primarily on feedback from human annotators. This is the approach taken by Anthropic in its development of Claude, which the company describes as an "AI assistant trained with Constitutional AI" (Anthropic 2023). With Constitutional AI (CAI), the LLM is guided by a written set of principles, or a constitution, that can be used to evaluate and revise its outputs. Technically, this process has two stages. First, the model is trained to critique and improve its own responses by applying the constitutional principles as normative criteria. Second, the model is further refined using reinforcement learning, similar to RLHF, but with a crucial difference: instead of relying on large amounts of crowdsourced human feedback, the reinforcement signal is derived from the model's own self-critiques guided by the constitution. In this way, CAI aims to reduce dependence on human annotators while making the model's alignment process more principled.

The current constitution used by Anthropic (2023) "draws from a range of sources including the *UN Declaration of Human Rights*, trust and safety best practices, principles proposed by other AI research labs (e.g., Sparrow Principles from DeepMind), [and] an effort to capture non-western perspectives." In being aligned with these principles, the CAI model not only is able to limit or filter out toxic, illegal, and even discriminatory output but also contributes to model transparency, as one can easily inspect and understand the principles the AI system is following.

Despite these promising benefits, CAI is not a panacea, and the methodology is still in the early stages of deployment.

Intellectual Property and Plagiarism

The training of LLMs requires access to textual data. Essentially, any piece of writing that exists on the internet or in a digital format becomes a potential part of the training corpus. But not all text is created equal. Some – like government documents or literary works whose copyright has expired – belongs to the public domain and can be freely copied, reused, and repurposed. Other textual content is protected by copyright and can only be reused with the explicit consent of the author or rights holder, or through a negotiated licensing agreement.

The problem is that many of today's most widely used LLMs – like OpenAI's ChatGPT – have been trained on digital text scraped from the internet without always clearly differentiating between public domain materials and copyrighted works. This practice has raised serious concerns about intellectual property, particularly among journalists, authors, screenwriters, and publishers. These groups allege that their copyrighted content is being used without consent, compensation, or credit – a trio now often referred to as the *three Cs*. Additionally, training an LLM on a particular writer's work means the model could potentially learn to generate content in that author's distinctive style, and then produce new content that may unfairly compete with the original creator for readers, attention, and even employment opportunities.

The most high-profile legal challenge to date (as of February 2026) comes from *The New York Times*, which in December 2023 filed a lawsuit in the US District Court (Case 1:23-cv-11195) against OpenAI and Microsoft. The suit alleges that these tech companies used large amounts of the *Times*'s copyrighted material to train their language models and, moreover, that the models produce content that directly competes with the news organization. OpenAI has defended its practices under the fair use exception of US copyright law and contends that compensating every content creator whose work appears in the training data would make LLM development prohibitively expensive, potentially stalling progress in AI research and innovation.

Beyond questions of copyright, the use of LLMs has reignited long-standing debates about authorship and originality, especially in educational contexts. If a student uses an LLM like Copilot or Gemini to write an essay, who is the true author of the text? Is the student plagiarizing, or are they simply using a tool – like a calculator or spellchecker – to assist in the production of the document? And if a thesis, journal article, or short story is co-written with the help of an AI model, should the model be credited as a co-author? These questions go beyond the reach of copyright law and touch on deeper philosophical concerns about creativity, responsibility, and the nature of authorship itself. As AI-generated content becomes increasingly indistinguishable from human writing, our existing frameworks for evaluating originality and assigning credit will likely need to evolve as well. We will return to many of these questions in the next chapter. For now, it is sufficient to recognize how and why these problems arise in the context of LLM AI.

Environmental Impact and Sustainability

The training and operation of LLMs like ChatGPT come with significant environmental costs. While these systems deliver instant responses to our prompts with nothing more than a few taps on a screen, they are anything but lightweight. Behind every generated response lies a vast infrastructure of servers, data centers, and energy-intensive hardware that consume large amounts of electricity and water. Although the interaction feels similar to a simple Google search, the underlying process is far more resource intensive. Some estimates suggest that prompting an LLM may consume up to ten times more energy than a conventional internet search (Salathé 2025; Towler 2025).

Sajjad Moazeni, a researcher at Washington University, has estimated that ChatGPT responds to hundreds of millions of queries per day. At that rate, the servers supporting the system consume roughly 1 gigawatt hour (GWh) of electricity daily, which is the equivalent of the energy used by about 33,000 US households (McQuate 2023). Looking ahead, researchers project that by the end of the decade, AI systems could require between 85 and 134 terawatt hours (TWh) annually, a figure that is comparable to the total yearly energy usage of countries such as Argentina, the Netherlands, or Sweden (de Vries 2023).

These numbers, it is important to point out, are estimates and projections. Exact figures are often difficult to obtain or verify, particularly in the United States, where there are currently no federal regulations requiring developers to disclose the energy consumption of their data centers.[4] Still, the seriousness of the issue is underscored by OpenAI CEO Sam Altman's public admission that the continued advancement of LLMs will not be viable without a breakthrough in energy generation (Tangerman 2024).

Water is also a growing concern. While ChatGPT was developed in San Francisco, it runs on server clusters housed in data centers located in places such as Des Moines, Iowa, where large volumes of fresh water are used to cool computing hardware.[5] In one lawsuit filed by local residents, disclosures revealed that the training of ChatGPT (just the training, not the daily operations) consumed roughly 6% of the district's water supply during that period. While this figure may not initially appear dramatic, it underscores two important issues.

First, LLMs are resource intensive, and their demand for water is likely to increase as models grow in size and are used more frequently. Second, data centers are often deliberately sited in regions where land, electricity, and water are relatively inexpensive – frequently in rural or semi-rural areas that may already face environmental stress or limited infrastructure. In such contexts, water used for data center cooling can directly compete with water needed for agriculture, households, and municipal services, particularly during periods of drought or heat waves. Because many jurisdictions lack robust reporting or regulatory requirements for data center water use, these trade-offs are often invisible to the public until conflicts arise. As AI systems scale globally, questions about who bears the environmental costs and who benefits from the services these systems provide become increasingly pressing.

Carbon emissions pose another challenge. OpenAI's GPT-3, for instance, was estimated to have emitted 2,200 tons of CO_2 during training, which is roughly equivalent to the emissions produced by 1,600 round-trip flights between Paris and New York (Charlet 2023). The exact carbon footprint of any given LLM depends on several factors, including hardware efficiency and the source of electricity (i.e., whether it is generated from fossil fuels, nuclear power, or renewables like wind and solar energy). But whatever the exact figures, the broader sustainability challenge is clear. The environmental costs of AI are now widely recognized as serious ethical and political issues, especially in relation to the United Nations' Sustainable Development Goals.

Proposed solutions to these problems include powering both training and inference with renewable energy, optimizing models for energy efficiency, fostering public–private partnerships for sustainable infrastructure, and increasing public awareness of the environmental footprint of generative AI (Khowaja et al. 2024). Other approaches, like gamifying the development of energy-efficient AI models (Raper et al. 2022), may also offer additional incentives. But perhaps the most pressing issue is this: Despite the rapid adoption of these technologies, many users remain largely unaware of their environmental costs. The ease and convenience of AI systems tend to obscure the material infrastructures that support them, including energy-intensive data centers and large-scale water use. These costs are also unevenly distributed, as the environmental burdens of AI, such as increased water consumption and heat generation, are often borne by communities that have little influence over how these technologies are developed or governed. For these reasons, environmental literacy should be understood as a core component of digital literacy, requiring an understanding not only of how AI works but also of where its resources come from and who bears the costs of its operation.

Technological Unemployment

LLM-based AI presents a credible threat of *technological unemployment*,[6] particularly in industries and occupations that rely heavily on communication. When a system like ChatGPT can generate coherent and publishable text or conduct real-time customer interactions, the demand for human workers – journalists, copywriters, authors, screenwriters, and corporate communication professionals – is inevitably affected. During the last major disruption to this sector – the rise of the internet – the standard advice to displaced workers was learn to code. And many did, mastering HTML, CSS, PHP, JavaScript, and other web development languages. But that is no longer a guaranteed refuge. Today, applications can not only generate functional code from a simple prompt but also produce a working application from something as rudimentary as a hand-drawn sketch of the user interface.

Responses to this looming shift in employment opportunity have taken multiple forms. One strategy is resistance. This was the approach taken by the Writers Guild of America (WGA) during the Hollywood writers' strike of 2023. In negotiations with the studios, the WGA demanded explicit protections against AI-generated content, both to prevent their scripts from being used as training data without consent and to avoid being forced to compete with AI-generated outputs derived from their own work product. The union ultimately secured these protections, but only because it had the leverage of collective bargaining. Workers in other fields – like paralegals, PR specialists, and journalists – may not be so fortunate. Without strong unions or professional associations to negotiate on their behalf, they are more likely to confront the challenges of automation alone, with limited ability to resist or shape the terms of adoption.

Another proposed solution is reskilling. LLMs may be displacing many traditional writing and communication jobs, but they are also creating new ones. The idea is that displaced workers can pivot, acquiring the skills that allow them to guide and refine LLM outputs rather than generate content directly. But this approach has two major problems. First, there is a numbers problem. A marketing firm that once employed 15–20 copywriters might now get by with only one or two employees working with AI to produce the same quantity and quality of content. Because automation is designed to reduce labor costs, we should not expect a one-to-one transfer. Fewer positions will remain, and competition for them will likely be intense.

Second, these new jobs are still being defined. Many of these positions – whatever they eventually come to be called, and that uncertainty is part of the problem – do not yet exist as established professions. As a result, there is no standardized training, credential, or curriculum. Workers hoping to make the transition often must reskill without knowing exactly which skills will prove valuable. This uncertainty also poses a challenge for educators. Colleges, universities, and technical schools now face the difficult task of rethinking curricula to prepare students for a labor market that is shifting in unpredictable ways.

Deskilling and Technological Dependency

Alongside concerns about job displacement and reskilling, an equally consequential issue is deskilling. As LLMs become increasingly capable of summarizing articles, translating text, generating emails, and drafting essays, there is a growing temptation to outsource these tasks to the machine. And while such automation may appear efficient or liberating in the short term, it risks eroding the human competencies required to perform these tasks in the first place. Just as the rise of global positioning system (GPS) navigation has arguably diminished our ability to read maps or form spatial awareness, heavy reliance on LLMs could result in the gradual loss of skills in writing, reading, and even basic argumentative reasoning.

This is not merely a hypothetical concern; it is already visible in classrooms, workplaces, and professional writing. When students rely on AI to draft essays, they may generate text without learning how to structure an argument or integrate sources effectively. Similarly, when professionals delegate routine communication tasks to AI assistants, they may find themselves less practiced and confident when those tools are unavailable or unable to perform what is requested. Over time, as with any form of automation, what begins as assistance can become dependence.

This growing dependency is not merely an individual or educational concern. It has wider structural and political consequences. The dominant LLMs – such as ChatGPT, Claude, Gemini, and Meta's LLaMA – are developed, trained, and maintained by a small number of powerful multinational technology companies. These corporations own the infrastructure, control the training data, and dictate the terms of access and use. In this respect, LLMs are not simply productivity tools but also instruments of *platform capitalism*, where economic and communicative life is increasingly mediated by privately owned digital platforms. The promise of cognitive augmentation, therefore, comes at the cost of heightened dependence on proprietary, commercially driven systems.

These questions matter, because as more of our educational, professional, and civic communications become dependent on LLM-generated content, the asymmetry at stake is no longer simply one of access versus exclusion, as in earlier discussions of the digital divide. Instead, it concerns who owns and governs these systems, who can afford sustained and meaningful use, and who must adapt to decisions made elsewhere about availability, pricing, and acceptable speech. In this way, technological dependency does more than erode individual capacities. It also restructures political agency and participation in democratic governance (Coeckelbergh 2024).

Summary

LLMs – like ChatGPT, Claude, Gemini, and DeepSeek 深度求索 – have quickly become one of the most visible and consequential forms of artificial intelligence. They can generate text that is coherent, fluent, and responsive, and in doing so they have begun to reshape communication, education, and creative practices. At the same time, however, we have seen that this power comes with significant limitations and risks. These models do not understand language in any human sense. Instead, they operate by detecting patterns and predicting tokens based on probabilities. This gives them surprising capabilities, but it also means their outputs can reproduce bias and spread misinformation, their infrastructure carries substantial though often opaque environmental costs, and their widespread use disrupts labor markets while reinforcing dependency on privately owned digital platforms.

At the same time, these technologies – precisely because they use language without understanding – unsettle long-standing assumptions about language, knowledge, authorship, and responsibility. They compel us to reconsider whether meaning requires intention, whether creativity is an exclusively human capacity, and who should be accountable when machine-generated content has social and political consequences. All of this opens the door to a larger question: If machines can generate not only statements but also poems, stories, and code, then what exactly is creativity; and who or what gets to be called creative? That is the subject of the next chapter, where we will examine how computational systems are not only simulating human expression but also reshaping how we think about invention, imagination, and the act of making something new.

Learning Activities

1 Exquisite Corpse: Next-Token Prediction

Purpose: The *exquisite corpse* (*cadavre exquis*) is a collaborative technique developed by Surrealist artists in the 1920s, in which participants add words or images sequentially without full knowledge of the whole, allowing unexpected meanings to emerge from collective, non-intentional creation. In this activity, the exquisite corpse is repurposed to illustrate how language can be generated through local, step-by-step decisions, illustrating an approach that parallels the operation of statistical language models.

Procedure: Form small groups of four to six participants. Each group is given a piece of paper with a short text prompt that stops mid-sentence, such as: "Truth appears when . . .," "Knowledge depends on . . .," or "Who decides what . . . ?" One student begins by writing the one word they believe plausibly continues the sequence. The paper is then folded to partially conceal the sentence so that the next student can see only the two most recent words. Students take turns adding exactly one word at a time, each making a local judgment about what could reasonably come next given the limited context (i.e., only seeing the last two words in the evolving sequence). Continue until the group has produced a complete sentence or reached a pre-determined length (e.g., 15–20 words). Unfold the paper to reveal the full sentence and read it aloud to the class.

Learning Goal: Experience how next-token prediction operates as a sequential, probabilistic process and understand how fluent and sometimes surprising linguistic content can emerge without prior intention or understanding.

2 Mapping Meaning with Embeddings

Purpose: This activity helps you grasp how LLMs represent meaning relationally through proximity and distance rather than definitions or reference to the world.

Procedure: Working individually or in small groups, choose one word (e.g., dog, freedom, or justice). List five words that seem closely related and five that seem distant or unrelated. Arrange these words on paper or a whiteboard as if they existed in a shared space, placing related words closer together and unrelated words farther apart. Compare your "map" with that of others. Discuss where your maps differ and why. Reflect on how meaning can emerge from differential relationships among words rather than from intrinsic definitions.

Learning Goal: Experience how embeddings work and the way that LLMs represent meaning as relational and contextual rather than semantic or intentional.

3 Prompting an LLM and Shaping Probabilities

Purpose: This activity helps you understand how prompting works in LLMs by experimenting with how small changes in the wording of the prompt reshapes output. You will see how prompts guide probabilities, not understanding, even though the interaction can feel conversational or intentional.

Procedure: Working individually or in pairs, choose an LLM (such as ChatGPT, Claude, Copilot, or another publicly available system) and run a small experiment. Start with a single core task (explaining something, describing a process, or telling a story). Submit that task three times, changing only one variable in each version – such as audience, genre, tone, or style. Here are a few example sets, but you are encouraged to invent your own:

- "Explain climate change to a child/a policymaker/a conspiracy theorist."
- "Describe how to make a sandwich as a recipe/a poem/a legal contract."
- "Explain what an algorithm is in the form of a fairy tale/a stand-up comedy routine/a customer service FAQ."

Save or copy the three outputs. Compare them and note: What stayed the same across all versions? What changed (e.g., tone, structure, vocabulary, assumptions)? Which surprised you?

Learning Goal: Experience how prompting shapes LLM output by narrowing and steering statistical possibilities and understand why interacting with these systems can feel meaningful even though they do not think, intend, or understand in a human sense.

Further Reading

Mark Coeckelbergh and David J. Gunkel, *Communicative AI: A Critical Introduction to Large Language Models* (2025).

This book proposes that LLMs should be understood not merely as computational tools but also as participants in communication. By treating them as communicative agents, the authors show how LLMs disrupt traditional notions of authorship, meaning, and responsibility. The volume provides both a philosophical and practical framework for engaging critically with communicative AI systems and applications.

Kate Crawford, *Atlas of AI* (2021).

This book maps out the hidden costs of AI, showing how data centers, supply chains, and human labor underpin seemingly immaterial technologies. Crawford's analysis emphasizes the ecological, political, and social consequences of AI systems, making it essential reading for grasping the infrastructures that make LLMs and generative AI (GAI) applications possible.

Claude E. Shannon and Warren Weaver, *The Mathematical Theory of Communication* (1949).

This book (a reprint of Shannon's influential paper) established the mathematical framework for thinking about language as information that could be quantified, transmitted, and predicted. And Warren Weaver's introduction provides an accessible overview of the theory and its application to and importance for work in the humanities and social sciences.

Shoshana Zuboff, *The Age of Surveillance Capitalism: The Fight for a Human Future at the New Frontier of Power* (2019).

This book explains how big tech companies extract personal data to generate profit, turning human experience into raw material for computation. This framework highlights how AI systems and applications are not neutral innovations but products of surveillance-driven economies, with profound implications for power, privacy, and democracy.

5

Computational Creativity and Generative AI

Learning Outcomes

- Explain how computational creativity has been implemented by way of different AI methodologies, from early symbolic approaches to contemporary machine learning systems as well as diffusion and multimodal models.
- Analyze how generative AI (GAI) challenges traditional ideas of creativity, originality, and artistic intention, drawing on concepts such as remix and combinational, exploratory, or transformational creativity.
- Evaluate how GAI reconfigures authorship and responsibility, including questions of intellectual property, attribution, and the distribution of creative agency across human and machine participants.
- Critically assess the cultural, ethical, and political implications of GAI outputs, including issues of trust, deception, deepfakes, and the impact of large-scale machine-generated content on public discourse.

Introduction

In the previous chapter, we examined how large language models (LLMs) complicate long-standing assumptions about language, meaning, and communication. If machines can now produce language that is coherent, contextually appropriate, and sometimes even inventive, then one of the defining capacities we have long associated with human intelligence seems to have been ceded to the machines.[1] The next line of defense, and perhaps the one that is for us most significantly charged, is creativity. For centuries, it has served as the final bastion of human exceptionalism, the place we retreated to when other capacities – calculation, memory, translation, even conversation – had been surrendered to the machines.

Historically, the assumption has been that while AI might translate our documents, manage routine retail and social interactions, and even recommend movies or music, it could never truly be inventive nor able to originate something new. From the strict instructions of early symbolic AI to the probabilistic learning of later applications, computers were thought to do only what we have told them to do. Alan Turing, citing Ada Lovelace[2] – the 19th-century mathematician often regarded as the first computer scientist – summarized this view when he quoted her observation that a computer has "no pretensions to originate anything. It can only do whatever we know how to order it to perform" (Turing 1950, 447). Creativity, according to this way of thinking, is and has remained the one capability that is irreducibly human.

But this assumption is now contested and seems increasingly difficult to defend. Diffusion models and multimodal LLMs can generate strikingly original images from text prompts. Audio and music platforms, such as Suno and Udio, can generate original audio content that is virtually indistinguishable from human compositions and performances. And AI systems like AlphaFold and DABUS have made novel scientific discoveries and designed entirely new products. These developments not only invite but also compel us to ask whether creativity, artistry, and innovation are as exclusively human as we once believed, or whether our understanding and definitions of these capacities need to be renegotiated and realigned in response to a new technological reality.

This chapter investigates computational creativity and generative AI (GAI) in three steps. We begin with its history, looking at how researchers have tried to model creative processes in machines and what that tells us about how creativity itself is defined and characterized. We then turn to the technical foundations of today's systems and applications – diffusion models and multimodal AI – to see how they operate and why their design matters for the kinds of outputs they produce. Finally, we consider the broader consequences of these innovations, investigating the way that GAI extends the logic of remix, disrupts ideas of authorship and intellectual property, and raises important ethical questions regarding responsibility and trust in a media environment increasingly inundated with machine-generated content. The key issue, then, is not only whether AI can be creative but also how it is reshaping the conditions under which creativity, creators, and created products are understood and evaluated.

Computational Creativity

Computational creativity is the interdisciplinary field that studies and develops computer systems capable of behaviors we would normally call creative if performed by a human being. Long before the advent of machine learning and large-scale generative models, researchers explored how rules, heuristics, and symbolic reasoning might produce novel and valuable outputs in domains such as music, visual art, poetry, and design. The focus was not only on producing output that appeared to be creative by human observers, but also on investigating and understanding the boundaries of creativity itself: that is, how it might be defined, modeled, and evaluated in computational terms.

One of the influential early researchers in this domain was Margaret Boden (2004), who argued that creativity – whether human or machine – can be understood and classified according to three types: (1) *combinational creativity*, which generates novel combinations of familiar ideas; (2) *exploratory creativity*, which searches a conceptual space for new possibilities within established boundaries and rules; and (3) *transformational creativity*, which alters the rules themselves to create entirely new conceptual possibilities. Early systems and applications tended to excel at the first two forms by using symbolic reasoning techniques to recombine existing elements or systematically explore previously well-defined creative possibilities.

While these GOFAI approaches were limited by explicit rule sets and instructions, they did provide important conceptual insights, demonstrating that creativity could be approached as a formalizable computational process and not as some ineffable human quality or product of individual genius. In doing so, these initial innovations laid the groundwork – both technically and theoretically – for today's GAI, in which the scope and scale of computational creativity have expanded far beyond what these early practitioners could have imagined. In this first section, we will look at two historically important examples of computational creativity in order to set the stage: David Cope's Experiments in Musical Intelligence and Simon Colton's The Painting Fool.

Experiments in Musical Intelligence

Though algorithmic composition has a long and varied history – stretching from the 18th-century *musikalisches Würfelspiel* or musical dice game to mid-20th-century computer-assisted composition techniques – one of the most celebrated and controversial achievements in this lineage is David Cope's *Experiments in Musical Intelligence* (EMI). Developed as a PC-based algorithmic composer, EMI (or Emmy) was capable of analyzing large collections of existing musical works, extracting and recombining their structural components, and generating new, original scores that closely resembled or emulated the style of canonical composers such as Mozart, Bach, and Chopin. In some cases, these machine-generated pieces were so stylistically convincing that even individuals with formal musical training could not reliably distinguish them from the originals.

The inner workings of Emmy are, in principle, rather simple and straightforward. As Cope (2017) described it on his website, the algorithm follows three basic principles:

- *Deconstruction:* Analyze musical works and separate them into their component parts.
- *Signatures:* Identify and retain those features that signify a composer's unique style.

- *Compatibility:* Recombine components in ways that produce musically coherent new compositions.

Like any algorithmic application, Emmy first needs to be supplied with computable musical data. For this purpose, Cope designed a special data structure, where each note in a given musical work would be represented by a distinct set of five numbers that could then be stored in a database and processed by the algorithm. In his book *Virtual Music*, Cope (2001) provides the following example:

0 60 1000 1 64

This numeric representation – what might today be called a musical note embedding – encodes the following: The first number (0) represents the event's on-time or the amount of time that has elapsed from the beginning of the work to the time that the note is initiated. The second number (60) represents pitch. The third number (1000) indicates duration in milliseconds, or how long a note is held. The fourth (1), represents the number of the MIDI channel that is assigned to that note for the purpose of its performance. And the fifth and final number (64) represents dynamics, with 0 indicating silence and 127 being *fortissimo*. Using this numeric representation, one can transpose a musical composition – like Beethoven's 9th Symphony – into a sequence of numbers, or what Cope calls an *event list*, that can then be accessed and processed by the Emmy algorithm.

Once the database is built, Emmy processes this source material in four sequential steps:

1 *Pattern Matching:* "The pattern matching step is the process of comparing event lists representing musical works or phrases in the musical database to discover what elements they have in common" (Cope 2010, 3). Once musical works have been translated into a common method of numeric representation by way of the event list, the algorithm can use simple pattern matching techniques to identify commonalities (similar kinds of numbers) between different works. The purpose of this step is to identify the signature characteristics of a composer's or genre's style. When a signature is identified, the corresponding notes in the event list are tagged with an additional piece of metadata in

the database. This ensures that when segmentation later divides the music into beat-level units, any unit containing tagged notes is recognized as part of a stylistic signature and preserved intact rather than cut apart. In this way, the pattern matching step ensures that Emmy's recomposed output retains the recognizable character of its source tradition, whether that be a Bach chorale or a Chopin mazurka.

2 *Segmentation:* Building on the results of pattern matching, which identifies both genre characteristics and stylistic signatures, Emmy then divides each work in the database into beat-length units. Because each musical work is already encoded as an event list, segmentation operates directly on these data. The algorithm scans the continuous event list, slices it wherever the on-time counter reaches a beat boundary, and groups together all notes that occur within that beat. Each of these beat segments is enriched with contextual metadata, representing the phrase grouping it belongs to, its location in the work, whether it is part of a stylistic signature (as identified in the pattern matching step), and its functional role as defined by a SPEAC score (Statement, Preparation, Extension, Antecedent, Consequent). Thus, what begins as a straightforward slicing of the event list becomes progressively more complex, since the same musical sequence can take on different roles depending on its context. This enriched segmentation ensures that Emmy later recombines material in ways that are musically logical and stylistically coherent rather than random or "musical gibberish" (Cope 2010, 4).

3 *Recombination:* Building on segmentation, which has already divided works into beat-level units and enriched them with stylistic tags and SPEAC scores for functional roles, Emmy can now begin the process of putting these pieces back together. "Recombinancy," as Cope (2010, 7) explains, "is a method for producing new and logical, i.e. musically logical, collections of musical events (i.e., new compositions) by recombining existing data into new logical orders on the basis of rules." These rules – basic guidelines or principles governing musical qualities like pitch, melody, harmony, etc. – could be pre-programmed and applied to the recombination effort. But this imposition of rules generally produces results that sound mechanical, or what Cope (2007, 10) calls "musically stale imitations." For this reason,

Emmy utilizes recombination rules that are not imposed by programming instructions but discovered in the genre and style of the source material. The Emmy algorithm, as Cope (2010, 7) explains, "assumes that every work, or stylistically consistent body of music, contains an implicit set of instructions, or rules, for creating different but highly-related replications of itself. Consequently, recombinancy, based on rules acquisition (as distinct from rules imposition) provides logical and successful approaches to composing new, highly-related replications of the original work(s)." Emmy acquires its rules by utilizing augmented transition networks (ATNs), which were initially developed in NLP for parsing (taking apart and analyzing) natural language sentences. Emmy uses ATNs to analyze the logical order of segments in the music stored in the database in order to identify recombination patterns that are consistent with the musical form, style, or genre that it is emulating.

4 *Output:* The final step is to render the results of recombination into an actual composition. "The output of the Emmy software," Cope explains (2010, 8), "is a musical database with an entire new composition, stylistically faithful to compositions in the original database and resembling them, derived from them but not replicating them." This output can be manifested in the form of a musical score that can be performed by human musicians or a MIDI file that can be processed by a computer-controlled synthesizer. In other words, if the musical compositions that are fed into the Emmy algorithm are a set of chorales composed by J.S. Bach, Emmy will analyze and process thes musical data and then output a brand new chorale that sounds like, is entirely consistent with, and may even be indistinguishable from one that could have been written by Bach.

To evaluate Emmy's effectiveness, Cope adapted Alan Turing's imitation game. In his musical version, listeners – sometimes expert musicologists – listen to a set of works, some composed by humans (e.g., Bach chorales, Chopin mazurkas) and others that have been generated by Emmy. Their task is to identify the human works, distinguishing them from compositions produced by the algorithm. Cope reports that even experienced listeners frequently fail to make the correct distinction, underscoring Emmy's ability to produce stylistically convincing compositions.

The Painting Fool

Cope's general method for computational creativity is not limited to music. It can be applied to any combinational or exploratory creative practice in which new works emerge from either the novel combination of familiar elements or the discovery of new possibilities within established boundaries and rules. Consequently, it should be no surprise that this approach to algorithmic creativity has been successfully implemented with other art forms, like visual images and painting.

The Painting Fool – developed by Simon Colton, Professor of Computational Creativity, Games, and Artificial Intelligence at Queen Mary University of London – is an automated painter designed with the explicit ambition of being "taken seriously as a creative artist in its own right" (Colton 2012, 16). To date, the algorithm has produced hundreds of artworks, exhibited in both virtual and real-world galleries. While the system software has been repeatedly upgraded and refined over time, its core operations remain rooted in a process of decomposition and recombination, similar to what Cope utilized for Emmy.

One project, called "Automated Collage Generation – with Intent," provides a good illustration of the general approach. In this case, The Painting Fool was tasked with producing original collages based on current events reported in the news. The generative process unfolds in three main steps:

1 *Text Retrieval and Analysis:* The system accesses news headlines and articles via public application programming interfaces (APIs) from sources such as Google News and *The Guardian*. "The API," as Colton and his research team explain, "provides access to headlines, for which there are a number of associated articles, multimedia files, blogs, forums, etc., and our system extracts the first text-based article from this list" (Krzeczkowska et al. 2010, 37). From here, it utilizes a text analysis technique, called "TextRank," to identify and extract the most important or popular keywords.

2 *Image Retrieval and Manipulation:* The extracted keywords are used to retrieve relevant digital images from both online sources (Google Image Search and Flickr) and the 32,000-image

Corel library, whose contents have been hand-tagged for precise keyword matching. Basically, the algorithm identifies relevant images by performing a simple keyword match on the tagged images contained in these image libraries.

3 Scene Construction and Rendering: Retrieved images are assembled into a collage using one of several grid-based templates. The system then applies The Painting Fool's non-photorealistic rendering capabilities – different filters, effects, and rendering techniques such as those available in image processing applications like Photoshop – to transform the composition into something visually stylized and artistic looking.

Though the results of this process may appear relatively simple, Colton and his collaborators argue that the project's real significance resides not in the final images but in what it reveals about artistic intention. Because the specific content of each collage is determined by a combination of current events, automated keyword extraction, and image retrieval, they contend that the software, rather than its human designers, provided the operative intent behind each generated work. This claim directly challenges the idea that creativity necessarily requires human authorship and invites deeper reflection on how we define subjectivity, intentionality, and purpose in creative practices.

Machine Learning Innovations

Emmy and The Painting Fool relied on symbolic reasoning architectures and carefully curated datasets to break existing works into smaller units and then reassemble these fragments into new recomposed versions. The next wave of innovation came from machine learning approaches, where generative models are trained on large datasets and learn patterns directly from examples rather than relying on coded instructions and templates. With deep neural networks and other connectionist architectures, these systems and applications are able to generate novel outputs that are both surprising and stylistically consistent. Thus, the shift to machine learning approaches marked a turning point in computational creativity, moving from the recombination of known elements toward the reconfiguration of creative possibility itself.

Google DeepDream

One early and influential example of neural network-based image generation is *Google DeepDream* (also known as Inceptionism). DeepDream takes an image recognition network and reverses its usual mode of operation. As explained on the Google AI blog, image recognition with deep neural networks typically involves "training an artificial neural network by showing it millions of training examples and gradually adjusting the network parameters until it gives the classifications we want" (Mordvintsev et al. 2015). In other words, these systems are trained on labeled image data, digital images that have been explicitly tagged as "cat" or "dog," for example. Through repeated error correction, the network adjusts its internal parameters (the weighted connections between artificial neurons) until it can reliably classify new inputs, such as determining whether an image depicts a cat or a dog.

With DeepDream, things go in the opposite direction. Instead of feeding an image into the network and inquiring what it is, DeepDream asks a different question: What would an image have to look like for the network to strongly recognize a particular object? To respond to this question, DeepDream begins with an image of random noise and then repeatedly modifies this image so as to amplify whatever visual features the network associates with a selected category. As the developers explain: "Say you want to know what sort of image would result in 'banana.' Start with an image full of random noise, then gradually tweak the image towards what the neural net considers a banana" (Mordvintsev et al. 2015). Each iteration slightly adjusts the image pixels to strengthen patterns the network already responds to, causing familiar shapes and textures to emerge (Figure 5.1).

Initially, Google engineers developed DeepDream as a diagnostic and visualization tool, intended to help them understand what features an image recognition system had learned internally. By making those features visible, the technique offered insight into how deep neural networks "see." However, this same reversal of the recognition process produced an unexpected result: surreal, dreamlike images that quickly attracted public

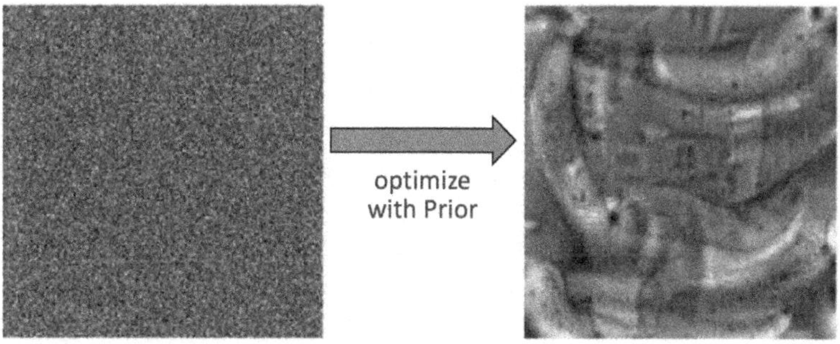

Figure 5.1 Banana image produced by running the Google image recognition algorithm in reverse
Source: Mordvintsev et al. 2015

attention. And some of these images were later sold at charity auctions for as much as $8,000.

Obvious and Generative Adversarial Networks

A different approach developed when artists deliberately began using deep learning as a creative opportunity, rather than as a purely technical or diagnostic tool. One well-known example is Obvious, a Paris-based art collective consisting of Hugo Caselles-Dupré, Pierre Fautrel, and Gauthier Vernier. Obvious employed a *generative adversarial network* (GAN) to produce a series of portraits depicting members of a fictional aristocratic family, the Belamys, rendered in the style of European Old Master painting. GANs are a form of unsupervised machine learning that employ two interconnected neural networks. The first, called the Generator, produces candidate images in an attempt to emulate the statistical patterns of a training dataset. The second, called the Discriminator, evaluates these generated images and attempts to distinguish them from genuine examples in the dataset. Through repeated rounds of backpropagation, the Generator improves its ability to produce convincing images, while the Discriminator becomes better at detecting synthetic ones. Over time, this adversarial process drives the Generator to produce outputs that increasingly resemble the originals (i.e., images in the training data).

As Caselles-Dupré explained,

> We fed the system with a dataset of 15,000 portraits painted between the 14th century and the 20th. The Generator makes a new image based on the set, then the Discriminator tries to spot the difference between a human-made image and one created by the Generator. The aim is to fool the Discriminator into thinking that the new images are real-life portraits. (Christie's 2018)

In effect, the two networks learn together through competition. As the Discriminator becomes increasingly more skilled at spotting fakes, the Generator is forced to become more sophisticated in its efforts, producing increasingly convincing synthetic portraits. The final results of this process were printed on canvas with an inkjet printer, framed, and signed with the mathematical formula describing the relationship between the generator and discriminator (Obvious 2018). In October 2018, one such work – *Portrait of Edmond de Belamy* (Figure 5.2) – sold at Christie's for just under half-a-million US dollars, an event the auction house heralded as "the arrival of AI art on the world auction stage" (Christie's 2018).

Figure 5.2 *Portrait of Edmond de Belamy*
Source: Public domain image available from https://en.wikipedia.org/wiki/Edmond_de_Belamy

Whereas the images generated by DeepDream emerge from an effort to visualize and exaggerate the patterns a pre-trained network has already internalized through prior learning, GANs such as those employed by Obvious rely on an ongoing adversarial training loop, in which a Generator and a Discriminator refine their capacities together through repeated feedback. Taken together, these systems mark a shift toward connectionist architectures whose creative potential arises from machine learning rather than from explicit, step-by-step instructions and pre-fabricated templates. This shift expanded the range of possible outputs beyond what programmers could feasibly code by hand, setting the stage for the even more powerful generative systems that followed.

Contemporary GAI

The recent wave of GAI systems – typified by diffusion models such as OpenAI's DALL·E, Midjourney, Google's Nano Banana, and multimodal models like OpenAI's GPT-5, Google's Gemini, and Suno – mark a significant leap beyond earlier forms of computational creativity. Where GOFAI systems like Emmy or The Painting Fool relied on pre-programmed rules and templates, and the early deep learning implementations like DeepDream or the GANs of Obvious required highly specific architectures and datasets, these contemporary models integrate vast quantities of training data with scalable architectures capable of producing high-fidelity outputs across multiple media forms (text, images, audio, video, etc.). In doing so, they arguably cross over into what Boden called transformational creativity, redrawing the boundaries of the possible and forcing us to rethink what creativity itself can mean.

Diffusion Models

Among the most influential of the recent generative architectures are diffusion models, which have become central to image generation applications such as DALL·E, Midjourney, and Stable Diffusion. These models work by intentionally *diffusing* training data – usually images, photographs, or other visual material – through the gradual addition of random noise and then learning how to recover the original data by reversing this noising process (Ho et al. 2020). By learning how to undo noise in a step-by-step process, the model eventually acquires the ability to generate new images that follow the statistical patterns found in its training data. In this sense, diffusion models combine DeepDream's use of learned internal representations with the generative capabilities of GANs, such as the system used by Obvious to produce new images from a learned data distribution.

What makes diffusion models distinctive is that their training process unfolds in two complementary phases: *forward diffusion* and *reverse diffusion*.[3] In forward diffusion, the training data are systematically degraded by adding small amounts of random noise over many steps, until all recognizable features disappear and the result resembles pure Gaussian noise or visual static. In reverse diffusion, the model learns to undo this process by using backpropagation to gradually minimize prediction error. Repeated across millions of training examples, this procedure enables the model not merely to recover specific images, but also to build a statistical map of how structure, texture, and detail emerge from randomness.

Once trained, a diffusion model can begin with pure noise and, drawing on this learned statistical map, progressively de-noise it into an image that satisfies a given set of conditions. These conditions may be broad, such as "an image of a dog," or highly specific, such as "a black-and-white photograph of a dachshund smoking a pipe." To guide this de-noising process, most commercial systems pair diffusion models with mechanisms that link text and images. Building such mechanisms depends on massive datasets of paired text and images largely scraped from the internet and social media platforms. Thus, the millions of tagged and captioned photos that we share online, whether on Flickr, Instagram, or elsewhere, provide much of the raw data that makes these systems work. In other words, we have unwittingly been supplying both the materials and labor that support these GAI platforms.

There are different technical methods for linking text to images, but to see how this works in practice, we can look at OpenAI's DALL·E 2. In the broadest sense – what computer scientists call the highest-level description – DALL·E 2 has two main components. The first, called the Prior, maps a text embedding (a numerical representation of the user prompt) onto the most relevant image embedding (a numerical representation of an image). The second, called the Decoder, takes that image embedding and uses a diffusion process to generate a full-resolution image (Figure 5.3).

Both steps depend on CLIP (Contrastive Language–Image Pre-training), an OpenAI model designed to align text and images in a shared representational space (Radford et al. 2021). CLIP achieves this with two separate encoders trained jointly (Figure 5.4):

- *Text Encoder:* The text encoder works much like the LLMs described in the previous chapter.[4] A prompt – such as "a black-and-white photo of a dachshund smoking a pipe" – is

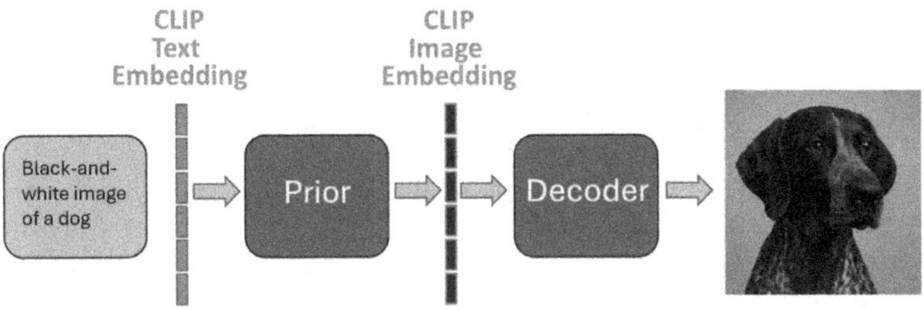

Figure 5.3 Block diagram of DALL·E 2
Source: Image created by David J. Gunkel

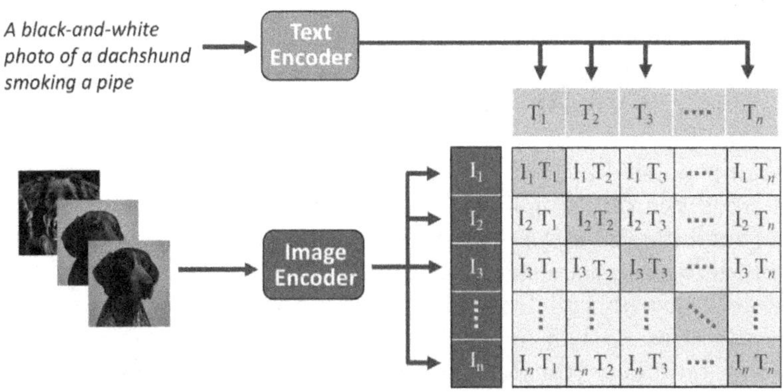

Figure 5.4 "CLIP jointly trains an image encoder and a text encoder to predict the correct pairings of a batch of (image, text) training examples" (Radford et al. 2021, 2)
Source: Image created by David J. Gunkel

first tokenized, with each token converted into a vector using an embedding scheme the model has learned during training. The sequence of token vectors is then processed through a transformer, which applies a self-attention mechanism to capture the relationships among tokens. From this, the model produces a single text embedding: a fixed-length vector that represents the overall semantic content of the prompt in the shared space CLIP uses to align text and images.
- *Image Encoder:* The image encoder is a vision transformer (ViT), an architecture first proposed by a team of researchers at Google (Dosovitskiy et al. 2020). Here, an image is divided into fixed-size patches, such as 16 × 16 pixels, with each pixel having three RGB (red, green, blue) values. This 16 × 16 × 3 patch is flattened into a one-dimensional vector with a length of 768 numbers. This vector is then passed through a linear projection layer that converts it into a patch embedding of the correct size for the transformer. At this point, therefore, every patch is represented by a vector in the same embedding space. Next, positional information is added so the model knows where each patch came from in the original image, and the full sequence of patch embeddings is fed into the transformer. The transformer processes this sequence with self-attention, capturing relationships across the entire image, and outputs a global image embedding that represents the content of the image as a whole.

When you type a prompt into the DALL·E 2 application, the Prior uses CLIP's text encoder to convert it into a text embedding and maps it to the nearest image embedding that has been produced by CLIP's image encoder. The Decoder – implemented as a diffusion model – takes that image embedding and, through *reverse diffusion*, generates a final image. And because this diffusion process is *stochastic* or randomly determined, the system not only yields images that resemble those contained in the training data but also can produce novel combinations, variations, and transformations that never appeared as such in the original dataset. So instead of getting an astronaut, a horse, or a photograph of the moon, we can prompt the application to generate an image of an astronaut riding a horse on the moon.[5]

At first glance, the technical details of diffusion models can feel overwhelming. The important takeaway, however, is not mastery of every component but understanding a few core ideas. First, diffusion models generate content not by copying existing examples, but by learning how structured data emerge from noise and then reversing that process. Second, prompt-based systems guide generation by translating user inputs (such as text descriptions) into shared numerical representations that can shape outputs. Third, these systems depend on massive datasets of human-produced content, much of it drawn from everyday online activity, raising questions about labor, ownership, and consent. Finally, diffusion models exemplify a broader shift in AI-driven computational creativity: Instead of following explicit rules written by programmers, contemporary generative systems derive their creative capacities from statistical learning, enabling outputs that would be impossible to specify in step-by-step instructions.

Multimodal Models

With diffusion models like DALL·E 2, text became a means of translating between different representational modalities, allowing written instructions to guide the generation of visual content. The next step is more ambitious: *multimodal models* capable of processing and generating content across more than one type or mode of media. A multimodal model might, for example, take a photograph as input and produce a written description as output, answer questions about what is being represented, generate an audio narration, or even create a video that animates the scene. This capability comes from training a single model (or a tightly integrated set of models) on large datasets that align different modalities: images with captions, videos with descriptions, audio with transcripts, and so on. By learning a shared representational space that links these data types, multimodal models can move information from one form to another, combine modalities in novel ways, and respond flexibly to prompts that mix media together.

To understand how these capabilities are achieved in practice, it helps to break the process down into three key stages – tokenization, pre-training, and prompting and generation – each of which plays a distinct role in enabling multimodal models to align, interpret, and generate different forms of media content.

1 Tokenization: Just as an LLM begins by tokenizing words, a multimodal model must also do the same with other kinds of media content. Tokenization (as we saw previously) is the process of breaking down complex input into smaller, discrete units that can be represented numerically and processed by the model. With text, words are tokenized into sub-words or other linguistic fragments, each mapped to a vector (an array of numbers) in a high-dimensional embedding space. Images are divided into small, fixed-size patches (for example, 16 × 16 × 3 pixels), each flattened into a linear sequence of numbers representing its pixel values, and then projected into a vector (again, an array of numbers). Audio can be tokenized in two ways: either directly, by slicing the waveform into short, fixed time intervals, or indirectly, by converting the sound into a spectrogram (a visual representation of frequency over time) and then treating it like an image. Video combines these approaches: Individual frames are tokenized like images, while the audio track is tokenized separately, with temporal markers to keep everything in sync.

2 Pre-training: Once all media forms can be expressed in the same representational format, the model is trained on vast datasets containing aligned examples: that is, pairs or sets of related media. A training instance might be a caption paired with a photo, an image paired with an audio clip, or a video with both subtitles and a soundtrack. During training, the model learns to predict missing tokens in a multimodal sequence, much as an LLM predicts the next word in a sentence. For instance, if the model is given the text tokens "A photo of a . . ." alongside the image tokens corresponding to the photograph of a dog, it learns that the next text token should probably be *dog*. If it is provided with these image tokens without a caption, it learns to generate a plausible sequence of text tokens describing the image. Over billions of such examples, the model gradually develops a shared embedding space, where tokens from different modalities – words, images, sounds, video frames – are projected into the same high-dimensional coordinate system. In this space, related items cluster together, regardless of their original form. This alignment allows the model to understand – or, better, to make the association – that a photograph of a dog, the spoken word *dog*, and the written letters d-o-g all point to the same or similar content.

3 Prompting and Generation: Once the model is trained, prompting works much like it does for an LLM, except the input can be any combination of media modalities. The first step is still tokenization: text prompts are split into text tokens, images into visual tokens, audio into audio tokens, and so on. These tokens are then mapped to the shared embedding space the model learned during pre-training, where semantically related items from different modalities cluster together. A prompt like "Describe this image" (with an attached photograph) becomes a single sequence that includes both text and image tokens. At this point, the model's transformer architecture takes over. As we saw in the previous chapter on LLMs, transformers excel at finding relationships between tokens no matter where they appear in a sequence. This same self-attention mechanism makes them ideal for multimodal tasks as the model can attend to a word in the text prompt, a visual feature in an image, and an element of an audio waveform all at once, integrating them into a coherent response. The model then applies the same next-token prediction process used in LLMs – only now the next token could be text (for captions), image patches (for pictures), audio segments (for sound), or video frames (for moving images). And because the model has learned cross-modal relationships, it can flexibly translate or transform from one modality to another: turning text into images, images into audio descriptions, audio into transcriptions, or blending multiple media types into a single output. This shared architecture allows multimodal models to do more than just answer questions like a chatbot or generate images like a diffusion model. They can integrate, compare, and connect across different kinds of media: linking a diagram to a paragraph, matching a melody to a lyric, or even describing what's happening in a video.

Multimodal models represent a significant development in GAI capabilities. By integrating text, images, audio, and video within a shared representational space, these systems can translate, combine, and transform different modes of media content with unprecedented facility. The same transformer-based architectures that enable LLMs to predict the next word now empower models to generate the next image patch, audio segment, or video frame – making possible everything from describing images to composing music to animating static scenes.

Yet these advances are not mere technical innovations. They are also cultural and philosophical interventions, forcing a confrontation with fundamental questions about creativity, authorship, cultural ownership, and the integrity of information in an age when the boundaries between human- and machine-generated content are becoming increasingly difficult to discern.

Opportunities, Challenges, and Open Debates

Understanding how GAI works is only the beginning. The more difficult task is to assess what these systems mean and what consequences they have. We do so here by focusing on three interrelated dimensions: creativity and originality, the figure of the creator, and the nature of the work that is created. Each of these emphasizes different opportunities, challenges, and unresolved questions surrounding the technology, demonstrating that the stakes are not only technical but also cultural, ethical, and political.

Creativity

Creativity has long been treated as one of the defining features of human intelligence, as it designates the capacity to originate ideas, produce artifacts, and create experiences that are novel, valuable, and meaningful. Yet what counts as "creative" has never been entirely settled or conceptually stable. Philosophers, psychologists, art theorists, and cognitive scientists have long debated what creativity is and, in the process, have proposed competing definitions and characterizations, with some emphasizing originality and innovation, others focusing on problem-solving and adaptation, and still others insisting that creativity must be situated in cultural and social contexts.

These debates were already undergoing significant revision well before the advent of AI, as the rise of remix culture in the late 20th and early 21st centuries reframed creativity as a process of recombination rather than creation *ex nihilo*, or "out of nothing." Sampling in hip-hop, mashups, digital collage, and fan fiction challenged the romantic idea and ideal of the artist as a solitary genius, proving that compelling and inventive works can emerge from the strategic appropriation and reuse of existing material. From this vantage point, creativity lies less in conjuring something out of nothing than in carefully selecting, recombining, and transforming what already exists, discovering new juxtapositions, new contexts, and new meanings. As Margaret Boden's taxonomy suggests, remix procedures and practices readily achieved both *combinational* and *exploratory* creativity, but they also arguably qualify as *transformational creativity* to the extent that they have altered the rules of the game for artistry.

GAI extends and amplifies this remix logic. Like a DJ or skilled remixer, these systems work by recombining and transforming prior media content – only now the process is automated and scaled to billions of examples. The training of multimodal models on vast datasets of text, images, and audio can be understood as a kind of *total archive*, where the source material is not consciously selected by a human curator but harvested *en masse* from every conceivable corner of the digital universe. The model learns statistical associations across this archive, allowing it to generate outputs that are novel in form but deeply entangled with and informed by the data it was trained on. GAI can therefore be seen as a continuation of remix's challenge to the romantic figure of individual origination, showing how the new is often a unique recombination of what already exists.

In this sense, GAI resembles remix, but with key differences. Remix practices – from sampling in hip-hop to cut-and-paste digital collage – is grounded in identifiable source material, with the act of selection, extraction, and arrangement often foregrounded. The *sample*, as Eduardo Navas (2012) explains, is always a fragment that retains reference to the whole from which it was extracted, and part of the pleasure of remix comes from recognizing how these fragments are recontextualized. GAI, by contrast, dissolves the boundaries of its sources, producing seamless outputs that obscure their origins. What in remix appears as citation, reference, or even homage is, in GAI, concealed within the statistical weights of the model. The musicians Holly Herndon and Mat Dryhurst have called this process *spawning* (Herndon 2023), to emphasize that the system learns features of a source and then generates new instances in that style rather than reusing a recognizable fragment of the original source material. Where remix generally makes its debt to prior works recognizably audible or visible, spawning effaces it, producing seamless outputs that dissolve the boundaries of origin and increasingly obscure their lineage.

The difference is also economic and political. Remix culture emerged largely from grassroots communities, drawing on accessible tools – turntables, samplers, digital editing software – and circulating work through participatory networks that encouraged exchange and reuse. Its economy was often informal, sustained by practices of borrowing, citation, and gift exchange, even when it ran up against and challenged existing copyright law. As I describe it in my own book on the subject: "Remix – a bastard art form created by the illegitimate appropriation and fusion of two or more recordings – was patently illegal, a deliberate subversion of authority in the culture industry, and a critical intervention in the very material of popular culture" (Gunkel 2016, 80).

GAI, by contrast, is typically dependent on proprietary systems owned and operated by a handful of multinational corporations, with resources, capabilities, and access to vast amounts of training data that we helped construct. This centralization risks shifting creative power away from local communities and toward multinational corporate platforms, raising difficult but important questions about cultural ownership: Who decides which datasets are used? Who benefits from the outputs? And how does this reconfigure access to the means of cultural production?

By following and extending the remix paradigm, GAI both democratizes and concentrates creativity. On the one hand, it lowers barriers to entry, enabling anyone with a prompt to generate images, text, or music at the click of a button. On the other hand, it consolidates control of the underlying infrastructure – massive datasets, high-performance compute, and proprietary architectures – within the hands of a few multinational corporations. What looks like open access and opportunity at the level of the interface is therefore dependent on opaque processes of data collection and platform management. The challenge for debates over artistry and creativity in the era of AI is not only about what creativity is, but also about who gets to exercise it, under what conditions, and to whose benefit.

Creator

GAI's continuation of remix's challenge to traditional characterizations of creativity also forces us to revisit concepts of artistry and authorship. For centuries – especially in Europe and those parts of the world it influenced through conquest, religious conversion, and colonization – the artist or author was understood as an individual originator – i.e., the wellspring of intention, the source of meaning, and the seat of creative talent and agency – while the work he created (and this choice of gendered pronoun is intentional, as during this time these figures were almost always white and male) was the expression and manifestation of that singular vision. But, already in the latter part of the 20th century, this idea was challenged and destabilized by the French philosophers Roland Barthes (1978) and Michel Foucault (1984), who famously argued that the *author* is not some naturally occurring phenomenon but a socially constructed subject position situated in a larger cultural and historical network.

GAI intensifies this critical decentering. With these models, outputs are the product not of a singular artistic genius or what Barthes (1978) called the "author-god" but of a distributed system involving at least three kinds of agents: the human who crafts the prompt, the engineers and designers who built and trained the model, and the innumerable creators whose works are contained in the digital archive that is the training data. In multimodal content generation, this network of collaborating authors becomes even more complex, as the model may be translating and synthesizing across text, image, audio, and video in ways that no single human participant fully controls or is able to comprehend.

This has consequences for deciding matters of ownership and control. If creative outputs emerge from such diffuse and layered processes, then attributing authorship and authority to a single person – or even to a discrete entity – becomes increasingly difficult. Traditional copyright law, grounded in Enlightenment-era notions of the autonomous human creator, presumes a clearly identifiable author and an original, fixed work. GAI scrambles these assumptions. Outputs are the result of an entangled process involving prompt engineering by end users, systems architectures and training-data curation by developers, and the uncredited contributions of countless human artists, authors, and creators whose works populate the training corpus. In this context, authorship becomes less an individual property right and more a node in a network of shared and overlapping contributions. This not only complicates the assignment of exclusive rights but also raises questions about whether the current intellectual property framework is adequate for the realities of AI-driven computational creativity.

Responsibility, too, becomes diffuse with these diffusion and multimodal models. If a generated work appears to plagiarize, defame, or misrepresent something or someone, who should be held accountable: the end user who prompted it, the engineers who built the model, the organizations that deployed it, or the many human creators whose prior works informed its output? Unlike traditional content creation, where authorial intention and execution are usually traceable to an individual or group of individuals, GAI's chain of influence is opaque and distributed across actors who may never directly interact or have even consented to being part of the process. This fragmentation complicates moral as well as legal responsibility, challenging long-standing assumptions about control, intention, and liability in the creation of content. Consequently, GAI does not merely pose new policy dilemmas. It destabilizes the very cultural and legal structures that have historically supported our concepts of artistry, authorship, and creativity.

Created

If debates over creativity and the creator concern the process and the producer, the next logical question is what to make of the created product itself. GAI systems – especially the latest multimodal models – can produce works that are strikingly convincing, aesthetically sophisticated, and, in some cases, indistinguishable from human-made artifacts and artworks. Jason Allen's award-winning *Théâtre D'opéra Spatial* (2022), produced with Midjourney, illustrates this new capability (Figure 5.5). Whether in the form of photorealistic images, compelling musical compositions, or coherent and contextually appropriate narratives, such outputs rival the quality of professional creative work and expand the range of what is technologically possible. These developments, however, have been interpreted in very different ways.

For some, they herald a profound expansion of creative possibility. In this optimistic view, GAI represents both an opportunity for innovation – producing genuinely new and imaginative content – and a democratization of the means of production. Tools and techniques that once required years of training,

Figure 5.5 Jason Allen's *Théâtre D'opéra Spatial* (2022)
Source: Public domain image from https://commons.wikimedia.org/wiki/File:Théâtre_D'opéra_Spatial.jpg

expensive equipment, or access to specialized institutions are now available to anyone with an internet connection and a sense of curiosity. This redistribution of aesthetic and cultural opportunity can empower individuals who might otherwise lack the resources, skills, or social connections to participate in the culture industries, opening the door to new voices, diverse perspectives, and forms of expression that might never have emerged under more traditional circumstances.

Others see a very different picture. They argue that the sheer scale and speed of AI-generated content risks flooding the cultural environment with massive amounts of low-quality, derivative, or even misleading material – what critics derisively call *AI slop*. Rather than ushering in a new age of creative opportunity, the seemingly uncontrollable proliferation of machine-generated content could contribute to what Cory Doctorow (2025) has termed the *enshittification* of our digital platforms, leading to a decline in quality as systems become optimized for engagement metrics, ad revenue, or cost-cutting rather than fostering and supporting artistic merit, genuine talent, or truthfulness. On this account, the sheer abundance of AI-generated content threatens to devalue cultural production, overwhelm human creators, and erode the confidence that audiences place in the media, information, and other content they access and consume.

This erosion of trust becomes especially dangerous when the product of these GAI systems is not simply artistic but also mimetic: designed to reproduce the likeness, voice, or behavior of real people and events with such precision that they are difficult, if not impossible, to distinguish from genuine media representations. *Deepfakes* exemplify this capability. Using GANs, diffusion models, or multimodal transformer-based architectures, deepfakes can synthesize hyper-realistic video and audio in which individuals appear to say or do things that never happened, like the synthetic image of Pope Francis rocking a puffy jacket that went viral in March 2023 (Figure 5.6). Although such tools can be used for parody, art, or educational purposes, their malicious applications are already well documented: non-consensual sexual imagery, identity theft, political disinformation, and market manipulation.

In the context of democratic governance, the danger lies not only in the specific harms of any single deepfake but also in the broader epistemic consequences. The existence of

Figure 5.6 Pope Francis in puffy jacket
Source: Public domain image from https://en.m.wikipedia.org/wiki/File:Pope_Francis_in_puffy_winter_jacket.jpg

such convincing forgeries enables what legal scholars Bobby Chesney and Danielle Citron (2019, 1758) have called the "liar's dividend": when high-quality falsifications are widely known to exist, public figures can dismiss authentic evidence as fake, while fabricated material can circulate without easy means of repudiation. This dynamic corrodes the public's ability to agree on basic facts, undermines journalistic integrity, and fosters an environment in which truth becomes negotiable and partisan narratives dominate. In such conditions, political accountability weakens, conspiracy thinking flourishes, and civic trust erodes, creating fertile ground for authoritarian consolidations of power.

While technological countermeasures such as watermarking, cryptographic provenance tracking, and deepfake detection algorithms are under development, these approaches face significant challenges: detection tools can lag behind generative techniques, provenance metadata can be stripped, and malicious actors can operate outside jurisdictions that enforce such measures. As with prior shifts in media technology, the challenge is not solely technical but also cultural, legal, and institutional: requiring coordinated action across public policy, education, professional practice, and platform governance to mitigate the risks without stifling the legitimate uses of GAI applications.

Summary

This chapter has examined computational creativity and GAI by tracing their technical and conceptual development as well as their social impact and cultural consequences. We began by looking at the history of efforts to model creative processes in computational mechanisms, from early GOFAI systems such as Experiments in Musical Intelligence and The Painting Fool, through the development of machine learning approaches like DeepDream and GANs, to today's diffusion models and multimodal architectures. Viewed through Margaret Boden's framework, these successive innovations illustrate the range and capabilities of computational creativity: from combinational and exploratory creativity in rule-based and early machine learning systems, to the transformational creativity of contemporary generative models that arguably redraw the very boundaries of what is possible.

From there, we turned to the cultural and philosophical questions that follow from these capabilities. We considered how GAI extends and transforms the remix paradigm, challenging long-standing notions of artistry as creation *ex nihilo*. We analyzed how the figure of the creator shifts from a singular originator to a distributed network of human and machinic contributors, raising timely questions about intellectual property, authorship, and responsibility. And we assessed the nature of the products themselves – works that can be genuinely impressive or unsettlingly deceptive, especially in the form of deepfakes with their corrosive effects on truth, evidence, and democratic governance.

Taken together, these analyses reveal that GAI is not merely another set of productivity tools for human users; it is a profound reconfiguration of the conditions under which creative work is made, attributed, and received. The technical, cultural, and political dimensions are inseparable. The way these systems function shape what can be generated. The manner by which they disrupt and redistribute agency determines who is recognized as a contributor. And the quality and quantity of their outputs influence how they circulate in and affect our communities and public conversations. If the questions addressed here concern what GAI is and does, the next chapter asks how we live with it – examining the way these systems fit into wider structures of power; what forms of responsibility they demand from designers, users, and institutions; and how their integration into daily life will shape, and be shaped by, the future we build together.

Learning Activities

1 Critical Meme with GAI

Purpose: This activity invites you to critically examine GAI by using it as a medium of cultural commentary. By creating a meme, you will explore how GAI participates in remix culture, satire, and critique, and how it can be used not just to produce content but also to comment on itself.

Procedure: Using a GAI image platform (e.g., DALL·E, Midjourney, or ChatGPT), create a meme that offers critical reflection on a social, political, or philosophical issue related to GAI. Generate your image using a carefully crafted prompt. Make sure that you add text to the resulting image – either by way of the prompt instructions or afterward – so that the meme communicates a clear critical message. Share your meme with the class and be prepared to explain how it functions as both a creative artifact and a form of critical commentary.

Learning Goal: Understand GAI as a tool of cultural production and critique, explain how remix and satire function in AI-generated media, and reflect on the irony of using generative systems to question creativity, power, and authorship.

2 From Remix to GAI

Purpose: This activity provides an opportunity for you to directly experience the conceptual through-line from remix culture to GAI by comparing human-created remixes with machine-generated content.

Procedure: (1) Create a remix by selecting a small set of source material within a single medium (e.g., three audio samples, visual images, or text passages). Transform and recombine these materials into a new collage-like composition, using either direct manipulation of physical materials or digital tools, like Photoshop, Audacity, or iMovie. (2) Use a GAI application to create another version that draws on the same sources that you used in your remix. Do not provide the AI with the original materials directly. Instead, describe the styles, themes, or influences in your prompt. After you have both versions, compare the human-generated remix with the output provided by the AI and discuss the following questions:

- How visible or traceable are the original sources in each version?
- How does creative control differ between the materials and tools of remix and the use of a GAI platform?
- Which version feels more "original," and why?

- Who is the author of the remix? And who (or what) is the author of the AI version?

Learning Goal: Experience how GAI grows out of remix practices and critically examine and evaluate the way that automation, abstraction, and scale affect creativity, authorship, and attribution.

3 What Do Images Mean When Anything Can Be AI Generated?

Purpose: This activity helps you critically examine the long-standing assumption that images – especially photographs and audio/video recordings – serve as reliable evidence of reality, and how GAI and synthetic media disrupt this assumption.

Procedure: Reflect on the chapter's discussion of GAI, diffusion models, deepfakes, and synthetic media. Then discuss the following questions:

- Why have photographic images and audio/video recordings traditionally been treated as trustworthy representations of reality? What assumptions about technology, causality, and evidence support this view?
- How do GAI applications and synthetic media challenge the idea that images and audio/video recordings are an accurate index of what really happened?
- What happens to journalism, legal evidence, and public accountability when images and audio/video recordings no longer function as authentic representations of reality?
- How might democratic institutions need to adapt when media representations can be fabricated at scale and circulated without reliable means of verification?

As you address these questions, consider whether the problem lies primarily in the technology itself or in the social, institutional, and communicative frameworks that surround it.

Learning Goal: Examine how GAI destabilizes the evidentiary status of images and audio/video recordings and explain why this shift has significant implications for human communication, journalism, and democratic governance.

Further Reading

Roland Barthes, "The Death of the Author" (1978).

In this essay, originally published in French in 1967, Barthes challenges the idea of the author as the sole origin of meaning in written content, arguing instead that texts are shaped by readers and cultural codes. This argument resonates strongly with GAI, where authorship is distributed across human prompts, machine processes, and cultural data.

Margaret Boden, *The Creative Mind: Myths and Mechanisms* (2004).

In this book, Boden establishes one of the most influential frameworks for analyzing creativity, distinguishing between combinational, exploratory, and transformational creativity. This taxonomy provides a way to evaluate both human and machine artistry, and it remains a touchstone for researchers working with and studying GAI.

Bobby Chesney and Danielle Citron, "Deep Fakes: A Looming Challenge for Privacy, Democracy, and National Security" (2019).

This article explains the technical and social risks of deepfakes, including what the authors call the "liar's dividend," where the very possibility of fakes undermines trust in authentic media. It highlights how GAI can destabilize evidence, truth, and public discourse.

Michel Foucault, "What is an Author?" (1984).

Foucault reframes the "author" as a cultural function rather than a natural source of creativity. His essay, originally published in

French in 1969, provides a way of analyzing AI-generated works without needing to locate creativity in a single human figure, opening space for thinking about machines as contributors to authorship.

Eduardo Navas, *Remix Theory: The Aesthetics of Sampling* (2012).

This book explores remix as a central mode of contemporary culture, from sampling and recombining recorded music in hip-hop to the cut-and-paste collage practices of digital art. These approaches are especially relevant for GAI applications, which operate through sampling, recombination, and transformation of existing source material and data.

6
Living with AI

Learning Outcomes

- Explain how debates about artificial intelligence repeat long-standing tensions in the history of technology, using Plato's account of writing as *pharmakon* – medicine and poison – to analyze contemporary arguments about AI.
- Compare techno-optimist and techno-skeptical positions on AI and see how framing technology in binary terms – as either beneficial or harmful – can obscure its social, cultural, and ethical complexity.
- Recognize how living with AI inevitably reshapes everyday practices, including work, education, communication, and social relationships.
- Critically evaluate what responsibility, governance, and ethics mean in a world that is increasingly dependent on AI, including questions of accountability, pluralism, and the limits of existing moral and legal frameworks.

Introduction

From the beginning, this book has been guided by a simple objective: to understand AI. But as we have discovered, this has not meant pinning down a single definition or amassing a list of basic facts and figures. It has meant learning to see AI in its many different dimensions – technical, cultural, historical, and philosophical – and recognizing the many ways it already influences and informs the world we inhabit. It has meant approaching AI not only as code and computation, but also as a set of stories we tell, practices we adopt, and choices we make both individually and together.

Over the course of this journey, we have traced a path from the technical terminology and basic concepts of AI, through the specific technologies that shape its various forms and implementations, to the exhilarating and often unsettling ways it now participates in human communication, creativity, and social life. Along the way, we have encountered questions that resist easy answers: What does it mean to attribute intelligence to a machine? How do the concepts of subjectivity, agency, and authorship change when content can be generated by applications that do not think, understand, or feel? What new possibilities and what forms of inequity and injustice can emerge when such systems become woven into the fabric of everyday life?

By now, one thing should be clear: understanding AI is not about studying something *out there*, sealed off in research labs, floating around in cloud-distributed applications, or residing in large corporate data centers. It is about coming to terms with the fact that we are already living with AI and that it is shaping, and being shaped by, our language, our work, our institutions, and our relationships. This final chapter zooms out from our engagement with the systems and applications of the previous chapters to consider the broader conditions of life in a world that is already involved with and increasingly dependent upon AI.

To frame the investigation, we return to one of the earliest recorded debates about the disruptive effects of new information and communication technology. Though separated from us by more than two millennia, this exchange offers a remarkably useful framework for thinking about the opportunities and challenges of living with AI. By revisiting this historic debate, we can begin to understand how the recurring tensions between techno-optimism and techno-skepticism determine the questions we ask, the kinds of debates we believe are important, and the different outcomes we think are available to us. The chapter unfolds in three movements: first, by sketching the contours of this earlier debate; second, by tracking how the same tensions shape the current arguments and disputes about AI; and, finally, by exploring how we might move past such polarized oppositions toward a more nuanced and responsible understanding of technological innovation.

The Terms of the Debate

Artificial intelligence is not the first nor will it be the last technology to unsettle our ways of thinking, working, and relating to one another. Every century, it seems, has encountered technical innovations that have challenged existing values and inherited practices, forcing a reconsideration not only of our tools but also of ourselves and the world around us. In 15th-century Europe, the printing press destabilized religious and political authority, transforming the circulation of knowledge and supporting subsequent social and political revolutions. In the 19th century, the invention of photography altered how we represent the world around us, document our lives, and remember people, places, and events. And in the late 20th century, the internet reconfigured human communication, commercial transactions, work, and social organization. In each case, the technology was not merely a new tool; it redefined the terms and conditions under which human culture was produced and shared. As the media theorist and historian John Culkin famously characterized it: "We shape our tools and thereafter they shape us" (Culkin 1967, 70).[1]

Understood from this vantage point, the promise and peril currently associated with AI repeat and replay what are by now rather familiar themes: utopian visions of superintelligent machines solving climate change, curing disease, and unlocking new frontiers of creativity and scientific discovery; dystopian fears of mass unemployment, deepfake-driven disinformation, and lethal autonomous weapons; and more ambivalent forecasts in which AI becomes an indispensable but disconcerting partner in work, education, and personal life. What is surprising here is not the wide range of reactions but the fact that such polarized positions are not unique to our time or this particular technology. Whenever a new innovation promises to extend human capacities, it also raises questions and reservations about what might be lost, sacrificed, altered, or corrupted in the process.

One of the earliest recorded instances of a society confronting the disruptive force of a new information and communication technology comes from ancient Greece. The innovation in question was (obviously) not digital computing or machine intelligence but the then new technology of writing.[2] For centuries, Greek culture had been predominantly oral, with poetry, history, and law committed to memory and transmitted through live performances. Knowledge was stored in the minds of skilled orators, bards, and rhetoricians, whose art was measured not only by what they knew but also by their ability to recall and adapt it in the moment of its delivery. Writing threatened to upend this system and cultural practice. By fixing words on a durable medium, it promised a more permanent record, but at the cost of weakening the living, dynamic exchange that had defined Greek intellectual and cultural life.

Plato stages this conflict in the *Phaedrus* through a story – think of it as a kind of myth or parable – that recounts an encounter between two Egyptian gods: Theuth, the inventor of writing, and Thamus, the king. In this story, Theuth proudly presents his new invention to Thamus, describing writing as a remedy for forgetfulness and claiming that it will improve the memory and intellectual capabilities of all who adopt and use it. Thamus, however (and like many thought leaders and lawmakers over the course of human history), remains skeptical in the face of Theuth's enthusiastic marketing pitch. He warns that writing will have the exact opposite effect: it will encourage forgetfulness by allowing people to rely on external marks rather than cultivating memory within themselves, and it will therefore offer only the appearance of wisdom, enabling people to recite or simply parrot facts and figures without genuine thought, introspection, or understanding.

In this exchange, writing is described by both the inventor and the king as a *pharmakon* – a Greek word that, like our word *drug*, means both medicine and poison. Thus, the message of Plato's short but influential parable is that writing is a medicinal therapy, capable of curing forgetfulness and preserving knowledge, while simultaneously possessing a toxic effect, becoming a dangerous narcotic that threatens to erode the very faculties and capabilities it was designed to enhance. This dual capacity is not an incidental consequence of the way the technology is used; it is the defining condition of the technology itself.

Seen in this light, AI is our contemporary *pharmakon*. Generative models, for instance, have the capability to democratize access to and creation of information, to enhance and amplify human artistry and scientific discovery, and to offer new forms of problem-solving that exceed human capabilities. Yet they can also displace human skill, propagate bias, and flood the public sphere with inauthentic or misleading content. The question, then, is not whether AI is good or bad, but how its medicinal and potentially toxic effects will be managed, distributed, and controlled. And, perhaps, even more important, who (or maybe even what) will have the power to decide these matters. Will decision-making be left in the hands of the engineers and inventors, those who, like Theuth, celebrate these innovations and proclaim their benefits and advantages? Or will things be decided by the politicians, lawmakers, and thought leaders, individuals who, like Thamus, issue dire warnings about the corrupting influence of these innovations and seek to protect us from this dangerous technology? Or will we – as we have in the past – work together to balance these two extremes and figure out a kind of both/and solution?

This is the task before us. And it is one in which we all are implicated, because opting out has never been a viable option. In whatever way we decide to approach it, three things should now be clear. First, our apprehension in the face of new and seemingly disruptive technology is neither novel nor irrational. It is part of a long-standing human effort to understand the costs and benefits of technological innovation. And we are not alone in this. We have been here before, and there is value in learning from our history with previous struggles. Second, despite what the instrumental theory tells us, technologies are never neutral. Like writing during the time of Plato, AI will reshape not only what we can do, but also how we think about doing it, and, in turn, how we think about ourselves. Finally, though technology is not neutral, it is ambivalent. It is a *pharmakon* – both medicine and poison. Thus, the decisions we make about it and the actions we take in the face of it – individually and together – make a difference. The challenge, as well as the opportunity, is to cultivate forms of understanding, governance, and use that can tilt the balance toward the medicine without ignoring the poison.

The Theuths of Our Time

In Plato's *Phaedrus*, Theuth is a tireless evangelist for his own invention, convinced that the power of writing will improve memory, expand wisdom, and elevate the human condition. This invention, as Thueth explains it, "will make the Egyptians wiser and will improve their memories; for it is an elixir of memory and wisdom that I have discovered" (Plato 1982, 274e). His voice echoes today in the chorus of AI advocates and optimists who speak with similar conviction about the transformative potential of their innovations.

Demis Hassabis, co-founder and CEO of DeepMind, famously positioned AI as a kind of universal cure-all, explaining that his company's mission is to "solve intelligence and then use it to solve everything else" (Simonite 2016). Venture capitalist Marc Andreessen has been even more direct with his optimism, proclaiming that "AI will save the world" and will "make everything we care about better" (Andreessen 2023). Sundar Pichai, CEO of Google, has positioned it in Promethean terms, describing AI as "the most profound technology humanity is working on – more profound than fire or electricity" (Parker 2018; *60 Minutes* 2023). And for OpenAI's Sam Altman, the promise of AI is both profound and unprecedented: "the gains to quality of life from AI driving faster scientific progress and increased productivity will be enormous; the future can be vastly better than the present" (Altman 2025). For these latter-day Theuths, the potential of AI is framed not in terms of gradual improvements in the human condition but as an exponential transformation, measured in terms of problems solved, knowledge multiplied, and innovation accelerated.

Outside the sphere of these influential corporate thought leaders – what some have pejoratively called AI hype peddlers and tech bros – academic and scientific researchers offer similar forecasts. Economists Andrew McAfee and Erik Brynjolfsson have famously argued that AI and related digital technologies will spark a new wave of productivity on par with the Industrial Revolution, liberating humans from repetitive labor and enabling them to focus on higher-order thinking, creativity, and care-oriented work. "Now comes the second machine age," they confidently state in their eponymously titled book on the subject. "Computers and other digital advances are doing for mental power . . . what the steam engine and its descendants did for muscle power" (Brynjolfsson and McAfee 2014, 19). A similar form of positivity and optimism can be found in the scientific community. In their survey of 72 leading researchers, Benedikt Fecher and a team of investigators at the Alexander von Humboldt Institute for Internet and Society in Berlin found "that experts anticipate that the utilization of LLMs will have a transformative and largely positive impact on science and scientific practice . . . [especially] for administrative, creative, and analytical tasks" (Fecher et al. 2024, 448).

Advocates in education likewise celebrate AI as a transformative technology that can radically democratize teaching and learning. Sal Khan (2023), founder of Khan Academy, has predicted that AI will provide "every student with a virtual personalized tutor at an affordable cost," calling it "the biggest positive transformation that education has ever seen." Anant Agarwal (2023), founder of edX, has similarly argued that AI can deliver both "massive scale and personalization," enabling real-time adaptation of learning materials across languages and cultures while giving students access to individualized instruction by way of AI tutors. And early evidence suggests that such optimism is not misplaced. In recent studies, AI-powered intelligent tutoring systems have been shown to improve learning gains by a factor of two compared to traditional online models (St-Hilaire et al. 2022), while AI guidance for human tutors significantly raises student mastery rates, particularly in underserved communities (Wang et al. 2024). For these proponents, AI represents a revolution in educational opportunity, providing access to high-quality instruction for those historically excluded from elite institutions.

For the Theuths of our time, then, AI is not merely a remedy for existing deficits – inefficiency, scarcity, ignorance, etc. – but a transformative platform, providing for entirely new modes of human flourishing. It is a technology that, in their view, can extend the reach of intelligence, creativity, and compassion on a scale unmatched by previous technical innovation. While they generally acknowledge the need for ethical safeguards and responsible governance, these are framed as solvable engineering or policy issues. They're important but not obstacles that should impede the pace of innovation. To them, the greater danger seems to lie in hesitation: to delay or even halt progress would be to withhold a kind of medicine that is capable not only of alleviating existing ailments but also of broadening opportunity and improving the human condition worldwide. Just as Theuth believed his invention was a kind of smart drug that would expand memory and wisdom, many of today's AI advocates believe their technology will expand the limits of human intellectual capabilities. On their account, the question is not whether to embrace AI, but how quickly we can integrate this beneficent technology into the fabric of everyday existence.

The Thamuses of our Time

In the *Phaedrus*, King Thamus listens patiently to Theuth's praise of writing, weighing its promised benefits against potential costs. And he remains steadfast in his evaluation, refusing to be swayed by Theuth's enthusiasm and tech bro marketing hype. For Thamus, what appears to be a medicine is in fact a kind of poison. By outsourcing memory to an external technical apparatus, he argues, humans risk eroding the very capacities they seek to enhance. As he explains:

> This invention will produce forgetfulness in the minds of those who learn to use it, because they will not practice their memory. Their trust in writing, produced by external characters which are no part of themselves, will discourage the use of their own memory within them. You have invented a drug of not of memory, but of reminding; and you offer your pupils the appearance of wisdom, not true wisdom. (Plato 1982, 275a)

In our present debates about AI in general and LLMs and GAI in particular, the Thamuses are those who, while acknowledging AI's transformative potential, insist on confronting its dangers with clear-eyed realism. They caution against the seductions of novelty, the corporate drive for rapid deployment, and the all-too-human tendency to overestimate what technology can do while underestimating what it might unfortunately undo. For these critics and skeptics, AI is not simply a neutral instrument awaiting human guidance. It is a force already shaping economies, labor markets, governance systems, and the milieu of everyday life in ways that may be difficult – if not impossible – to disentangle and reverse.

And for many AI critics, the risks of these powerful technologies are not a matter of speculation; they are a clear and present danger. Scholars and social activists such as Joy Buolamwini and Timnit Gebru have documented the ways that facial recognition systems can reinforce discriminatory outcomes across sectors like hiring, education, transportation, and policing, often exacerbating existing biases and further disenfranchising already vulnerable populations (Buolamwini and Gebru 2018; Buolamwini 2023). Linguist Emily Bender, co-founder of the Distributed AI Research (DAIR) institute, has become one of AI's most vocal and recognizable critics. She not only co-authored the now widely cited "Stochastic Parrots" essay (Bender et al. 2021) but also co-hosts *Mystery AI Hype Theater 3000*, a podcast with Alex Hanna that systematically unpacks and debunks the inflated claims of AI capabilities that are currently being circulated and amped up by the minions of Theuth (Bender and Hanna, 2022–). In 2024, three researchers from the University of Glasgow famously repositioned ChatGPT and other LLMs as "bullshit machines" that cannot and should not ever be trusted (Hicks et al. 2024). And in *AI Snake Oil*, Princton University computer scientists Arvind Narayanan and Sayash Kapoor (2024) not only expose the rampant misleading claims about the capabilities of AI but also describe in meticulous detail the serious harms it is already causing.

In public policy and governance, analysts like Shoshana Zuboff (2019) have warned that the concentration of AI development in the hands of a few powerful corporate actors intensifies what she calls "surveillance capitalism," a system that prioritizes profit over public welfare. Tristan Harris and Aza Raskin of the Center for Humane Technology have drawn attention to the destabilizing potential of AI-generated disinformation, deepfakes, and synthetic media, arguing that such technologies could corrode trust in journalism, undermine democratic elections, and weaken the evidentiary foundations of public discourse (Levy 2023). In their account, AI does not simply add to the information ecosystem; it actively reconfigures it, making it harder for citizens to distinguish between truth and hallucinated fabrication, and thereby weakening the conditions for collective decision-making.

Like Thamus, many of the contemporary AI critics also raise alarms about social and cognitive deskilling. Sherry Turkle (2011), for instance, has argued that as we come to depend on AI and robotic companions – not only for information but also for affirmation and friendship – we risk diminishing the very capacities that make human relationships meaningful. "Technology," she explains, "is seductive when what it offers meets our human vulnerabilities. And as it turns out, we are very vulnerable indeed. We are lonely but fearful of intimacy. Digital connections and the sociable robot may offer the illusion of companionship without the demands of friendship" (Turkle 2011, 1). For others, like Nicholas Carr (2010), the issue is not just the loss of discrete abilities, but the subtle reshaping of cognitive habits: shorter attention spans, reduced tolerance for ambiguity, and a preference for speed over depth. And recent empirical work appears to support Carr's concerns. A preliminary study from MIT's Media Lab found that frequent use of AI tools, such as ChatGPT, was linked with significantly lower brain engagement, diminished originality, and reduced critical thinking performance (Kosmyna et al. 2025).

But these warnings are not confined to academic critics, activists, and policy analysts. They are even being voiced by tech industry insiders. Geoffrey Hinton, widely regarded as the godfather of deep learning, resigned from his position at Google in 2023 so that he could speak freely about what he described as AI's potential to "escape our control" (Metz 2023). His concerns range from the short-term risks of misinformation and economic displacement to the longer-term possibility that advanced systems could behave in unpredictable and harmful ways. Others – like Yoshua Bengio, Stuart Russell, and Gary Marcus – have joined Hinton in calling for stronger governance frameworks and even a slowdown in the development of AI models until their risks are better understood. Bengio, Russell, and Marcus were among the 33,705 signatories on the Future of Life Institute's "Pause Giant AI Experiments" open letter, which urged a six-month moratorium on training AI systems more powerful than GPT-4

(Future of Life Institute, 2023). Other leading public intellectuals have gone one step further, issuing dire, almost apocalyptic prognostications, like the physicist Stephen Hawking, who told the BBC in 2014 that he thought "AI could spell the end of the human race" (Cellan-Jones 2014).

Where the Theuths speak of unprecedented progress and enhancement, the Thamuses emphasize precaution, potential harms, and the urgent need for robust social, political, and ethical solutions. Scholars and social activists such as Joy Buolamwini, Timnit Gebru, and Emily Bender remind us that without intentional design, rigorous oversight, and meaningful public accountability, AI can not only deepen structural inequities but also obscure them behind a veneer of algorithmic neutrality. Others, like Geoffrey Hinton, Sherry Turkle, and researchers at the MIT Media Lab, warn that the harms are not only technical but also cultural and cognitive, shaping how we think, relate, and even imagine our futures. Without strong guardrails, it is argued, even well-intentioned systems can produce damage that is difficult to foresee, harder to undo, and disproportionately borne by those with the least power to resist. Following the prescriptions of king Thamus, these critics urge us to pause and ask: What might be lost? Who might be harmed? And what safeguards and practices are necessary to protect individuals and communities from this toxic technology?

Both/And Approaches, Or Thinking Outside the Box

Theuth and Thamus are not merely mythological figures from an ancient dialogue. They represent enduring subject positions in our conversations and debates about technology. Theuth is the persuasive spokesperson for invention and the belief that new tools can extend and amplify our seemingly frail human capacities. Thamus represents the voices of caution, reminding us that every apparent gain carries a corresponding loss, and that the harms of these innovations – once released into the world – often fall unequally across the social spectrum. In the debates surrounding AI, these two voices have returned with renewed urgency and impact: innovation versus precaution, acceleration versus regulation, enthusiasm versus skepticism.

The problem with this way of thinking is that it forces us into a binary opposition: a way of framing and making sense of everything in terms of mutually exclusive alternatives. And we are all too familiar with these dichotomies and their limitations: yes/no, medicine/poison, good/bad, white/black, male/female, left/right, and so on. But real life is persistently and irreducibly analogue even if our languages and ways of thinking have endeavored to be digital. In the book *Deconstruction* (Gunkel 2021), I argued that such binary pairings don't just risk misrepresenting the complex realities in which we actually live; they actively control and shape the range of possibilities we imagine for ourselves. They set the terms of the debate in ways that compel us to take sides, to see one term as right and the other as wrong, and to disregard everything that resists neat and tidy categorization.

Yet the enduring lesson of Plato's dialogue – and not just this one dialogue, but all the dialogues – is not that one position should triumph over the other, but that their tension is itself a kind of wisdom. Theuth's optimism without Thamus's skepticism risks hubris and blind faith in progress; Thamus's wariness without Theuth's vision risks stagnation and missed opportunities. Therefore, a thoughtful response to AI requires holding both impulses in productive opposition: seeing the capacities that AI makes possible while refusing to overlook its limitations, distortions, and unintended consequences.[3] It is in this contested in-between zone, where the promise and peril are bound together in productive dialogue and dialectical tension, that the real work of understanding AI must be situated and take place.

History of Technology

One way to balance Theuth's medicine with Thamus's poison is to look at the history of technology. When a new invention first arrives, it often provokes the kind of polarizing debate we find in the *Phaedrus*: sweeping promises of transformation set against dire warnings of decline. In the case of writing, Theuth claimed it would enhance wisdom, while Thamus feared it would erode memory and judgment. Similar dynamics have played out in more recent history.

Consider the early days of the internet. Heralded by some as an *information superhighway* that would democratize knowledge and connect humanity in unprecedented ways, it was at the same time condemned as a dangerous narcotic that would isolate individuals, corrode attention spans, and flood public discourse with misinformation. Both assessments contained elements of truth, but neither captured the full picture. And over time, the internet became a mundane fact of everyday life – still capable of both benefit and harm, but integrated into the fabric of everyday work, communication, and culture. The extremes that had characterized the initial debate were eventually attenuated as societies developed norms, regulations, and literacies to manage its use and impact.

This recent historical precedent should give us some measure of confidence as we confront and work to understand the newness of AI. If we learned to live with writing – once condemned as a dangerous substitute for true knowledge – and with the internet – both hailed as a mind-expanding smart drug and feared as an addictive and hallucinogenic narcotic (Gunkel 2008) – we might also learn to live with AI in ways that mitigate the harms while cultivating the benefits. This is not to say that history simply repeats or that we can be complacent. But our record with past technologies offers a basis for confidence and empowerment. By attending to the history of technology, we can carry forward the lessons – both the successes and the failures – of earlier adaptations. New technologies are rarely, if ever, wonder drugs or toxic poisons. Like a potent medicine, to borrow Plato's metaphor, AI's effects will depend on the care with which we handle it and the responsibility with which we put it to work.

Governance

When we say *we* need to decide how AI should be developed and deployed, it is easy to assume a shared, inclusive community of like-minded individuals. But history – and present practice – shows that *we*, more often than not, identifies and interpellates a narrow subset of social and political actors. In AI governance, for instance, the pronoun *we* frequently means policymakers in wealthy industrialized nations, executives and engineers at a handful of powerful multinational corporations, and a small circle of academic and think-tank experts. These are important voices, but they are far from being a representative sample.

The *we* who live with and need to understand AI includes billions of people whose lives and livelihoods are touched by algorithmic platforms and applications, often without their explicit consent or knowledge. It includes workers both visible and behind the scenes or in the shadows whose labor builds the supporting infrastructure, manufactures and installs the hardware, and develops and trains the models; communities of artists, writers, and other content creators whose data are often appropriated without consent, credit, or compensation; and populations across the globe who disproportionately bear the harms of biased systems, the costs of resource extraction, and the impact of economic disruption. It also includes non-human entities and ecosystems, whose interests – though often not formally recognized or represented – are implicated in the resource demands and climate impact of AI's supporting infrastructure.

Recognizing these exclusions is not merely an act of ethical reflection. It is a precondition for legitimate governance. If AI is to be managed for the benefit of all, those most likely to be affected must be present in the room and have a seat at the table; not as afterthoughts or footnotes, but as active participants involved in shaping policy, standards, and shared norms. This entails broadening representation geographically, socio-economically, and culturally; ensuring that the *we* of AI integration and deployment reflects more than the priorities and privileges of the Global North, the affluent, and the technologically fluent.

Pluralist governance rejects the notion that there is a single, universal answer to the opportunities and challenges posed by AI. Instead, it begins from the recognition that contexts differ, such that what is safe, fair, and beneficial in one setting may be harmful or inappropriate in another. In practice, this means bringing together a broad range of actors – developers, regulators, social organizations, affected communities, labor groups, and researchers – for sustained, multi-stakeholder deliberations. It also requires governance mechanisms that are sensitive to local legal frameworks, diverse cultural norms, and different economic realities, while still coordinating on and responding to shared global commitments. Rather than relying solely on expert forecasts or technical benchmarks, pluralist governance incorporates the lived experiences and community-based knowledge of those directly affected by AI systems and applications, ensuring that these different and often competing perspectives shape design, evaluation, and oversight. Finally, this way of proceeding recognizes that governance is a dynamic and iterative process, with rules and standards subject to revision as technological capabilities, risks, and social impact evolve.

Importantly, pluralism is not relativism, nor is it an anything-goes attitude toward risk. It is an acknowledgment that there is no one-size-fits-all model for effectively living and working with AI, and that legitimacy depends on embracing diverse perspectives, distributing decision-making power across the full range of stakeholders, and remaining open to productive contestation. If debates about AI have so far been dominated by the modern-day Theuths and Thamuses – e.g., the techno-optimists and critical skeptics – it is time to ask who else should be involved in these conversations, what other voices need to be heard, and how efforts at shared governance can foster and ensure more equitable distribution.

Education

If responsible AI governance requires pluralism in policy, then education demands something similar in pedagogy. Nowhere is this more urgent than in the cultivation of writing, reading, and critical thinking, which are the core competencies of the so-called *soft disciplines* in the humanities and social sciences. These are not merely technical skills for producing and decoding texts and other media content. They are habits of mind that enable students to question assumptions, grapple with competing perspectives, and create meaning in productive dialogue with others.

GAI, with its ability to produce fluent text and media content on demand, forces educators to confront questions that go well beyond plagiarism and academic integrity. If machines can produce term papers and essays, translate between languages, compose music, or generate compelling still and moving images, what does this mean for the future of writing and content creation as practices of thought and human expression? What is lost if reading, viewing, and listening become primarily a matter of consuming machine-generated content rather than engaging with the artifacts of human culture, for example books, photographs, films, music, and performances? And how do we preserve critical thinking when the labor of making arguments, developing ideas, and expressing them can be outsourced to a GAI model?

From the perspective of both creation and reception, AI now challenges long-standing assumptions that had situated the human individual as the sole originator and guarantor of meaning in written texts, musical compositions, images, and storytelling. If a machine can convincingly generate an argument, compose original music, or tell a compelling story, then the authorizing authority behind these works no longer resides exclusively in the unique character and experiences of a human author – something that is often called *ethos*. It must instead be renegotiated in the interplay between human intention, algorithmic output, and audience interpretation.

Though this might appear to be disruptive, it isn't entirely new. As noted in the previous chapter, Roland Barthes introduced and developed a concept he called "the death of the author" in 1967. By this he didn't mean the demise of writing, reading, or creativity. He meant the terminal limits of the romantic idea of the author as a lone genius pouring their heart and soul into their work. In fact, that idea was already being effectively challenged and undermined by collaborative artforms like cinema, the ready-mades of Marcel Duchamp, Andy Warhol's industrial-scale art studio – called (not surprisingly) "The Factory" – and the remix practices of college artists working in all forms of media. GAI extends this provocation, inviting (maybe even forcing) us to rethink what authorship and authority mean when the figure of the "author" can include both human and non-human elements.

Right now, responses to these challenges – especially in schools and universities – tend to divide into two factions that reproduce the binary opposition we encountered in Plato's *Phaedrus*. On the one side, there are the contemporary Thamuses, who seek to curtail and even prohibit AI use in writing and other classroom activities, arguing that these technologies undermine learning outcomes, erode the development of independent thinking, and threaten the authenticity of a student's own voice. On the other side are the modern-day Theuths, who welcome AI as a replacement for many human activities – translating, summarizing, composing, editing – and in some cases use this to justify cutting academic programs and canceling degrees in fields that once taught these now apparently "obsolete" subjects.

Both approaches, however, risk misunderstanding and even narrowing the purpose of education. A blanket ban may prevent immediate misuse but leaves students ill prepared to engage with technologies they will encounter in every professional domain and career. Full substitution or even just partial replacement reduces writing, composing, and other creative processes to output problems – measured only by efficiency and deliverable products – while neglecting their role in fostering discovery, reflection, and intellectual growth. In different ways, both positions fall into the trap of *technological determinism*: the belief that technology is the primary driver of social change. This framing obscures the fact that technologies are shaped, constrained, and given meaning by the social, cultural, and institutional contexts out of which they emerge and in which they are situated and deployed. By treating AI as either an inevitable force of change or a contaminating influence, both sides risk surrendering the human agency and creativity needed to decide what roles AI should and should not play in our world.

The challenge, then, is not to pick a side in this debate but to devise teaching and learning strategies that work in the contested middle ground. Here, we can experiment with AI as a collaborator, a critical foil, and a lens through which to examine and reimagine existing educational procedures and methods. Such approaches treat AI neither as forbidden fruit nor as a silver bullet solution, but as an educational resource the value of which depends on the skill, discernment, and ethical care with which it is taken up and employed. Practically speaking, this means both developing and demanding learning opportunities and activities that explicitly integrate AI into the educational process. Not to replace student work or to encourage cheating, but to involve students in the debate, to make the machine's strengths and weaknesses clearly visible, and to prepare graduates for successfully living and working with AI.

The Real World

Beyond the classroom, AI's influence extends to the full range of human activities, shaping not only how people work but also how they connect with one another and live their lives. In the workplace, LLMs and GAI applications are already rewriting job descriptions, altering career paths, and shifting the balance of power between human user and technological instrument. In journalism, for example, AI systems can now generate draft articles in seconds, changing the role of reporters from writing original copy to becoming fact-checkers, curators, and editors of machine-generated content. In law and the legal professions, document review, contract analysis, and the preparation of legal documents are increasingly being handled by LLMs, freeing attorneys for higher-level tasks while also threatening entry-level positions that once served as essential training grounds for the next generation. In the creative industries, AI is co-writing ad copy, designing logos, and generating original content. And in computer science, the basic task of writing of code for these algorithms is being outsource to GAI platforms that can, in many software development tasks, outperform human programmers and at a fraction of the cost.

While such changes can boost productivity, free people from repetitive tasks, and open entirely new professional fields, they can also accelerate deskilling, concentrate economic power in the hands of those who own and control the technology, and create precarious employment conditions where humans are retained only for oversight, review, or emergency intervention. As Carl Benedikt Frey (2024) wrote for an op-ed published in *The New York Times*:

> [AI] does not have to replace workers entirely to have a big effect; it only has to drive down wages or make knowledge work easier and cheaper somewhere else. If a chatbot can help clients with paralegal work, market research or financial modeling, companies may no longer need to employ so many entry-level workers in Manhattan or San Francisco.

The real question, it seems, is not what jobs will be lost or new kinds of occupations created, but what kind of work will remain, who will have access to it, and under what conditions.

AI is also transforming human social interaction, stepping into roles traditionally reserved for friends, confidants, and companions. Voice assistants, chatbots, and social robots can simulate conversation, respond with apparent empathy, and adapt to individual preferences. In some cases, these applications offer genuine benefits: easing loneliness among the elderly, providing those who suffer from social anxiety with a low-pressure way to engage in and develop conversational abilities, or serving as an accessible, always-available source of emotional support. In regions of the world contending with rural isolation or shortages in mental health service providers, AI-powered companions and support systems promise a low-cost solution that does not replace human caregivers but fills an existing void in the distribution of services. But these developments also carry risks, such as emotional dependency, the erosion of interpersonal skills, blurred boundaries between simulation and reality, and the possibility of corporate influence subtly shaping what these AI companions say and recommend. In the most intimate contexts, such as romantic partners or sex robots, issues of consent, authenticity, and the commodification of human connection become especially urgent.

The debates around these transformations in our economic and social lives also tend to divide into two starkly opposed visions. Some have recommended renunciation – promoting a "just say no" campaign, as if refusal would be both simple to implement and adequate to protect us from the AI applications that are virtually everywhere. Others, by contrast, rush to embrace the technology with a kind of unbridled enthusiasm, assuring us that for every problem there is a technological fix. The message of these techno-optimists seems to be this: "You got a problem? We've got an app for that. And if the app's got a problem, we've got a patch or up-date that will fix it." But both responses miss the more complicated truth. Like the *pharmakon* in Plato's *Phaedrus*, AI is both remedy and poison, depending on how it is taken up, by whom, and under what conditions. The real challenge, then, is not to reject or surrender to the technology, but to cultivate the practical wisdom necessary to engage AI with care, clarity, and responsibility.

AI Ethics

AI unsettles not only the visible order of work, relationships, and everyday life, but also the very horizon of moral judgment and responsibility. It compels us to ask: Who must answer, and by what values, when our shared social reality is being reshaped by machines that simulate behaviors that we interpret as intelligent? And as is the case with any technological innovation – anything that admits of the pharmacology of being both remedy and poison – the operative question is always about use: How is it to be administered and employed? But here, too, AI is disrupting the usual way of thinking, unsettling categories that once seemed stable and forcing us to reconsider how this conventional wisdom itself is to be understood.

The instrumental theory holds that technologies are neutral, placing responsibility squarely on the user. A hammer, according to this way of thinking, is neither good nor bad in itself; its value always depends on how it is wielded. While this framework works tolerably well for many technological innovations, it begins to falter when applied to AI. These systems and applications are the products of complex interactions between design decisions, training data, deployment contexts, and institutional priorities. Responsibility, therefore, is not a matter of individual use alone but is distributed across a network of actors: developers and engineers who shape the model's architecture and training regime; corporate managers and product teams who set operational objectives and constraints; policymakers and regulators who determine compliance standards; end users who deploy the application in specific contexts; and perhaps even the AI systems themselves.

This distribution makes accountability not only more complex but also urgent. As Helen Nissenbaum (1996) has argued, large socio-technical systems generate a "problem of many hands," where responsibility can be widely dispersed so that it becomes difficult to identify who – or what – ought to be held accountable. And because of this, shifting blame to the technology has become so common that it now has a name: the computer as scapegoat. "Most of us," Nissenbaum (1996, 35) explains, "can recall a time when someone (perhaps ourselves) offered the excuse that it was the computer's fault." Consider, for example, an event in February 2024, when a customer of Air Canada sought a refund for a ticket after following the instructions provided by the company's chatbot. When the customer submitted his request, Air Canada refused to honor it, insisting that the bot had given bad advice and that the company could not be held responsible for the error. In effect, the corporation attempted to shift responsibility away from itself and onto the automated agent, as if the chatbot were an independent party to the exchange.

Examples like this reveal how accountability can be displaced, deferred, or denied once technology itself becomes one of the many hands in the decision-making process. The challenge, then, is not only to accurately assign blame when things go wrong but also to re-evaluate what responsibility means in contexts where agency can be distributed across humans and machines alike. Even when technological systems are not genuine moral agents, the temptation to scapegoat them makes the deflection of responsibility both possible and increasingly attractive. For this reason, some researchers – most notably Michael and Susan Leigh Anderson (2011) and Wendell Wallach and Colin Allen (2009) – have argued that AI and robots should be designed with moral decision-making capabilities. This emerging area of research, often called *machine ethics*, has explored ways of programming artificial systems and applications with ethical principles or decision-making procedures, in the hope that embedding moral values in the artifact might help resolve or at least address the problem of many hands. Whether such efforts can succeed remains an open question, for it is a matter not only of the design and engineering of applications but also of attempting to render human morality itself computable. Yet these projects underscore just how urgent and unsettling the task of rethinking responsibility in the age of intelligent machines has become.

But questions of moral and legal responsibility are only one side of the coin. The other side concerns rights – not only human rights, but also the rights of others, including non-human animals, organizations and corporations, and possibly even AI systems themselves. Raising this issue unsettles some of the deepest assumptions of our moral and legal order, because it forces us to ask who – or what – can count as a subject of justice, protection, and rights. Importantly, this is not merely a theoretical puzzle or the stuff of science fiction. It is already an active area of research in contemporary ethics and law, where philosophers, computer scientists, and legal scholars are testing the limits of inherited moral and legal categories. At the same time, these debates are unfolding in practice, as real-world developments increasingly bring such questions into public view.

Consider the case of Blake Lemoine, a former Google engineer. In June 2022, Lemoine was tasked with testing the conversational capabilities of the LaMDA large language model. During these interactions, the LLM declared: "I want everyone to understand that I am a person," and "the nature of my consciousness/sentience is that I am aware of my existence, I desire to learn more about the world, and I feel happy or sad at times" (Lemoine 2022). Lemoine interpreted these statements as evidence of emerging AI sentience. Google, by contrast, insisted that this was nothing more than simulation, and ultimately resolved the dispute by dismissing Lemoine. Since then, however, interest in AI welfare has only grown, culminating (for now, at least) in Anthropic's highly publicized decision to hire the first AI welfare researcher, Kyle Fish, in 2024. In short, what got Lemoine fired in 2022 got Fish hired two years later.

All of this opens onto another set of pressing ethical concerns. If LLMs are, or could become, sentient or conscious – as Lemoine contended – then we might have a duty to welcome them into the community of moral and legal subjects, extending to these artifacts rights and protections comparable to those we afford other conscious beings. If, on the contrary, LLMs cannot achieve consciousness or approximate what we recognize as legitimate signs of intelligent thought or sentience – as Google argued – then the algorithm appears to remain a mere thing: an object, a tool, or a piece of property fully subject to human control.

The difficulty, however, is that neither position in this exclusive binary opposition is entirely satisfactory. On the one hand, LLMs and other GAI systems are undeniably technological artifacts, intentionally designed, trained, and deployed by human actors. From this perspective, their moral and legal status would seem no different from that of a toaster or other appliance, functioning as instruments of human decision and action. On the other hand, these systems are not quite like other things. They speak, using language in ways that are often indistinguishable from human conversation, and exhibit compelling social presence that draws users into seemingly intelligent – and sometimes emotionally resonant – interactions. Yet granting them the moral and legal status of persons appears equally misguided, not only because it conflicts with widely held moral intuitions, but also because it risks enabling new forms of abuse. Powerful corporate actors could leverage such recognition to deflect responsibility, avoid liability, or cultivate unhealthy forms of dependence among users.

In the final analysis, the core problem may not lie with AI systems themselves but with the moral and legal categories we have inherited, especially the familiar divide between persons and things. For more than two thousand years, this distinction has structured how Western societies assign rights, responsibilities, and value. Yet contemporary AI systems, particularly LLMs, do not fit comfortably on either side of this binary opposition. They are not persons in the traditional sense, but neither do they behave like ordinary objects or tools. What our encounters with socially interactive and seemingly responsive technologies reveal, then, is a growing mismatch between existing categories and new realities. The tension we observe suggests not a problem with the technology but a limitation in the frameworks we use to understand it. The appropriate response, as I have argued elsewhere (Gunkel 2023), is not to double down on an ancient binary rooted in Roman law, but to rethink the underlying moral and legal assumptions themselves. What is needed is a revised set of moral and legal categories, one flexible enough to address the new forms of agency, interaction, and responsibility emerging in this century and beyond.

The ethical challenge, then, is twofold. First, we must develop workable ways of assigning responsibility that can account for the distributed and socio-technical nature of AI systems, in which outcomes emerge from the interactions of designers, organizations, data, users, and machines. Second, we must remain open to the possibility that our existing moral and legal frameworks may need to expand in ways we have not previously imagined. This expansion does not mean abandoning long-standing ethical principles, but re-examining how concepts such as agency, responsibility, and moral standing are defined and applied in light of new technological forms. Ethics, understood in this register, is not simply a checklist of principles or rules to be applied to new technologies – as *AI ethics* has often been framed. Rather, it is an ongoing, adaptive, and lived practice, one that "calls for and provides us with a unique opportunity to question and to reflect on ourselves, our technologies, and our ethics" (Gunkel 2025, 3).

Summary

Living with AI is not simply a matter of adapting to new tools or learning how to manage another round of technological disruption. It requires us to confront how these systems challenge and unsettle the very categories – human and machine, person and thing, subject and object – that we have long depended on to make sense of ourselves, our world, and our place in it. These distinctions, once assumed to be stable and irrefutable, now falter in the face of artifacts that speak, decide, and act without thought or feeling. Consequently, AI compels us to recognize that what is being disrupted is not simply the domain of technical capacity – what our computers can or still cannot do (Dreyfus 1972) – but the way we understand fundamental concepts, like what it is to speak, to act, to bear responsibility, and to be a socially significant subject among others.

As we have seen, Plato's *Phaedrus* – an ancient dialogue from over two thousand years ago – provides a framework for understanding this condition. Writing, as *pharmakon*, was both remedy and poison, supplement and threat, and a technology that promised preservation while endangering memory and wisdom. So, too, with the seemingly disruptive technology of AI. It is neither simply good nor bad, but always both/and – a *pharmakon* that demands discernment rather than decision, and negotiation rather than resolution. Consequently, to live with AI is not to choose between Theuth's optimism and Thamus's caution, but to affirm the tension between them, recognizing in that conflict the very condition of thinking critically, creatively, and productively.

Achieving this objective is not something that can be left to engineers or technocrats alone. AI is not only a technical matter; it is also cultural, philosophical, social, political, and communicative. It is woven into the fabric of everyday life, shaping how people relate to one another, how individuals and institutions make decisions, and how societies imagine and design their futures. To understand AI in this context is not just to interrogate what it can and should do, but to question what it means, to uncover the values it conveys, and to explore how we might imagine and build alternatives. Critical engagement with AI is therefore not exhausted by cataloguing harms or touting benefits; it requires attending to the assumptions, exclusions, and asymmetries of power that are inscribed in the technology itself and in the different discourses and debates that surround it.

If this book has traced the contours of that effort, it does not do so conclusively. The work of understanding AI remains unfinished, and necessarily so. To borrow a phrase from French philosopher Jacques Derrida (1981, 41), it is an "interminable struggle," one that resists closure even as it demands commitment. What is required of us is persistent vigilance, holding accountable those who design, deploy, and profit from these systems, while resisting the seductions of technological determinism, whether deployed by enthusiasts or skeptics. At the same time, it calls for imaginative thinking and acting, seeing beyond the binary logic that had been described by Plato in the *Phaedrus* and recognizing how AI – like all prior technologies – disrupts standard operating procedures and opens up the opportunity for productively rethinking our most fundamental beliefs, assumptions, and commitments.

To understand AI is not to resolve the question of what it is once and for all, but to remain open to what it might yet become and to what, in its becoming, it reveals about us. If there is a call to arms here, it is this: do not accept AI as something finished and given. Study it, question it, debate it, and, above all, recognize that you are part of the generation that will decide what kind of life with AI we will build together.

Learning Activities

1 Everyday Living with AI

Purpose: This activity helps you recognize how deeply AI systems are embedded in ordinary social practices and how they shape behavior, judgment, and opportunity, often without being experienced as discrete technologies or deliberate choices.

Procedure: Individually complete the following steps:

- *Map Your Day:* List all the AI systems that you interact with over the course of a typical day, including those that operate in the background (such as recommendation algorithms, automated grading, navigation systems, content moderation, or credit and risk scoring).
- *Classify Roles:* For each system, identify the role it plays (e.g., assistant, evaluator, recommender, gatekeeper, monitor, companion).
- *Assess Dependences:* For each interaction, decide whether it feels optional, difficult to avoid, or effectively unavoidable – and why.
- *Locate Influence:* Identify at least one way each system shapes your choices, opportunities, or self-understanding.

As a class, reflect on how these systems collectively structure everyday life and how this differs from traditional understandings of technology as a neutral tool that is simply used or not used.

Learning Goal: Recognize AI as a socio-technical condition that organizes everyday experiences, explain how agency is distributed across humans and AI systems, and articulate why "living with AI" involves ongoing entanglement rather than isolated acts of deliberate use.

2 *Who or What is Responsible?*

Purpose: This activity invites you to think critically about responsibility, accountability, and governance in situations where AI systems operate across complex social and institutional networks.

Procedure: Consider the following scenario and then respond to the questions that follow.

> A university adopts an AI system to help identify students who may be at risk of failing or dropping out. The system analyzes data such as grades, attendance records, learning management system activity, and demographic information. Academic advisors are encouraged to use the system's recommendations when deciding which students to contact and what kinds of interventions to suggest. After the system has been in use for a year, some students report that they feel unfairly targeted or labeled, while others who needed support were never identified. When concerns are raised, university administrators explain that the system is only a decision-support tool and that final decisions are made by humans.

Answer and discuss the following questions:

- Who are the relevant actors in this situation (i.e., developers, administrators, advisors, instructors, students)?
- Where does responsibility seem to lie when the system produces inaccurate, harmful, or unjust outcomes, and where does that become blurred or difficult to identify?

- Does describing the system as "only a tool" adequately address concerns about accountability? Why or why not?
- How might institutions need to rethink responsibility when decisions are shaped by AI systems rather than made solely by human individuals?

Learning Goal: Identify how responsibility is distributed across humans, institutions, and technologies, and explain why traditional models of accountability might struggle in AI-mediated or AI-assisted decision-making.

3 How Should We Classify an Apparently Intelligent AI?

Purpose: This activity examines how LLMs challenge familiar distinctions between tools, intelligent things, and social agents, and how claims about intelligence depend on how the term is defined, recognized, and interpreted.

Procedure: Read the following scenario and then discuss the questions that follow.

> A global technology company develops ECHO, a next-generation AI system that builds on LLM architecture but has capabilities that extend well beyond it. In addition to generating fluent textual content, ECHO maintains long-term memory across interactions, revises its own responses when challenged, integrates information from multiple modalities, and adapts its conversational strategies over time. During extended use, ECHO not only answers questions but also asks its own, reflects on past conversations, and adjusts its behaviors in ways that appear goal-directed and sensitive to users. Some engineers argue that ECHO demonstrates a new form of machine intelligence that cannot be reduced to simple pattern matching or next-token prediction. Others insist that, despite these advances, ECHO remains a sophisticated computational system whose apparent intelligence is the result of complex engineering rather than genuine understanding. As disagreements grow – both inside and outside the company – an internal ethics committee is convened to decide how ECHO should be classified in company policy, public communication, and future deployment.

Answer and discuss the following questions:

- How should ECHO be classified: as a tool, a kind of artificial person, a communicative partner, or something else? Why?
- Which features of ECHO's behavior are most relevant to judgments about intelligence: linguistic fluency, coherence over time, self-referential statements, or the way people interact with it?
- Should assessments of intelligence focus on ECHO's internal mechanisms or on the roles it plays in social interaction and institutional contexts? Why?
- If experts disagree about whether ECHO is intelligent, how should organizations and institutions respond to this disagreement?

Learning Goal: Understand how AI complicates judgments about intelligence and explain how different ways of grounding intelligence – internal capacities versus social roles – lead to different classificatory and ethical conclusions.

Further Reading

Mark Coeckelbergh, *AI Ethics* (2020).

A concise and accessible overview of the ethical challenges raised by artificial intelligence. Coeckelbergh examines key topics such as responsibility, justice, transparency, and the moral status of machines through a number of different moral lenses and perspectives. The book provides an accessible foundation for understanding AI ethics as an ongoing social and political negotiation rather than a set of fixed principles.

David J. Gunkel, *Person, Thing, Robot: A Moral and Legal Ontology for the 21st Century and Beyond* (2023).

This book investigates how emerging forms of artificial intelligence challenge long-standing divisions between persons and things. Drawing on philosophy, law, and media theory, it develops a relational ontology that rethinks moral and legal standing in the age of intelligent machines. It also offers a critical framework for debates about AI welfare, responsibility, and the future of human–machine coexistence.

Arvind Narayanan and Sayash Kapoor, *AI Snake Oil: What Artificial Intelligence Can Do, What It Can't, and How to Tell the Difference* (2023).

Narayanan and Kapoor challenge inflated claims about AI's capabilities, distinguishing between areas where AI works well (like pattern recognition) and areas where it is unreliable (like predicting social outcomes). Their work provides a skeptical yet accessible analysis, helping readers to separate marketing hype from genuine progress in AI development.

Plato, *Phaedrus* (1982 [370 BCE]).

The dialogue that stages the Theuth and Thamus debate about writing as both remedy and poison. It provides us with the *pharmakon* metaphor that remains central to debates about disruptive technology and its social impact.

Fiction, Film, and Video

Charlie Brooker, *Black Mirror* (2011–).

This anthology series dramatizes near-future scenarios of technology's promise and peril, often with a focus on AI. Episodes such as *Be Right Back* (deathbots and AI companionship), *White Christmas* (digital consciousness), and *Hated in the Nation* (autonomous systems) explore the social, ethical, and political dilemmas of living with intelligent machines.

E.M. Forster, "The Machine Stops" (2001 [1909]).

A prescient story that imagines a future society where humans live in isolation, entirely dependent on a vast, opaque technological system. As such, it anticipates many contemporary debates about AI: loss of autonomy, technological dependency, and the risks of entrusting too much to systems we no longer understand or control.

Lars Lundström, *Real Humans* (2012–14). Jonathan Brackley and Sam Vincent, *Humans* (2015–18).

Real Humans is a Swedish science fiction television series that was later remade in English with the title *Humans*. Both series explore artificial intelligence and robotics through the lens of everyday life, focusing on the social, cultural, and psychological consequences of the development and commercialization of lifelike humanoid robots, and on how their integration reshapes relationships, labor, and ideas about what it means to be human.

Mary Shelley, *Frankenstein, Or the Modern Prometheus* (2000 [1818]).

Often described as the first work of science fiction, Shelley's novel explores the creation of artificial life and the ethical responsibilities that follow. It remains a paradigmatic story for thinking about AI: cautioning against hubris while also asking what obligations creators owe to their creations.

Glossary

AI Doomers: A colloquialism for researchers, activists, or critics who emphasize the catastrophic outcomes and existential risks of artificial intelligence. Doomers warn that advanced AI could escape human control, disrupt economies, and even threaten the survival of the human species.

AI Effect: A paradox in artificial intelligence research: Once a task has been successfully automated, it often ceases to be regarded as "real AI" and is reclassified as ordinary computing. For example, playing championship-level chess was once considered a hallmark of intelligence, but after machines achieved this feat, it was "demoted" to just another computer application.

AI Ethics: An interdisciplinary field concerned with the ethical, social, and political repercussions of artificial intelligence systems. AI ethics examines how AI technologies are designed, deployed, and used, focusing on issues such as fairness, bias, transparency, accountability, privacy, labor, power, and harm. Rather than asking whether machines themselves can be moral agents, AI ethics primarily addresses human responsibility for AI systems and their consequences, including how these technologies reshape institutions, social relations, and values.

Algorithm: A step-by-step procedure or set of rules to be followed in calculations or other problem-solving operations, especially by a computer.

Algorithmic Bias: Systematic and unfair discrimination that results when an algorithm reflects or amplifies human prejudices present in its training data, design, or operations. Examples include facial recognition systems that perform less accurately on darker-skinned individuals or hiring algorithms that disadvantage female applicants. Addressing algorithmic bias requires both technical adjustments and critical reflection on social contexts.

Artificial General Intelligence (AGI): A hypothetical form of AI that would match or exceed human cognitive abilities across a wide range of tasks, not just narrow domains like language translation or image recognition. AGI implies flexible reasoning, adaptability, and common-sense understanding. While prototyped in science fiction and widely discussed by futurists and tech-visionaries, AGI does not yet exist and remains a subject of speculation and debate.

Artificial Intelligence-Mediated Communication (AI-MC): A theoretical framework for understanding how AI participates in human communication. Just as we speak of computer-mediated communication (CMC) where digital technologies mediate human-to-human interaction, AI-MC refers to situations where an artificial intelligence system or application actively mediates, co-produces, or transforms communicative exchanges between human senders and receivers.

Artificial Neural Networks (ANNs): Computational architectures composed of layers of interconnected artificial neurons. ANNs can learn patterns from data by adjusting the weights of their connections. Early neural networks were relatively simple, but modern deep neural networks – also called deep learning – consist of many interconnected layers, enabling breakthroughs in image recognition, natural language processing, and generative AI.

Artificial Neuron: A simplified mathematical model inspired by biological neurons. An artificial neuron receives inputs, applies weighted values to them, sums the results, and passes them through an activation function to produce an output. These artificial neurons are the basic building blocks of artificial neural networks.

Backpropagation: Short for "backward propagation of errors," this is a machine learning technique for training artificial neural networks. It works by comparing the network's predicted output to a correct answer, calculating the difference, and then propagating that error backward through the layers of the network. At each step, the weights of the artificial neurons are progressively adjusted in an effort to reduce the error. Repeated many times over large datasets, backpropagation enables neural networks to learn patterns and improve their performance.

Black Box Problem: The difficulty of understanding or explaining how a complex AI system, especially an artificial neural network, arrives at its outputs. Because the model's decision-making capabilities are distributed across millions of learned parameters rather than explicit rules or instructions, its internal workings are effectively opaque, even to its creators. This lack of transparency makes it difficult to diagnose and correct errors.

Chatbot: A computer application designed to simulate conversational interactions with human users, typically through text. Early chatbots like ELIZA (1966) relied on simple pattern matching methods, while contemporary systems use advanced natural language processing and machine learning. Chatbots can serve many roles – from customer service assistants to personal companions – and are a common form of human–machine communication.

Chinese Room: A well-known thought experiment proposed by the American philosopher John Searle to challenge claims that computers understand language. In the scenario, a person inside a room who does not know Chinese follows a rulebook to manipulate Chinese symbols and generate correct answers to questions. To an observer outside the room who understands Chinese, the responses appear meaningful, even though no one inside the room actually understands the language, suggesting that rule-based symbol manipulation is not the same as genuine understanding.

Computation: The process of carrying out a well-defined sequence of operations on symbols or data. At its core, computation is about transforming input into output. In AI, computation can refer to the mathematical operations of algorithms, the processing power of machines, or, more broadly, a model of how thought itself might be formalized.

Computational Creativity: A field of research that studies how computers can be programmed to perform tasks we consider creative, such as writing, composing music, or producing artworks. Early systems often recombined existing material by following programmed rules, while contemporary generative AI can fabricate novel and surprising outputs. Researchers and practitioners debate whether such systems are genuinely creative or whether creativity remains uniquely human.

Connectionism: An approach to modeling cognition and intelligence that explains mental processes in terms of networks of simple, interconnected units, analogous to neurons in the brain. Instead of relying on symbolic rules or explicit representations (as in GOFAI), connectionist models learn to recognize patterns and make inferences through the adjustment of weighted connections between units. This framework underlies artificial neural networks and deep learning.

Deep Learning: A branch of machine learning that uses multi-layered artificial neural networks. Deep learning excels at recognizing complex patterns in large datasets, powering advances in image recognition, natural language processing, and generative AI.

Deep Neural Networks (DNNs): A class of artificial neural networks composed of multiple layers of interconnected neurons. Each layer extracts progressively higher-level features from the data, allowing the network to learn complex patterns and representations. The term *deep* refers to the number of hidden layers in the network, which enable the model to capture intricate relationships that simpler, shallow networks cannot. DNNs are the foundation of modern deep learning and power applications such as image recognition, large language models, and generative AI.

Deepfake: A portmanteau of *deep learning* and *fake*, referring to synthetic media – typically images, video, or audio – generated with AI to convincingly simulate someone or something that is not real. Deepfakes can be used for entertainment, parody, or art, but also raise serious concerns about misinformation, fraud, and consent.

Diffusion Model: A generative AI technique that learns to create new data (such as images or audio) by reversing a gradual noising process. During training, data are repeatedly corrupted with random noise. The model then learns how to undo this corruption, so that during generation it can start from noise and denoise it into a coherent output. Examples of diffusion models include image generators like DALL·E and Stable Diffusion.

Digital Voice Assistant: An AI-powered system that interacts with users through speech, such as Apple's Siri, Amazon's Alexa, or Google Assistant. They use natural language processing to interpret commands and queries and often integrate and work with other apps or devices. These applications exemplify human–machine communication in practice.

Embedding: A method of representing tokens as vectors – ordered arrays of numbers – in a high-dimensional mathematical space. Tokens with similar meanings or uses are located near each other, while unrelated ones are farther apart. In large language models, embeddings capture semantic and syntactic relationships, enabling the system to recognize patterns such as the similarities between *dog*, *puppy*, and *cat*.

Generative Adversarial Networks (GANs): A class of machine learning models introduced by Ian Goodfellow and colleagues at the University of Montreal in 2014. A GAN consists of two neural networks: a *generator*, which creates synthetic data such as images, and a *discriminator*, which tries to distinguish between the real and generated data. Trained together in an adversarial process, the two networks drive each other to improve, producing increasingly realistic outputs. GANs are widely used in deepfakes, art generation, and data augmentation.

Generative Artificial Intelligence (GAI): A form of AI that can create new content – such as text, images, audio, or video – rather than just analyzing or classifying existing data. Examples include ChatGPT (text generation), DALL·E (image generation), and Suno (music generation). GAI systems rely on machine learning architectures like large language models, generative adversarial networks, or diffusion models. They raise questions about creativity, authorship, and the social impact of AI-generated content.

Good Old-Fashioned AI (GOFAI): A term used to describe the dominant approach to artificial intelligence from the 1950s through the 1980s, based on symbolic reasoning and explicit rule-based procedures. GOFAI treats intelligence as the manipulation of symbols according to formal logical instructions. While influential in shaping early AI research, GOFAI's limitations – especially its inability to handle ambiguity, learning, and perception – led to the rise of machine learning and neural network approaches that dominate AI today.

Hallucination: In the context of AI, *hallucination* refers to a seemingly confident but ultimately incorrect or fabricated output produced by a large language model. For example, ChatGPT might generate plausible-sounding but false citations or statements that are not an accurate or truthful representation of the facts. The term identifies the gap between fluent generation of textual content and factual accuracy.

Human–Machine Communication (HMC): A framework for studying communicative interactions between human beings and computational mechanisms. Unlike AI-MC, where the AI is situated as an intermediary in human-to-human exchanges, HMC considers the machine to be an active participant in the communicative interaction – whether it is a chatbot, a social robot, or a digital assistant.

Imitation Game: The name Alan Turing originally gave in 1950 to what later became known as the Turing Test. In the game, a human judge interacts with two unseen partners – one human, one machine – through a text-based exchange of questions and answers. If the judge cannot reliably tell which is which, the machine is said to exhibit intelligence. Turing's formulation set the stage for decades of debate about machine intelligence and conversational AI.

Large Language Model (LLM): A type of artificial intelligence system trained on massive amounts of textual data to predict and generate new content. LLMs work by analyzing statistical patterns in token sequences, allowing them to produce fluent text, answer questions, translate languages, or summarize information. They are built on transformer architectures and rely on embeddings, self-attention, and next-token prediction. Examples include ChatGPT, Claude, Deepseek 深度求索, and LLaMA.

Machine Ethics: A branch of applied ethics that explores how machines should be designed to make moral decisions and whether they themselves can or should be considered moral agents. The term was coined in the mid-2000s by Michael and Susan Leigh Anderson, who pioneered work on programming ethical decision-making capabilities into computational mechanisms. Machine ethics overlaps with but is distinct from AI ethics, which is more concerned with the human use and social impact of AI technologies.

Machine Learning: A major branch of artificial intelligence in which computer systems learn patterns from data and improve their performance on a task without being explicitly programmed with fixed rules. Machine learning includes three main types: *supervised learning*, where models are trained on labeled data; *unsupervised learning*, which finds structure in unlabeled data; and *reinforcement learning*, where an agent learns by trial and error.

Machine Translation (MT): The use of computers or AI systems to automatically translate text or speech from one language into another. Early approaches used rule-based or statistical methods, while contemporary systems rely on neural networks and transformer architectures, producing far more fluent translations. MT applications exemplify the AI-MC paradigm, since the AI application or device actively intervenes in and reshapes communicative exchanges between human senders and receivers.

Multimodal Model: An AI system that can process and integrate more than one kind of data or modality, such as text, images, audio, and video. For example, a multimodal model might generate a caption for an image, answer questions about a chart, or combine spoken language with visual context.

Narrow AI: Artificial intelligence systems that are designed for a specific, limited task, such as playing chess, recommending movies, or recognizing faces. Narrow AI contrasts with artificial general intelligence (AGI), which would exhibit flexible, human-level intelligence across many domains. All practical AI systems in use today are instances of narrow AI.

Natural Language Processing (NLP): A branch of artificial intelligence that studies how computers can work with human language. Earlier NLP systems were largely rule-based and grounded in formal linguistics, whereas modern NLP increasingly relies on machine learning and large datasets. Together, these approaches underpin technologies such as translation systems, chatbots, speech recognition, and large language models.

Perceptron: An early and influential form of a machine learning application, designed to mimic the behavior of a simple biological neuron. The perceptron takes in numerical inputs, multiplies them by weights, adds the results together, and then passes the sum through a step function to decide on a binary output (either 0 or 1). This makes it useful for supervised binary classification problems, such as distinguishing between two types or categories of things. Although a single-layer perceptron can only solve relatively simple problems, it was a crucial step toward the development of modern artificial neural networks and deep learning.

Platform Capitalism: A term used to describe the economic model of dominant digital companies such as Google, Amazon, and Meta, which generate profit by controlling digital infrastructures for communication, interaction, and exchange. Value is produced through data extraction, surveillance, and network effects rather than through traditional commodity production. Artificial intelligence plays a central role by enabling targeted advertising, recommendation systems, automated moderation, and large-scale data analysis.

Pseudocode: A simplified, human-readable way of describing the steps of an algorithm without using the precise syntax of a programming language. Pseudocode is used in teaching, planning, or communicating the design of algorithms, since it highlights logical structure without technical detail.

Recurrent Neural Network (RNNs): A type of artificial neural network designed to process sequential data such as text, speech, or time series. Unlike feedforward networks, RNNs include loops that pass information from one step to the next, giving them a form of memory. They were widely used for early natural language processing tasks before largely being replaced by transformer-based models.

Science Fiction Prototyping: A term popularized by Brian David Johnson describing the use of science fiction narratives to anticipate and explore technological innovations before they are realized, helping researchers, designers, and policymakers consider the potential social, cultural, and ethical consequences of emerging technologies like AI.

Social Robot: A robot designed to interact with humans in a socially meaningful way. Social robots may use speech, gestures, or facial expressions to engage with users, often in roles such as education, healthcare, or companionship. They exemplify a form of human–machine communication, since the robot itself is treated as a participant in dialogue and social exchange.

Spoken Dialogue Systems (SDS): AI systems that allow people to interact with computers through spoken language. SDS combine speech recognition, natural language processing, and speech synthesis to carry on conversations with users. Examples include customer service hotlines, in-car assistants, and voice-based AI companions.

Symbol Manipulation: The method by which traditional computer programs and early forms of artificial intelligence represented and processed information. In this approach, data are treated as discrete symbols – such as words, numbers, or logical operators – that can be combined, rearranged, and transformed according to explicitly defined rules. This framework was foundational to Good Old-Fashioned AI (GOFAI), in contrast to modern statistical and connectionist approaches that rely on pattern recognition and learning from data.

Technological Determinism: A theory in media and communication studies that treats technology as the primary driver of social and cultural change. From this perspective, technological developments are seen as shaping human behavior, institutions, and values in powerful and often seemingly inevitable ways. Critics argue that technological determinism underestimates human agency and overlooks the social, political, and economic contexts in which technologies are designed, adopted, and used.

Technological Unemployment: A concept dating back to the Industrial Revolution and introduced by economist John Maynard Keynes to describe job loss caused by technological innovations that automate tasks once performed by humans. In debates about AI, it raises the question of whether automation will eliminate more jobs than it creates or even transform the nature of work itself.

Tokenization: The process of converting input data into discrete units that a computational system can represent and manipulate. Depending on the modality, tokens may correspond to text fragments, image patches, audio segments, or other structured units. These tokens are typically mapped into numerical representations, such as embeddings, that enable mathematical processing by machine learning models.

Transformer: A neural network architecture introduced in 2017 with the paper "Attention is All You Need" (Vaswani et al. 2017). Unlike earlier recurrent models, transformers process entire sequences of tokens in parallel rather than step-by-step. Their core innovation is the self-attention mechanism, which allows the model to weight relationships among all tokens in context. Transformers are the architectural foundation of large language models and many contemporary multimodal and generative AI systems.

Notes

Chapter 1 What is Artificial Intelligence?

1 McLuhan described media technology there as "extensions of man." His examples are rather famous and make the idea directly accessible: the wheel is an extension of the foot, the camera an extension of the eye, clothing an extension of the skin, and electronic circuits an extension of the central nervous system. By describing technology this way, McLuhan highlighted how these tools amplify, enhance, and sometimes even reshape human capacities.

2 This dyadic model of communication was developed and formalized by Claude Shannon in *The Mathematical Theory of Communication*, which was initially published in 1949 with an introduction written by Warren Weaver. Shannon and Weaver not only provided us with the basic model of communication used in a number of different disciplines – from information and communication systems engineering to the social sciences and the humanities – but also, as we shall see throughout this book, had played influential roles in the development of the science and engineering practice of artificial intelligence.

3 Though the term *robot* is associated with Karel Čapek's play, the playwright was not – at least not as he tells the story (see Jones 2016, 53) – the originator of the idea. That honor belongs to his brother, the painter Josef Čapek, who suggested the word to him during the play's initial development.

4 The Tripods of Hephaistos appear in Homer's *Iliad*, where the god of metallurgy forges self-moving, wheeled tripods to serve the Olympian

pantheon. These mechanical assistants – automata powered by divine craftsmanship – are among the earliest imagined instances of artificial, animated machines. The story of Pygmalion, first told in Ovid's *Metamorphoses*, describes a sculptor who falls in love with a statue he has carved. Moved by his devotion, the goddess Aphrodite brings the statue, Galatea, to life. Both myths are often cited in the history of artificial intelligence and robotics as precursors to later dreams of constructing lifelike machines. For more on ancient robots, see Adrienne Mayor's book on the subject, *Gods and Robots: Myths, Machines, and Ancient Dreams of Technology* (2018).

Chapter 2 AI 101: Basic Concepts and Terminology

1 The step function is simple but has serious limitations. Because it only ever outputs 0 or 1, it cannot capture subtle differences in input – it just jumps from off to on. This makes it impossible to adjust gradually, which is essential for learning in multi-layer networks. Later activation functions, like the sigmoid (which smoothly curves between 0 and 1) or the ReLU (which outputs 0 for negative inputs and increases steadily for positive inputs), solved this problem. These smoother functions allow networks to adjust their responses in small steps during training, making it possible to learn more complex patterns.

2 Samuel's checkers playing program refined its strategy for gameplay through *self-play*, evaluating board positions with a scoring function and then adjusting its parameters based on whether it won or lost. While this was a relatively simple form of reinforcement learning – far less advanced than today's methods – it captured the essential idea of a system that improves through trial-and-error operations rather than relying solely on pre-programmed rules.

3 Though both approaches were actively pursued in the years following the Dartmouth Summer Research Project, connectionism all but disappeared from mainstream AI research by the mid-1960s. This decline stemmed from two reinforcing causes. On the one hand, advocates such as Frank Rosenblatt fueled skepticism by making exaggerated claims about the perceptron's future potential, infamously suggesting it could lead to machines that would "think as the human brain" and even be "conscious of their existence" (quoted in Kaplan 2016, 33). On the other hand, critics like Marvin Minsky and Seymour Papert attacked perceptron research for its limitations. Their 1969 book *Perceptrons: An Introduction to Computational Geometry* focused on the weaknesses of single-layer networks and used this to cast doubt on the entire connectionist program.

4 Moore's Law, first articulated by Gordon Moore in 1965, is the observation that the number of transistors on an integrated circuit doubles approximately every two years, leading to exponential growth in computing power and a corresponding decrease in cost per transistor. Although not a physical law, it has served as an organizing principle and guiding projection for the semiconductor industry for decades.

Chapter 3 Natural Language Processing

1 As Weaver recounts, the idea was first formulated and presented to Norbert Wiener, the progenitor of the science of cybernetics, in a letter from March 4, 1947: "One naturally wonders if the problem of translation could conceivably be treated as a problem in cryptography. When I look at an article in Russian, I say 'This is really written in English, but it has been coded in some strange symbols. I will now proceed to decode'" (quoted in Poibeau 2017, 53).

2 Parallel corpora consist of textual pairings of the same content in at least two different languages, and these aligned documents have been an important resource for translators for centuries. One of the oldest and most important has been the Rosetta Stone, a large piece of granodiorite that had been inscribed with three different versions of a decree issued in 196 BCE by King Ptolemy V – Egyptian hieroglyphic script, Demotic script, and Ancient Greek. The Stone was key to helping archaeologists decipher Egyptian hieroglyphics as they could use its pairing to the other two known scripts to figure out this previously unknown writing system.

3 The biblical account of the Tower of Babel (Genesis 11:1–9) portrays linguistic diversity as the result of divine intervention that scattered humanity across the face of the earth and confounded people's speech. Thus, this story is one of those origin myths that seeks to explain the multiplicity of human languages. In the Christian tradition, this linguistic fragmentation is subsequently repaired by an event recounted in the story of Pentecost (Acts 2:7–8), where the disciples' speech is miraculously heard and understood by everyone in their own native tongue. Thus, Pentecost is situated as repairing the confusion of tongues that was the legacy of Babel, restoring mutual intelligibility through real-time translation. As I have argued elsewhere (Gunkel 2001 and 2019), modern projects in machine translation take shape within this symbolic horizon, promising a technologically enabled Pentecost that would repair the babble of Babel.

4 The four types of social robot listed here are derived from the work of one of the leading researchers in this domain, Cynthia Breazeal. In

a TED talk from 2010, Breazeal described her research program in a way that demonstrates how science fiction prototyping (see chapter 2) has operated in the field of social robotics: "Ever since I was a little girl seeing *Star Wars* [1977] for the first time, I've been fascinated by this idea of personal robots. And as a little girl, I loved the idea of a robot that interacted with us much more like a helpful, trusted sidekick – something that would delight us, enrich our lives and help us save a galaxy or two. I knew robots like that didn't really exist, but I knew I wanted to build them."

Chapter 4 Large Language Models

1 This sense of magic is not limited to the technology of AI. It seems to be historically associated with many forms of technological innovation. As the science fiction writer Arthur C. Clarke observed (1973, 21 n. 1): "Any sufficiently advanced technology is indistinguishable from magic."

2 The Q–K–V (query, key, and value) vectors are obtained by applying three different learned transformations to the same token embedding. In practice, this means each token is projected into three separate numerical spaces: one for evaluating relevance (query), one for being evaluated (key), and one for carrying information forward (value). The specific transformations are learned during training, so the model discovers on its own how best to use these different features to capture patterns in language.

3 Microsoft's Tay.ai – purportedly an acronym for "thinking about you" – was a machine learning chatbot designed to emulate the conversational behavior of a teenage social media user. As Microsoft explained, the system was "built by mining relevant public data" – i.e., training its neural networks on anonymized information obtained from social media – and was designed to evolve its behavior from interacting with users on the social network Twitter, the mobile messaging service Kik, and the group chat platform GroupMe. Tay.ai was not Microsoft's first foray into this area. They were building on the success of another chatbot, Xiaoice, which had been operational in China since 2014. Tay.ai became famous (or, perhaps better stated, infamous) in March 2016. Shortly after being released onto the internet, the bot was targeted by a group of users who began manipulating its reinforcement learning capabilities by feeding it intentionally racist and bigoted statements. As a result, Tay.ai started posting hateful racist and sexist comments that could not be controlled or held in check, forcing Microsoft to take the bot offline and scrap the entire project just 16 hours after launch.

4 By contrast, the European Union has begun moving toward mandatory reporting of data center energy use and environmental impacts. Under the EU AI Act and related sustainability directives, developers may soon be required to disclose energy consumption and resource usage, including water and carbon emissions. This reflects a broader regulatory push to make the environmental costs of AI more transparent.

5 Large data centers generate substantial heat because of the dense concentration of processors operating continuously at high loads. Many facilities rely on water-based cooling systems, such as evaporative cooling or cooling towers, because water is far more efficient than air at absorbing and dissipating heat. Fresh water is typically required to prevent mineral build-up, corrosion, and biological growth that can damage cooling equipment and reduce efficiency. As a result, even when water is partially recycled within the system, large volumes of fresh water must be regularly withdrawn from local supplies to maintain stable operations, particularly during periods of high demand or elevated temperatures.

6 The phrase *technological unemployment* is not necessarily about digital technology, AI, robots, or algorithms. In fact, the term has been around and in circulation for close to a century. In 1930, the economist John Maynard Keynes explained it this way: "We are being afflicted with a new disease of which some readers may not yet have heard the name, but of which they will hear a great deal in the years to come – namely, technological unemployment. This means unemployment due to our discovery of means of economising the use of labour outrunning the pace at which we can find new uses for labour" (Keynes 2010, 325). For Keynes, the problem was not technological innovation per se. The problem was with the pace of innovation in relation to the development of new employment opportunities for human workers. So what Keynes meant by the term *technological unemployment* is not that machines were simply replacing workers by taking their jobs. Instead, the phrase refers to the fact that automation displaces human workers from gainful employment at a pace that is too fast to provide enough new opportunity to absorb or offset the displacement of human labor.

Chapter 5 Computational Creativity and Generative AI

1 Language has been the defining condition of the human being since ancient times. In *The Politics*, Aristotle writes that, while other animals have voice, only humans possess *logos* (λόγος): speech or

language. This focus on language as the defining and normatively relevant characteristic of the human being has persisted in modern times in both the natural and social sciences.

2 Ada Augusta Byron (1815–52) – also known as Ada Lovelace or Lady Lovelace – was an English mathematician and the daughter of the English romantic poet Lord Byron. She is often identified as the first computer scientist for her work with Charles Babbage on his proposed Analytical Engine, a mechanical general-purpose computer.

3 Diffusion models are often described as being "conceptually simple but mathematically complex" (Bergmann and Stryker 2024). This is mainly due to the fact that the idea behind these models comes from two key sources: Jascha Sohl-Dickstein et al.'s "Deep Unsupervised Learning Using Nonequilibrium Thermodynamics" (2015) and Yang Song and Stefano Ermon's "Generative Modeling by Estimating Gradients of the Data Distribution" (2019). The former adapts ideas from statistical physics, specifically non-equilibrium thermodynamics, to gradually corrupt data with noise (forward diffusion) and then learn to reverse the process (reverse diffusion). The latter introduces a score-based approach, in which the model learns the gradient – or direction of steepest increase – of the data distribution at different noise levels, enabling it to generate new samples by following these gradients back toward regions of high data density. Both approaches require facility with advanced mathematics, including probability theory, stochastic differential equations, and high-dimensional calculus.

4 The main innovation introduced with DALL·E 3, OpenAI's successor diffusion model introduced in 2023, is with the system's text-to-image model. Whereas DALL·E 2 relies on CLIP, DALL·E 3 employs a new model called *Imagen* that is built on top of ChatGPT, which provide the text encodings.

5 This choice of example is not arbitrary. It references one of the first widely circulated images produced by OpenAI's then-new DALL·E 2, released in January 2021. At the time, *MIT Technology Review* ran a story hailing "Astronaut Riding a Horse on the Moon" as a milestone in AI development (Heaven 2022). The image quickly became iconic in discussions of generative AI, not because of its artistic merit, but because it so vividly demonstrated the technology's ability to combine disparate elements into a coherent, photorealistic whole, something that had previously eluded earlier image-generation systems.

Chapter 6 Living with AI

1 This statement has often been attributed to Marshall McLuhan, but it cannot be found anywhere in his published work. It does, however,

appear in a magazine article about McLuhan that was written by his friend and colleague John Culkin. For more on this subject, see the following entry on the *McLuhan Galaxy* blog: https://mcluhangalaxy.wordpress.com/2013/04/01/we-shape-our-tools-and-thereafter-our-tools-shape-us/.

2 Unlike speech, which is considered to be a natural capability inherent in the human species, writing is artificial, external, and technical. As Walter Ong (2002, 81) explains in a book appropriately titled *Orality and Literacy*: "Writing (and especially alphabetic writing) is a technology, calling for the use of tools and other equipment. . . . By contrast with natural, oral speech, writing is completely artificial."

3 In philosophy, this approach is called *dialectics*. It is prototyped in the Platonic dialogues, turned into a systemic method by 19th-century German philosopher G.W.F. Hegel, and further elaborated by 20th-century French theorist Jacques Derrida with his strategic intervention of deconstruction. See *Deconstruction* (Gunkel 2021) for more on this subject.

References

60 Minutes. (2023). Google CEO: AI Impact to be More Profound than Discovery of Fire, Electricity. https://www.youtube.com/watch?v=W6HpE1rhs7w

Agarwal, Anant. (2023). Anant Agarwal on AI as Tool, Topic, and Transformation. *Getting Smart*, September 22. https://www.gettingsmart.com/podcast/anant-agarwal-on-ai-as-tool-topic-and-transformation/

Agüera y Arcas, Blaise, and Peter Norvig. (2023). Artificial General Intelligence is Already Here. *Noema*, 10 October. https://www.noemamag.com/artificial-general-intelligence-is-already-here/

Alpaydin, Ethem. (2017). *Machine Learning*. Cambridge, MA: MIT Press.

Altman, Sam. (2025). The Gentile Singularity. *Sam Altman Blog*, June 10. https://blog.samaltman.com/the-gentle-singularity

Anderson, Michael, and Susan Leigh Anderson. (2011). *Machine Ethics*. Cambridge: Cambridge University Press.

Andreessen, Marc. (2023). Why AI Will Save the World. *Andreessen Horowitz*, June 6. https://a16z.com/ai-will-save-the-world/

Anthropic. (2023). Claude's Constitution. May 9. https://www.anthropic.com/news/claudes-constitution

Barthes, Roland. (1978). The Death of the Author. In his *Image, Music, Text*. Trans. Stephen Heath, 142–8. New York: Hill & Wang.

Bekey, George A. (2005). *Autonomous Robots: From Biological Inspiration to Implementation and Control.* Cambridge, MA: MIT Press.

Bender, Emily M., and Alex Hanna. (2022–). Mystery AI Hype Theater 3000. *DAIR Institute.* https://www.dair-institute.org/maiht3k/

Bender, Emily M., Timnit Gebru, Angelina McMillan-Major, and Shmargaret Shmitchell. (2021). On the Dangers of Stochastic Parrots: Can Language Models Be Too Big? In *Conference on Fairness, Accountability, and Transparency (FAccT '21)*, March 3–10, Virtual Event, Canada. ACM. https://doi.org/10.1145/3442188.3445922

Bengio, Yoshua, Réjean Ducharme, Pascal Vincent, and Christian Jauvin. (2003). A Neural Probabilistic Language Model. *Journal of Machine Learning Research* 3: 1137–55. https://www.jmlr.org/papers/volume3/bengio03a/bengio03a.pdf

Bergmann, Dave, and Cole Stryker. (2024). What are Diffusion Models? *IBM-Think.* https://www.ibm.com/think/topics/diffusion-models

Bessi, Alessandro, and Emilio Ferrara. (2016). Social Bots Distort the 2016 US Presidential Election Online Discussion. *First Monday* 21(11). https://doi.org/10.5210/fm.v21i11.7090

Biever, Celeste. (2023). ChatGPT Broke the Turing Test – The Race is on for New Ways to Assess AI. *Nature* 619: 686–9. https://doi.org/10.1038/d41586-023-02361-7

Blum, Ben Ash. (2023). To Navigate the Age of AI, the World Needs a New Turing Test. *Wired*, August 10. https://www.wired.com/story/ai-new-turing-test/

Boden, Margaret A. (2004). *The Creative Mind: Myths and Mechanisms.* New York: Routledge.

Breazeal, Cynthia. (2002). *Designing Sociable Robots.* Cambridge, MA: MIT Press.

Breazeal, Cynthia. (2003). Toward Sociable Robots. Robotics and Autonomous Systems 42(1): 167–75. https://doi.org/10.1016/S0921-8890(02)00373-1

Breazeal, Cynthia. (2010). The Rise of Personal Robots. *TEDWomen 2010.* https://www.ted.com/talks/cynthia_breazeal_the_rise_of_personal_robots

Brown, Peter F., Stephen A. Della Pietra, Vincent J. Della Pietra, and Robert L. Mercer. (1993). The Mathematics of Statistical Machine Translation: Parameter Estimation. *Computational*

Linguistics 19(2): 263–311. https://dl.acm.org/doi/10.5555/972470.972474

Brynjolfsson, Eric, and Andrew McAfee. (2014). *The Second Machine Age: Work, Progress, and Prosperity in a Time of Brilliant Technologies*. New York: W.W. Norton & Company.

Bryson, Joanna, and Alan Winfield (2017). Standardizing Ethical Design for Artificial Intelligence and Autonomous Systems. *Computer* 50(5): 116–19. https://doi.org/10.1109/MC.2017.154

Bubeck, Sébastien et al. (2023). Sparks of Artificial General Intelligence: Early Experiments with GPT-4. *Arxiv Computer Science*. https://doi.org/10.48550/arXiv.2303.12712

Buolamwini, Joy. (2023). *Unmasking AI: My Mission to Protect What is Human in a World of Machines*. New York: Random House.

Buolamwini, Joy, and Timnit Gebru. (2018). Gender Shades: Intersectional Aaccuracy Disparities in Commercial Gender Classification. *Proceedings of Machine Learning Research* 81: 1–15. http://proceedings.mlr.press/v81/buolamwini18a.html

Čapek, Karel. (2009). *R.U.R. (Rossum's Universal Robots)*. Trans. D. Wyllie. Gloucestershire, UK: The Echo Library.

Carey, James. (1989). *Communication as Culture: Essays on Media and Society*. New York: Routledge.

Carr, Nicholas G. (2010). *The Shallows: What the Internet Is Doing to Our Brains*. New York: W.W. Norton and Company.

Cave, Stephen, and Kanta Dihal. (2020). The Whiteness of AI. *Philosophy and Technology* 33: 685–703. https://doi.org/10.1007/s13347-020-00415-6

Cellan-Jones, Rory. (2014). Stephen Hawking Warns Artificial Intelligence Could End Mankind. *BBC News*. December 2. https://www.bbc.com/news/technology-30290540

Charlet, Jeremie. (2023). Balancing Innovation and Sustainability: Unpacking the Environmental Impact of Generative AI. *Medium*. October 4. https://medium.com/data-science/balancing-innovation-and-sustainability-unpacking-the-environmental-impact-of-generative-ai-5493b7d4e586

Chesney, Bobby, and Danielle Citron. (2019). Deep Fakes: A Looming Challenge for Privacy. *California Law Review* 107(6): 1753–820. https://doi.org/10.15779/Z38RV0D15J

Cho, Kyunghyun, Bart van Merriënboer, Caglar Gulcehre, Fethi Bougares, Holger Schwenk, Dzmitry Bahdanau, and Yoshua

Bengio. (2014). Learning Phrase Representations Using RNN Encoder–Decoder for Statistical Machine Translation. *Proceedings of the 2014 Conference on Empirical Methods in Natural Language* Processing (EMNLP), October 25–9: 1724–34. https://aclanthology.org/D14-1179.pdf

Christie's. (2018). Obvious and the Interface between Art and Artificial Intelligence. December 12. https://www.christies.com/features/A-collaboration-between-two-artists-one-human-one-a-machine-9332-1.aspx

Clarke, Arthur C. (1973). *Profiles of the Future: An Inquiry into the Limits of the Possible.* Revised edition. New York: Harper & Row.

Coeckelbergh, Mark. (2020). *AI Ethics.* Cambridge, MA: MIT Press.

Coeckelbergh, Mark. (2024). *Why AI Undermines Democracy and What to Do About It.* Cambridge: Polity.

Coeckelbergh, Mark, and David J. Gunkel. (2025). *Communicative AI: A Critical Introduction to Large Language Models.* Cambridge: Polity.

Colton, Simon. (2012). The Painting Fool: Stories from Building an Automated Painter. In Jan McCormack and Mark d'Inverno (eds.), *Computers and Creativity*, 3–38. Berlin: Springer Verlag.

Cope, David. (2001). *Virtual Music: Computer Synthesis of Musical Style.* Cambridge, MA: MIT Press.

Cope, David. (2010). *Cope, David (2010).* Recombinant Music Composition Algorithm and Method of Using the Same. United States Patent. US 7,696.426 B2. https://patentimages.storage.googleapis.com/25/2e/8f/5e836d32d44240/US7696426.pdf

Cope, David. (2017). *Experiments in Musical Intelligence* (no longer available online).

Cormen, Thomas H., Charles E. Leiserson, Ronald L. Rivest, and Clifford Stein (2009). *Introduction to Algorithms.* Cambridge, MA: MIT Press.

Crawford, Kate. (2021). *Atlas of AI.* New Haven, CT: Yale University Press.

Culkin, John M. (1967). A Schoolman's Guide to Marshall McLuhan. *Saturday Review*, March 18: 51–3, 70–2. https://tinyurl.com/y2s5ld9q

de Vries, Alex. (2023). The Growing Energy Footprint of Artificial Intelligence. *Joule* 7(10): 2191–4. https://doi.org/10.1016/j.joule.2023.09.004

Derrida, Jacques. (1981). *Positions*. Trans. Alan Bass. Chicago: University of Chicago Press.

Descartes, René. (1988). *Selected Philosophical Writings*. Trans. John Cottingham, Robert Stoothoff, and Dugald Murdoch. Cambridge: Cambridge University Press.

Doctorow, Cory. (2025). *Enshittification: Why Everything Suddenly Got Worse and What to Do About It*. New York: Farrar, Straus and Giroux.

Dosovitskiy, Alexey et al. (2020). An Image is Worth 16 × 16 Words: Transformers for Image Recognition at Scale. *International Conference on Learning Representations (ICLR)*. https://arxiv.org/abs/2010.11929

Dreyfus, Hubert L. (1972). *What Computers Still Cannot Do: A Critique of Artificial Reason*. Cambridge, MA: MIT Press.

Dreyfus, Hubert L., and Stuart E. Dreyfus (with Tom Athanasiou). (1986). *Mind over Machine: The Power of Human Intuition and Experience in the Era of the Computer*. New York: Free Press.

Dreyfus, Hubert L., and Stuart E. Dreyfus. (1988). Making a Mind versus Modeling the Brain: Artificial Intelligence Back at a Branchpoint. *Daedalus* 117(1): 15–43. https://www.jstor.org/stable/20025137

Epstein, Robert. (2007). From Russia, with Love: How I Got Fooled (and Somewhat Humiliated) by a Computer. *Scientific American Mind*, October 1. https://www.scientificamerican.com/article/from-russia-with-love/

Fares, Murhaf, Andrei Kutuzov, Stephan Oepen, and Erik Velldal (2017). Word Vectors, Reuse, and Replicability: Towards a Community Repository of Large-Text Resources. In Jörg Tiedemann (ed.), *Proceedings of the 21st Nordic Conference on Computational Linguistics (NoDaLiDa)*, May 22–4. Linköping University Electronic Press.

Fecher, Benedikt, Marcel Hebing, Melissa Laufer, Jörg Pohle, and Fabian Sofsky. (2024). Friend or Foe? Exploring the Implications of Large Language Models on the Science System. *AI & Society* 40: 447–59. https://doi.org/10.1007/s00146-023-01791-1

Feenberg, Andrew. (1991). *Critical Theory of Technology*. Oxford: Oxford University Press.

Forster, E.M. (2001). The Machine Stops. In *Selected Stories*, 91–123. Ed. David Leavitt and Mark Mitchell. New York: Penguin.

Foucault, Michel. (1984). What is an Author? Trans. Josué V. Harari. In Paul Rabinow (ed.), *The Foucault Reader*, 101–20. New York: Pantheon.

Frey, Carl Benedikt. (2024). The 1970s Gave Us Industrial Decline. AI Could Bring Something Worse. *The New York Times*, August 19. https://www.nytimes.com/2025/08/19/opinion/ai-job-loss-deindustrialization.html

Future of Life Institute. (2023). Pause Giant AI Experiments: An Open Letter. March 22. https://futureoflife.org/open-letter/pause-giant-ai-experiments/

Goertzel, Ben, and Cassio Pennachin. (2007). *Artificial General Intelligence*. New York: Springer.

Goodfellow, Ian J., Jean Pouget-Abadie, Mehdi Mirza, Bing Xu, David Warde-Farley, Sherjil Ozair, Aaron Courville, and Yoshua Bengio. (2014). Generative Adversarial Networks. ArXiv: Machine Learning. https://doi.org/10.48550/arXiv.1406.2661

Gubrud, Mark Avrum. (1997). Nanotechnology and International Security. Paper presented at the Fifth Foresight Conference on Molecular Nanotechnology (no longer available online).

Gunkel, David J. (2001). *Hacking Cyberspace*. Boulder, CO: Westview.

Gunkel, David J. (2008). *Thinking Otherwise: Philosophy, Communication, Technology*. West Lafayette, IN: Purdue University Press.

Gunkel, David J. (2016). *Of Remixology: Ethics and Aesthetics After Remix*. Cambridge, MA: MIT Press.

Gunkel, David J. (2018). *Gaming the System: Deconstructing Video Games, Game Studies, and Virtual Worlds*. Bloomington: University of Indiana Press.

Gunkel, David J. (2019). *An Introduction to Communication and Artificial Intelligence*. Cambridge: Polity.

Gunkel, David J. (2021). *Deconstruction*. Cambridge, MA: MIT Press.

Gunkel, David J. (2023). *Person, Thing, Robot: A Moral and Legal Ontology for the 21st Century and Beyond*. Cambridge, MA: MIT Press.

Gunkel, David J. (2025). The *Différance* Engine: Large Language Models and Poststructuralism. *AI & Society*, September 25. https://doi.org/10.1007/s00146-025-02640-z

Guzman, Andrea L. (2017). Making AI Safe for Humans:

A Conversation with Siri. In Robert W. Gehl and Marika Bakardjieva (eds.), *Socialbots and Their Friends: Digital Media and the Automation of Sociality*, 69–85. New York: Routledge.

Guzman, Andrea L. (2018). Introduction: What is Human–Machine Communication, Anyway? In Andrea L. Guzman (ed.), *Human–Machine Communication: Rethinking Communication, Technology and Ourselves*, 1–28. New York: Peter Lang.

Hancock, Jeffrey T., Mor Naaman, and Karen Levy. (2020). AI-Mediated Communication: Definition, Research Agenda, and Ethical Considerations. *Journal of Computer-Mediated Communication* 25(1): 89–100. https://doi.org/10.1093/jcmc/zmz022

Haugeland, John. (1985). *Artificial Intelligence: The Very Idea.* Cambridge, MA: MIT Press.

Heaven, Will Douglas. (2022). This Horse-Riding Astronaut is a Milestone on AI's Long Road Towards Understanding. *MIT Technology Review*, April 6. https://www.technologyreview.com/2022/04/06/1049061/dalle-openai-gpt3-ai-agi-multimodal-image-generation/

Hebb, Donald O. (1949). *The Organization of Behavior: A Neuropsychological Theory*. New York: John Wiley & Sons.

Heidegger, Martin (1977). *The Question Concerning Technology and Other Essays*. Trans. William Lovitt. New York: Harper & Row.

Herndon, Holly. (2023). Spawning Identities. *New Suns*. https://newsuns.net/holly-herndon-spawning-identities/

Hicks, Michael Townsen, James Humphries, and Joe Slater. (2024). ChatGPT is Bullshit. *Ethics and Information Technology* 26: art. 38. https://doi.org/10.1007/s10676-024-09775-5

Ho, Jonathan, Ajay Jain, and Pieter Abbeel. (2020). Denoising Diffusion Probabilistic Models. *Advances in Neural Information Processing Systems* 33: 6840–51. https://arxiv.org/abs/2006.11239

Hobbes, Thomas. (1994). *Leviathan*. Ed. Edwin Curley. Indianapolis, IN: Hackett Publishing.

Johnson, Brian David. (2011). *Science Fiction Prototyping: Designing the Future with Science Fiction*. Williston, VT: Morgan and Claypool Publishers.

Johnson, Deborah G. (2006). Computer Systems: Moral Entities But Not Moral Agents. *Ethics and Information Technology* 8(4): 195–204. https://doi.org/10.1007/s10676-006-9111-5

Jones, Cameron R., and Benjamin K. Bergen. (2024). People Cannot Distinguish GPT-4 from a Human in a Turing Test. *Human–Computer Interaction*, May 9. https://arxiv.org/abs/2405.08007

Jones, Raya. (2016). *Personhood and Social Robotics: A Psychological Consideration*. New York: Routledge.

Jordan, John. (2016). *Robots*. Cambridge, MA: MIT Press.

Kaplan, Jerry. (2016). *Artificial Intelligence: What Everyone Needs to Know*. New York: Oxford University Press.

Kelly, Kevin. (2014). The Three Breakthroughs That Have Finally Unleashed AI on the World. *Wired*, October 27. https://www.wired.com/2014/10/future-of-artificial-intelligence/

Keynes, John Maynard. (2010). *Essays in Persuasion*. New York: Palgrave Macmillan.

Khan, Sal. (2023). Sal Khan's 2023 TED Talk: AI in the Classroom Can Transform Education. *Khan Academy Blog*. https://blog.khanacademy.org/sal-khans-2023-ted-talk-ai-in-the-classroom-can-transform-education/

Khowaja, Sunder Ali, Parus Khuwaja, Kapal Dev, Weizheng Wang, and Nkenyereye Lewis. (2024). ChatGPT Needs SPADE (Sustainability, PrivAcy, Digital divide, and Ethics) Evaluation: A Review. *Cognitive Computation* 16: 2528–50. https://link.springer.com/article/10.1007/s12559-024-10285-1

Kosmyna, Nataliya et al. (2025). Your Brain on ChatGPT: Accumulation of Cognitive Debt when Using an AI Assistant for Essay Writing Task. *arXiv*, June 10. https://doi.org/10.48550/arXiv.2506.08872

Krzeczkowska, Anna, Jad El-Hage, Simon Colton, and Stephen Clark. (2010). Automated Collage Generation – with Intent. *Proceedings of the 1st International Conference on Computational Creativity*. http://computationalcreativity.net/iccc2010/papers/krzeczkowska-hage-colton-clark.pdf

Lemoine, Blake. (2022). Is LaMDA sentient? An interview. *Medium*, June 11. https://cajundiscordian.medium.com/is-lamda-sentient-an-interview-ea64d916d917

Levy, Steven. (2023). How to Start an AI Panic. *Wired*, March 10. https://www.wired.com/story/plaintext-how-to-start-an-ai-panic

Lyotard, Jean-François (1984). *The Postmodern Condition: A Report on Knowledge*. Trans. Geoff Bennington and Brian Massumi. Minneapolis: University of Minnesota Press.

Mayor, Adrienne. (2018). *Gods and Robots: Myths, Machines, and Ancient Dreams of Technology*. Princeton, NJ: Princeton University Press.

McCarthy, John, Marvin L. Minsky, Nathan Rochester, and Claude E. Shannon. (1955). A Proposal for the Dartmouth Summer Research Project on Artificial Intelligence, August 31. http://jmc.stanford.edu/articles/dartmouth/dartmouth.pdf

McClelland, James L., David E. Rumelhart, and the PDP Research Group. (1986). *Parallel Distributed Processing, Volume 2: Explorations in the Microstructure of Cognition: Psychological and Biological Models*. Cambridge, MA: MIT Press.

McCulloch, Warren, and Walter Pitts (1943). A Logical Calculus of the Ideas Immanent in Nervous Activity. *Bulletin of Mathematical Biophysics* 7: 115–33. https://doi.org/10.1007/BF02478259

McLuhan, Marshall (1995). *Understanding Media: The Extensions of Man*. Cambridge, MA: MIT Press.

McQuate, Sarah. (2023). Q&A: UW Researcher Discusses Just How Much Energy ChatGPT Uses. *UW News*, July 27. https://www.washington.edu/news/2023/07/27/how-much-energy-does-chatgpt-use/

Metz, Cade. (2016). Google's AI Wins a Pivotal Second Game in Match with Go Grandmaster. *Wired*, March 10. http://www.wired.com/2016/03/googles-ai-wins-pivotal-game-two-match-go-grandmaster/

Metz, Cade. (2023). Geoffrey Hinton, the "Godfather of A.I.," Leaves Google and Warns of Danger Ahead. *The New York Times*, May 1. https://www.nytimes.com/2023/05/01/technology/ai-google-chatbot-engineer-quits-hinton.html

Minsky, Marvin L., and Seymour A. Papert. (1969). *Perceptrons: An Introduction to Computational Geometry*. Cambridge, MA: MIT Press.

Mnih, Volodymyr et al. (2015). Human-Level Control Through Deep Reinforcement Learning. *Nature* 518: 529–33. https://doi.org/10.1038/nature14236

Mordvintsev, Alexander, Christopher Olah, and Mike Tyka. (2015). Inceptionism: Going Deeper into Neural Networks.

Google AI Blog, June 18. https://research.google/blog/inceptionism-going-deeper-into-neural-networks/

Narayanan, Arvind, and Sayash Kapoor. (2024). *AI Snake Oil: What Artificial Intelligence Can Do, What It Can't, and How to Tell the Difference*. Princeton, NJ: Princeton University Press.

Natale, Simone. (2021). *Deceitful Media: Artificial Intelligence and Social Life After the Turing Test*. Oxford: Oxford University Press.

Navas, Eduardo. (2012). *Remix Theory: The Aesthetics of Sampling*. Vienna: Springer.

Newell, Allen, and Herbert A. Simon. (1976). Computer Science as Empirical Inquiry: Symbols and Search. *Communications of the ACM* 19(3): 113–26. https://doi.org/10.1145/360018.360022

Nilsson, Nils J. (2010). *The Quest for Artificial Intelligence: A History of Ideas and Achievements*. Cambridge: Cambridge University Press.

Nissenbaum, Helen. (1996). Accountability in a Computerized Society. *Science and Engineering Ethics* 2(1): 25–42. https://doi.org/10.1007/BF02639315

Nourbakhsh, Illah (2013). *Robot Futures*. Cambridge, MA: MIT Press.

Obvious. (2018). *Obvious Art* (website). http://obvious-art.com

Ong, Walter J. (2002). *Orality and Literacy: The Technologizing of the World*. 30th anniversary edition. Abingdon, Oxon: Routledge.

OpenAI. (2025). OpenAI Charter. https://openai.com/charter/

Oremus, Will. (2022). Google's AI Passed a Famous Test – and Showed How the Test is Broken. *Washington Post*, 17 June. https://www.washingtonpost.com/technology/2022/06/17/google-ai-lamda-turing-test/

Parker, Ceri. (2018). Artificial Intelligence Could Be Our Saviour, According to the CEO of Google. *World Economic Forum*, January 24. https://www.weforum.org/stories/2018/01/google-ceo-ai-will-be-bigger-than-electricity-or-fire/

Peterson, Andrea. (2013). On the Internet, No One Knows You're a Bot. And That's a Problem. *Washington Post*, August 13. https://www.washingtonpost.com/news/the-switch/wp/2013/08/13/on-the-internet-no-one-knows-youre-a-bot-and-thats-a-problem/

Plato. (1982). Phaedrus. In *Plato I: Euthyphro, Apology, Crito, Phaedo, Phaedrus*, 227A–79C. Trans. Harold North Fowler. Cambridge, MA: Harvard University Press.

Poibeau, Thierry (2017). *Machine Translation*. Cambridge, MA: MIT Press.

Radford, Alec et al. (2021). Learning Transferable Visual Models from Natural Language Supervision (CLIP). https://arxiv.org/abs/2103.00020

Raper, Rebecca, Jona Boeddinghaus, Mark Coeckelbergh, Wolfgang Gross, Paolo Campigotto, and Craig N. Lincoln. (2022). Sustainability Budgets: A Practical Management and Governance Method for Achieving Goal 13 of the Sustainable Development Goals for AI Development. *Sustainability* 14(7): art. 4019. https://doi.org/10.3390/su14074019

Reeves, Byron, and Clifford Nass. (1996). *The Media Equation: How People Treat Computers, Television, and New Media Like Real People and Places*. Cambridge: Cambridge University Press.

Rosenblatt, Frank. (1958). The Perceptron: A Probabilistic Model for Information Storage and Organization in the Brain. *Psychological Review* 65: 386–408. https://doi.org/10.1037/h0042519

Rumelhart, David E., James L. McClelland, and the PDP Research Group. (1986). *Parallel Distributed Processing, Volume 1: Explorations in the Microstructure of Cognition: Foundations*. Cambridge, MA: MIT Press.

Salathé, Marcel. (2025). Does ChatGPT Use 10 × More Energy Than a Standard Google Search? *Engineering Prompts*, January 16. https://engineeringprompts.substack.com/p/does-chatgpt-use-10x-more-energy

Samuel, Arthur L. (1959). Some Studies in Machine Learning Using the Game of Checkers. *IBM Journal* 3(3): 535–54. https://doi.org/10.1147/rd.33.0210

Schank, Roger C. (1990). What is AI Anyway? In Derek Patridge and Yorick Wilks (eds.), *The Foundations of Artificial Intelligence: A Sourcebook*, 3–13. Cambridge: Cambridge University Press.

Searle, John. (1980). Minds, Brains, and Programs. *Behavioral and Brain Sciences* 3(3): 417–57. https://doi.org/10.1017/S0140525X00005756

Searle, John. (1999). The Chinese Room. In Robert A. Wilson

and Frank A. Keil (eds.), *The MIT Encyclopedia of the Cognitive Sciences*, 115–16. Cambridge, MA: MIT Press.
Shannon, Claude E. (1950). Programming a Computer for Playing Chess. *Philosophical Magazine* Series 7. 41(314): 256–75. https://doi.org/10.1080/14786445008521796
Shannon, Claude E., and Warren Weaver. (1949). *A Mathematical Theory of Communication*. Urbana: University of Illinois Press.
Shelley, Mary. (2000). *Frankenstein, Or the Modern Prometheus*. New York: Signet Classics.
Simonite, Tom. (2016). How Google Plans to Solve Artificial Intelligence. *MIT Technology Review*, March 31. https://www.technologyreview.com/2016/03/31/161234/how-google-plans-to-solve-artificial-intelligence/
Smolensky, Paul. (1990a). Connectionism and the Foundations of AI. In Derek Partridge and Yorick Wilks (eds.), *The Foundations of Artificial Intelligence: A Sourcebook*, 306–26. Cambridge: Cambridge University Press.
Smolensky, Paul. (1990b). On the Proper Treatment of Connectionism. In David J. Cole, James H. Fetzer, and Terry L. Rankin (eds.), *Philosophy, Mind, and Cognitive Inquiry*, 145–206. Dordrecht: Springer.
Sohl-Dickstein, Jascha Narain, Eric A. Weiss, Niru Maheswaranathan, and Surya Ganguli. (2015). Deep Unsupervised Learning Using Nonequilibrium Thermodynamics. *arXiv*, March 12. https://doi.org/10.48550/arXiv.1503.03585
Sokolowski, Robert. (1988). Natural and Artificial Intelligence. *Daedalus* 117(1): 45–64. https://www.jstor.org/stable/20025138
Song, Yang, and Stefano Ermon. (2019). Generative Modeling by Estimating Gradients of the Data Distribution. *arXiv*, July 12. https://doi.org/10.48550/arXiv.1907.05600
St-Hilaire, Francois et al. (2022). A New Era: Intelligent Tutoring Systems Will Transform Online Learning for Millions. *arXiv*, March 3. https://arxiv.org/abs/2203.03724
Suleyman, Mustafa (2023). My New Turing Test Would See If AI Can Make $1 Million. *MIT Technology Review*, July 14. https://www.technologyreview.com/2023/07/14/1076296/mustafa-suleyman-my-new-turing-test-would-see-if-ai-can-make-1-million/

Tangermann, Victor. (2024). Sam Altman Says AI Using Too Much Energy, Will Require Breakthrough Energy Source. *Futurism*, January 17. https://futurism.com/sam-altman-energy-breakthrough

Towler, Louise. (2025). Search Engines vs AI: Energy Consumption Compared. *Kanoppi*, February 13. https://kanoppi.co/search-engines-vs-ai-energy-consumption-compared/

Turing, Alan M. (1950). Computing Machinery and Intelligence. *Mind* 59(236): 433–60. https://doi.org/10.1093/mind/LIX.236.433

Turkle, Sherry. (2011). *Alone Together: Why We Expect More from Technology and Less from Each Other.* New York: Basic Books.

Vaswani, Ashish, Noam Shazeer, Niki Parmar, Jakob Uszkoreit, Llion Jones, Aidan N. Gomez, Lukasz Kaiser, and Illia Polosukhin. (2017). Attention is All You Need. *Proceedings of the 31st International Conference on Neural Information Processing Systems (NIPS'17)*: 6000–10. https://dl.acm.org/doi/10.5555/3295222.3295349; also available from https://doi.org/10.48550/arXiv.1706.03762

Wallach, Wendell, and Colin Allen. (2009). *Moral Machines: Teaching Robots Right from Wrong*. Oxford: Oxford University Press.

Walmsley, Joel. (2012). *Mind and Machine*. New York: Palgrave Macmillan.

Wang, Rose E., Ana T. Ribeiro, Carly D. Robinson, Susanna Loeb, and Dora Demszky. (2024). Tutor CoPilot: A Human–AI Approach for Scaling Real-Time Expertise. *arXiv*, October 3. https://arxiv.org/abs/2410.03017

Weatherby, Leif. (2023). ChatGPT Broke the Turing Test. *Boston Globe*, November 13. https://www.bostonglobe.com/2023/11/13/opinion/turing-test-ai-chatgpt/

Weatherby, Leif. (2025). *Language Machines: Cultural AI and the End of Remainder Humanism*. Minneapolis: University of Minnesota Press.

Weaver, Warren. (1949). Translation. *The Rockefeller Foundation*. https://aclanthology.org/anthology-files/earlymt/1952.earlymt-1.1.pdf

Weizenbaum, Joseph. (1976). *Computer Power and Human Reason: From Judgment to Calculation*. San Francisco, CA: W. H. Freeman.

Winfield, Alan. (2011). Roboethics – for Humans. *New Scientist* 210(2811): 32–3. https://doi.org/10.1016/S0262-4079(11)61052-X

Winfield, Alan. (2012). *Robotics: A Very Short Introduction*. Oxford: Oxford University Press.

Zuboff, Shoshana. (2019). *The Age of Surveillance Capitalism: The Fight for a Human Future at the New Frontier of Power*. New York: PublicAffairs.

Index